About One Plus One

The Authors

The authors of this review, Dr Lester Coleman and Fiona Glenn are respectively Head of Research and Research Officer at One Plus One.

One Plus One

One Plus One is the UK's leading relationships research organisation. We investigate what makes relationships work – or fall apart – and make the findings accessible to practitioners, policy makers, the media and the public.

Our team of researchers, practitioners, and information specialists work together to create a wide range of evidence based and innovative resources tailored to the needs of those working with families in both the statutory and voluntary sectors.

Acknowledgements

The authors would like to thank colleagues at One Plus One who greatly assisted in the production of this review, especially Penny Mansfield (Director), Justine Devenney (Head of Dissemination and Policy) and Laura Dimmock (Information Officer).

We are also thankful for the support provided by members of One Plus One's Research Committee who shared expert opinion and valuable comments on early drafts - Professor Paul Black, Professor Kath Kiernan, Professor Susan Golombok and Professor Sir Michael Rutter.

We are grateful to Pamela Meadows (National Institute for Economic and Social Research) who contributed substantially to the chapter on the issues to consider in estimating the economic costs of couple relationship breakdown. We are also appreciative of the numerous researchers who responded to our requests for their published articles as well as those in press.

Finally, we also thank the Department for Children Schools and Families for funding provided through the Children and Young People's Fund Strategic Grant.

Foreword

Many people hold strong views about marriage and divorce based on religious beliefs or ideology, but One Plus One sought, instead, to approach the topic of the effects of couple relationship breakdown on the basis of a dispassionate, thoughtful, critical assessment of the evidence. We are delighted, therefore, to publish this excellent review, which does just that. The aim was not a technical treatise, but rather a readable account that would be accessible to a wide audience. It is scholarly, however, in the important sense of being firmly based on research evidence and sensitive to the crucial methodological considerations.

Many people hold strong views about marriage and divorce based on religious beliefs or ideology, but One Plus One sought, instead, to approach the topic of the effects of couple relationship breakdown on the basis of a dispassionate, thoughtful, critical assessment of the evidence. We are delighted, therefore, to publish this excellent review, which does just that. The aim was not a technical treatise, but rather a readable account that would be accessible to a wide audience. It is scholarly, however, in the important sense of being firmly based on research evidence and sensitive to the crucial methodological considerations.

The enduring importance of the topic reflects the fact that humans are social beings; committed partnerships are an intrinsic part of human functioning and breakdown in those partnerships constitutes a major source of stress throughout the whole of the life span. The contemporary relevance is underlined by the declining rate of marriage, the widening range of other forms of couple relationships, and the very high rate of couple relationship breakdown. The prime focus is on the psychological and physical consequences of relationship breakdown for the two adults concerned and for their children. The key questions concern the frequency, severity, pattern and duration of adverse effects. To what extent are these universal and inevitable and to what extent do people vary in the extent to which they are affected? The focus on the couple and their children does not imply a lack of concern for the others involved. Thus, grandparents are also very much part of the situation, both as possible buffers and supports and as fellow sufferers, but they are largely outside the scope of this review.

On the face of it, the questions seem deceptively simple. Surely, it is just a matter of quantifying the various outcomes following couple relationship breakdown? Unfortunately, that is not so. To begin with, associations cannot be assumed to reflect causal influences. For example, might the apparent ill-effects of the breakdown really be a function of the sorts of people who have fragile relationships? Alternatively, might the supposed effects be a consequence of associated features (such as conflict and discord) rather than the breakdown as such? Even more basically, could the assessment of consequences reflect biases in measurement? Although longitudinal studies on their own do not solve the problem of causal inference, nevertheless they are much more powerful than cross-sectional studies. Accordingly, the review places most weight on longitudinal studies spanning the period before and after the relationship breakdown.

The review notes the substantial associations between relationship breakdown and worsening of physical and psychological health – especially in the early years after the relationship breakdown. It is noted that the finding of the overall better health of the married (as compared with the divorced or single) is dependent on the marriage relationship being of high quality. In other words, there is much to be said for interventions that can improve couple relationships sufficiently to prevent breakdown. On the other hand, maintaining a hostile, unloving, relationship 'for the sake of the children' is not usually a good solution.

Adverse effects on the children are well documented but there are similar questions about whether the main risk stems from the stresses of the breakdown or from the multiple associated adversities. It is clear that conflict is a key issue but it reflects a process that usually begins before the breakdown and, all too often, continues long after the breakdown. But, importantly, it seems that it is not so much conflict as such that is harmful, but how it is dealt with.

Does the major increase over time in the rate of divorce mean that the ill-effects are less now that couple relationship breakdown is so common? The finding that the adverse effects seem as marked as ever suggests that the risks stem, not from the atypicality, but rather from other key features of the family situation. It is noteworthy, too, that the risks for the children seem to be greater when there are multiple experiences of parental relationship breakdown.

Despite the evidence that ill-effects for both the adults and the children of couple relationship breakdown are common and substantial, the findings also show the marked heterogeneity in people's responses. That raises the critical question of what are the moderating factors? The evidence is not as decisive as we would like but the suggestion is that aspects of the parent-child relationship are operative as one of multiple moderators. As researchers have long noted, the relationship between any pair of individuals in a family is likely to involve repercussions for others in the family groups.

In seeking to understand the processes involved, it is essential to determine what sorts of people, from what sorts of background, in what sorts of social circumstances are likely to suffer a breakdown in a hitherto committed relationship? Findings indicate that both an unusually early age at marriage (or cohabitation leading to children being born), and coming from a family in which the individual's parents' marriage broke down, are relevant. In addition, however, it cannot be assumed that either cohabitations or marriage have the same meaning, or carry the same expectations, as in previous generations.

The review seeks to bring together the implications for interventions both with respect to the couple relationship and the parent-child relationships – recognising the importance of connections between the two. In addition, attention needs to be paid to poverty and disadvantage as factors predisposing to breakdown and as moderators of the effects of breakdown.

The report does not provide, nor could it provide, a simple remedy for all the problems, but what it does do is provide the evidence and the concepts that need to be considered when dealing with policy and practice. Furthermore, it provides good guides on what might be done to alleviate the problems. It makes for a thought-provoking, as well as helpful, read.

Michael Rutter, Professor of Developmental Psychopathology at the Institute of Psychiatry, Trustee of One Plus One and chair of its Research Committee.

Contents

Executive summary

Introduction

This literature review provides an understanding into the consequences of couple relationship breakdown for adults and children. The review outlines the consequences on the physical and psychological health and well-being of adults and children, includes recent statistical data on couple relationships, and outlines factors that need to be considered when estimating the economic costs associated with couple relationship breakdown. The review also addresses the dilemmas in interpreting the data (e.g. attributing outcomes that are an effect rather than a cause of the relationship breakdown), details factors that are associated with an increased likelihood of relationship breakdown, explores the theoretical and empirical mechanisms seeking to explain the consequences of relationship breakdown, and outlines why some people fare worse than others when couples part. The latter is especially relevant when understanding how to protect and improve outcomes for adults and children when breakdown occurs. By providing such an understanding, this review will be relevant for a broad audience to include researchers, policy-makers, practitioners and students working in the field of parenting, families and couple relationships.

Couple relationship breakdown is more frequent in today's society. It is estimated that 45% of marriages will end in divorce. Alongside declining rates of marriage and more recent reductions in divorce, the married population are arguably becoming more homogenous than ever. This review includes the breakdown of a range of couple relationship statuses (where possible), and thus reflects the changes in relationship formation that have been evident over the last 40 years or so. Recent increases in the numbers of people cohabiting, relationships described as 'closely involved', and children raised by 'single-parent' families support these trends. This increased fragility and diversity of family forms, in tandem with a growing political interest illustrates the timely production of this review.

This review is underpinned by recognising that strengthening couple relationships has profound benefits for adult and child well-being, as well as improved parenting. In acknowledging the detrimental effects of relationship breakdown, this review is able to provide support for developments in policy and practice that can either help prevent relationship breakdown (where appropriate) or minimise the negative effects on adults and children when the relationship is irretrievable. It is important to emphasise that there is convincing evidence that some relationships can be repaired, improved and prevented from breaking down.

The primary focus of this review is on assessing the impacts of couple relationship breakdown on the physical and psychological health of adults and children. Although reference to relationship conflict and relationship support interventions are made, for more comprehensive reviews in these two areas readers are referred to studies cited in the main body of the report.

Presenting the evidence from this review has involved a number of complex issues. One central to this study has been assessing the precise contribution that couple relationship breakdown has on the reported impacts. The key to establishing whether the association between relationship breakdown and outcome is causal, is to assess the extent to which 'selection' effects are occurring. Selection bias occurs when comparing samples (e.g. married and divorced) that differ in a number of ways (e.g. history of mental health problems) such that any reported impacts that are directly attributed to the breakdown are difficult to discern. The possibility of reverse causation, for example alcohol use causing relationship breakdown rather than vice versa, and the inability to rule out other influences such as behaviour, genetics and personality, bring further complications. In appreciation of these complexities, priority in this review has been given to prospective longitudinal cohort studies where, essentially, sample members serve as their own control group with the impact of relationship breakdown observed by comparing outcomes pre- and post-breakdown. Reference in the review is also made to the role of multiple measures, innovative designs and statistical advances that can help unravel some of these complex issues and forge conclusions with more certainty over whether relationship breakdown is causally associated with outcomes.

Main findings

The review has generated a great number of insights into the effects of couple relationship breakdown. With Chapters 1 and 2 providing an important context to the report, including the latest statistics on family formation and dissolution, the following presents a synopsis of the headline findings derived from the remaining chapters. The chapter headings are used to guide readers towards more substantive evidence in the full review:

Chapters 3 and 4 (adult impacts)

1. There is an unequivocal association between couple relationship breakdown and adult ill-health. Mortality statistics for England and Wales (in 2007) show elevated mortality rates for non-married (single, widowed and divorced) males and females, compared to those married, for all age groups between 25 and 64 years. From middle age (late 40's onwards) the single (never married) group show the highest rates of mortality. Evidence of a causal relationship between relationship status and the mortality statistics cannot be confirmed.

2. Overall, the elevation of mortality rates among unmarried groups is greatest among men of all ages. Office for National Statistics (ONS) data from England and Wales show that, between the ages of 30 and 50, single men have death rates about three times that of married men, and single women have rates about double those of married women. There is also evidence of an 'accumulative effect', with the strength of these mortality associations increasing by number of years non-married.

3. Associations between marital status and general health status and more specific health conditions such as Coronary Heart Disease (CHD) and raised blood pressure are also evident, with more detrimental outcomes among the non-married groups. The same association applies to the greater involvement in health-damaging behaviours. Studies indicate that the emotional and social 'protective effect' of marriage operates over and above selection effects (of people being selected out of marriage due to their poor health status) in explaining these health differences.

4. Couple relationship breakdown is associated with poorer adult mental health. Some research suggests that these impacts are observed from two years prior to breakdown, with a peak at the time of separation. This is then followed by a drop in psychological strain over the following two years to a lower level than observed before the separation (indicating a relief from stress over the longer-term). However, these findings are not consistent with some research showing poorer mental health outcomes over the long-term following divorce or separation. This may be partly due to differences in the ways mental health is measured.

5. In studying couple relationships and health, it is clear that the marriage must be of a high quality to be advantageous. Indeed, evidence suggests that the health outcomes for some single people may be more positive than those reporting unhappy marriages. Therefore, preventing relationships from breaking down (where appropriate) and improving relationship satisfaction are both important in maintaining the well-being of adults and children.

Chapters 5 and 6 (child impacts)

6. Evidence from extensive reviews of other studies has reported strong associations between couple relationship breakdown and poor child outcomes. These include: poverty and socio-economic disadvantage (especially), physical ill-health, psychological ill-health,

lower educational achievement, substance misuse and other health-damaging behaviours, and behavioural problems including conduct disorder, anti-social behaviour and crime. Longitudinal, cohort studies have shown that these effects may be long-term for some children, and include socio-economic disadvantage in later life, cohabitation or marriage at an early age, teenage pregnancy, and increased risk of their own marital breakdown.

7. These negative impacts of relationship breakdown on children are far from universal. The majority of children are able to adjust to a changing situation after a period of instability whilst others are less fortunate with negative impacts extending into adulthood.

8. The impact of multiple relationship transitions are particularly detrimental to children. Changes in family structure (e.g. from marriage to divorce, to remarriage, involving new half-siblings, etc.) may be more disruptive to children than maintaining a stable family structure, even if that is with a single parent. The effects are also considered to be accumulative, with the increased number of transitions leading to more negative consequences for children. Of those experiencing parental separation for the first time, younger children have a greater potential to face multiple transitions (because of their age) compared to older children.

9. Studying the effects of conflict illustrates that couple relationship breakdown should be viewed as a 'process' with events prior, during and after the breakdown affecting the impacts. There is unequivocal evidence highlighting the detrimental impact of adult relationship conflict and distress on children (that may precede a separation as well as continue afterwards). However, research also indicates that it is not necessarily whether parents are in conflict that is key, but how this conflict occurs and is managed. For example, 'destructive' conflict (e.g. physical violence) can be particularly harmful to children, although 'constructive' conflict (e.g. mild conflict effectively resolved) can be important in children learning how to resolve disputes in an effective manner. Similarly, unresolved conflict that involves children as messengers or recipients of negative information is particularly harmful.

10. Paradoxically, divorce following low pre-divorce conflict, compared to high pre-divorce conflict, has been shown to be more detrimental to the health and well-being of children. This is because low levels of conflict often mean children have little time to anticipate the relationship breakdown, and may result in some children blaming themselves for the separation. Therefore, even though relationships with least conflict may have a greater chance of reconciliation or a less stressful separation, they may result in more harm for children. Consequently, although interventions need to foster a continued parent-child relationship to alleviate the impact of relationship breakdown, they also need to consider ways in which children perceive and attribute the conflict and breakdown.

11. Although divorce is more common nowadays, there is evidence suggesting that the adverse outcomes for adults and children are still equally apparent. This contradicts the argument that increasing divorce rates diminish the negative impacts in line with reduced stigma and greater acceptance of relationship breakdown. Furthermore, the difference in adult mortality rates by marital status, in England and Wales, has actually increased since divorce has become more common.

Chapters 7 and 8 (additional issues and explanations)

12. The dissolution of a relationship results in the loss of the protective benefits from being in a partnership (such as effects on physical and psychological health), as well as in further strains associated with the process of separation. This is illustrated by research showing that never-married women report less detrimental health outcomes in terms of psychological and physical health compared to those who have experienced the stressful events of divorce or separation. However, this does not apply when observing mortality data that show single, never-married people, reporting higher death rates from middle age onwards in comparison to those who were married, divorced or widowed.

13. There are a number of moderating factors[1] that can influence the impact of couple relationship breakdown and explain why, for some, the impacts are worse than for others. For children, these include:
    - parenting quality;
    - financial resources;
    - maternal mental health;
    - children's age (older children tend to face more problems adjusting to new family forms than younger children, although for a younger child who cannot recognise the distress, the removal of one parent may cause confusion and anxiety, and lead to self-blaming);
    - sex of child (mixed evidence);
    - pre-divorce conflict (high levels are detrimental to children although low levels may mean children have little time to anticipate the separation);
    - communication between parent and child about the separation;
    - child's relationship and contact with both parents after separation;
    - supportive family members;
    - new family setting after separation;
    - whether one parent is re-partnering at any one time (rather than at the same time) with the latter presenting greater difficulties.

    Moderating factors affecting the impact on adults include social and economic support, ability to forgive, and consideration of who initiated the separation.

14. When considering the moderating factors that may influence how much children are affected by relationship breakdown, there is a strong case for all being mediated to some extent through the parent-child relationship. Therefore, good and effective parenting, although not always possible, may be one of the most potent means of reducing the negative impacts on children. In addition, with the unequivocal link between couple relationship satisfaction and supportive parenting, the role of strengthening couple relationships (including new, post-separation relationships) in order to minimise the impacts on children is clear. In view of these various risk and protective factors, there is a powerful argument that the way a family functions, rather than the family type, may be more important in shaping child outcomes.

15. Review evidence on the predictors of relationship breakdown suggests that demographic factors (especially those more volitional) are more predictive of marital breakdown compared to socio-economic factors. These factors are: early age at

1 Moderating factors affect the direction and/or strength of the relation between, in this instance, relationship breakdown and its impacts. Essentially, they can exacerbate or protect people from the effects of relationship breakdown.

marriage, pre-marital conception, pre-marital cohabitation, previous partnership breakdown, and parental divorce. The latter is particularly important and maintains a predictive effect when controlling for early age at partnership, premarital cohabitation and premarital childbearing.

16. Evidence from prospective longitudinal designs shows that the transition to parenthood is associated with relationship breakdown. The impacts are reported to have increased in contemporary samples due to the greater contrast between the lifestyle and choices open to young childless adults compared to those available to parents of young children. Reasons for the decline in relationship satisfaction through new parenthood include less time together, increased sleeplessness, increased depression (including post-natal depression), and increased fatigue. Protective factors include high pre-pregnancy relationship satisfaction, planned rather than unplanned pregnancy, and a low-demanding and fretful baby.

Chapter 9 (estimating the economic costs of relationship breakdown)

17. Women in Britain are 40% more likely to enter poverty if they divorce than if they remain married. Their income falls by an average of 17% after divorce, with a larger decrease among younger women, particularly mothers, and a smaller decrease among older women. Relative to married and cohabiting families, single-mother families are also found to be the most economically disadvantaged although subsequent partnerships can change the financial outlook.

18. The main economic outcomes of couple relationship breakdown can be summarised as: financial costs in terms of legal fees; moving; the need to maintain two households rather than one; additional childcare costs; impact on employment and earning prospects; impact on disposable income; and impact on services supporting the detrimental health and social impacts of couple relationship breakdown.

19. From an alternative perspective, it is important to note that some groups benefit from the costs of couple relationship breakdown. Divorce lawyers, mediators, counsellors and estate agents derive income from the consequences of couple relationship breakdown. This income generation should also be considered when establishing the financial impacts of divorce at a national level.

Implications of the review for practice, policy and research

The resounding conclusion from this review is that the association between couple relationship breakdown and disadvantage is evident through a wide range of health and socio-economic indicators. There are a number of ways in which this has clear implications for practice and policy. Key points to note include:

- couple relationships can be strengthened and that breakdown, in some cases, can be prevented;
- the opportunities available to minimise the burden on adults and children when breakdown occurs (in light of factors that moderate the impacts);
- the importance of maintaining relationship quality; and
- recognition of opportune moments where relationship strain is more pronounced (e.g. transition to parenthood, the birth of a disabled child, etc.).

This review supports the case for more investment to help strengthen family relationships and to minimise the burden when relationship breakdown does occur. Helping adults to become more informed about couple relationships (e.g. expected transitions and changes), the increased ability (of practitioners and couples) to identify relationship difficulties at an early stage, and the provision of appropriate and accessible support where applicable, are leading requirements.

A further theme central throughout this review is evidence for the link between couple relationships and parenting. Poor quality couple relationships are associated with poor parenting and consequently poor quality parent-child relationships. Conversely, children raised by parents (including those previously separated or divorced) reporting high relationship quality and satisfaction tend to have high levels of well-being. Also, improvements in co-parenting (supporting a partner during parenting) have been shown to improve partner and parent-infant relationships and their well-being. Collectively, this evidence demonstrates the need for parenting interventions that emphasise the importance of the couple relationship in improving adult and child outcomes.

These main findings have highlighted a number of areas requiring further research.

- Research to investigate more precisely why couple relationships break down or why contemporary relationships show more fragility. Although it is clear that attitudes to marriage have changed with shifts in the 1960s and 1970s from the 'companionate' marriage to the more 'individualized' marriage of modern day, the attitudinal and personality-based origins of couple relationship breakdown, relative to the broader socio-demographic predictors, are still under-researched.
- Understanding more about the relationship support needs and unique experiences of population subgroups, for example, teenage parents or those of 'mixed' heritage, is essential in providing tailored support.
- Evaluating the effectiveness of preventative relationship support programmes on couple relationship quality requires expansion, especially in the UK. Research is required among more ethnically diverse, disadvantaged and relationship- distressed couples. More research is also required to understand how changes in relationship quality occur in order to inform even more effective interventions.

Perhaps most critically of all, research evidence demonstrating the effectiveness of relationships skills programmes has rarely extended beyond 12 months and so the long-term effectiveness of these programmes is, as yet, unknown.

- Given the changing nature of relationship formation, there is a need to develop measures of relationship satisfaction and quality that reflect contemporary trends. Such measures could also help practitioners quickly and opportunistically assess the relationship support needs of adults and help examine the impact of any support provided.
- With the association/causation complexities between couple relationship breakdown and impact outlined earlier, there is a need to assess, through advanced research designs and statistical techniques, the ways in which evidence of causation can be derived with more certainty.

Conclusion

Although the evidence demonstrating the impact of couple relationship breakdown is highly complex, the overriding conclusion is the association it has with adult and child disadvantage. This association remains strong despite the fact that divorce and separation is widespread in today's society with research showing that the negative impacts have not diminished through time. Rather, the increased exposure of adults and children to couple relationship breakdown means that more people are affected compared to those of a previous generation. Hence the urgent need to increase the policy recognition of promoting family functioning and stability.

Indeed, while much of the evidence of impacts is relatively well established, arguably one of the more innovative strands for practice and policy has been the increased understanding of the factors known to prevent long-term detrimental outcomes for children in particular. With couple relationship breakdown becoming more widespread, and the impacts not thought to diminish through time, establishing the protective factors for adults and children is a necessity for ongoing research and practice developments in this field. The recent policy directive from the Dept. for Children, Schools and Families (DCSF), 'The Children's Plan: One Year On' (DCSF, 2008b), outlines the importance of minimising harmful outcomes as a priority for 2009:

"Introduce new ways to support parents at times when their relationships come under strain, and give more support to children when family relationships break down" (DCSF, 2008b, p.7).

Although the 'protection' offered by couple relationships (in terms of social support, companionship and intimacy) has been shown to explain the association between relationship breakdown and health over and above selection effects, the relative contribution of this to economic support still remains unanswered. The issue of poverty and economic resource remains central to our understanding of the impacts of relationship breakdown. There is a case for well-being being affected mostly by a decline in economic resources which, in turn, have arisen from relationship breakdown. At the time of writing, the recession and rising unemployment and financial stress among many families is most pertinent to this conclusion.

Although many factors may affect well-being, some of which are unknown and unmeasured, the role of poverty and financial disadvantage must not be understated. Research has shown that financial capability (often reduced following a separation) acts as a powerful protective factor against the potential harmful outcomes from relationship breakdown. With positive parenting, linked to the quality of the couple relationship, offering an additional protective factor, family functioning and within-family effects (from finance and parenting especially) may be particularly significant in shaping the outcomes when couples part. Moreover, although the impact of couple relationship breakdown can be considered detrimental as an 'average effect' (which may disguise instances of differing impacts), the financial situation and positive parenting are important influences on adult and child outcomes that must be integrated in any related practice and policy.

Chapter 1
Introduction to the impact of couple relationship breakdown

This introduction specifies the aim of the report, defines a 'couple relationship' and 'breakdown', and outlines the types of data under review. It presents the context brought to this report through previous research, the current political climate and related developments in practice. Finally, the chapter outlines some of the complexities recognised in developing this report (at the outset rather than as an afterthought), and how these are used to prioritise evidence.

1.1 Aim of the report

The aim of this report is to provide up-to-date information on the impact of couple relationship breakdown on:

- adults (Chapters 3 and 4);
- children (Chapters 5 and 6);
- related issues, such as mechanisms behind the impacts and variation in outcomes (Chapters 7 and 8); and
- factors influencing the economic costs (Chapter 9).

To further establish the context to the review, Chapter 2 presents some introductory data highlighting trends in relationships and breakdown in the UK.

The scope of this report is purposively broad and, as such, will be relevant to anyone interested in couple relationships. It will be of interest to researchers, students, policy-makers and a whole host of practitioners working in the field of parenting and couple relationships. This interest will be fuelled by the compelling evidence that, in the majority of instances, relationship breakdown has a negative impact on couples, children and the wider society. Therefore, this report will be of use to those requiring an evidence-base to support the case for improving relationship quality and preventing relationship breakdown where this is appropriate and achievable. Naturally, this report may also be of interest to couples and parents, and others in the wider public. With the strong policy focus on improving child outcomes (see later), this report makes an important contribution by outlining evidence demonstrating that relationship stability and quality is a strong contributory factor in maintaining child well-being. Note that this report focuses on the consequences of couple relationship breakdown, although some reference to the effects of relationship conflict will also be included.

The report presents evidence ranging in depth to accommodate different degrees of interest. The executive summary presents a concise, accessible account of the report, presenting key findings and conclusions and backed by references cited numerically. Key findings are also presented in bullet points at the end of each chapter. Note that with priority afforded to UK data, with significant contributions from the rest of Europe, the US and Australasia, the primary interest will be for people from these countries.

As a final point to this section, it is also important to note that the authors of this report, and One Plus One as an organisation, not intend to moralise about relationships, and the work is not reflected by a particular moral or faith-based perspective. By contrast, it is the intention to present conclusions based on the balanced and thorough assessment of the available evidence.

1.2 How we define a 'couple relationship'

In this report we define a 'couple relationship' as a personal connection between two adults that usually involves an emotional, romantic and/or sexual component. The couple relationships encompassed in this report include those where there is a sense of mutual obligation and commitment. In its simplest of applications, this definition includes those who are married and excludes those who have a platonic relationship. In this manner, a 'couple relationship' also includes those who are cohabiting as well as those who are romantically involved but who are not living together.

However, providing such a definition to include relationships outside of marriage brings with it a number of complexities. There are two points to note in connection to this. Firstly, although often grouped together, the relationships between cohabiting partners may range in duration, stability and commitment. For example, the expectations of an ongoing, long-term committed relationship may be vastly different for teenagers cohabiting for one or two years, compared to older adults who have children together and have lived together for many years (Mansfield,1996). Clearly, the impacts of the relationship breakdown among these groups who cohabit may be vastly different. Secondly, the recent emergence of the 'closely involved' category (termed 'visiting' in US research) provides an additional dimension. These include relationships among people who are not living together and, in similar fashion to the cohabiting relationships, the impact of the relationship breaking down may vary in this group. Those 'closely involved' may include those with marriage-like responsibilities as well as those consenting the relationship in purely sexual terms, or those just dating or 'seeing each other' and those just starting a new relationship. The range in relationship types (which may produce different impacts upon breakdown) within those who cohabit or who are 'closely involved' is the main point to observe here. The notion of grouping these diverse relationship forms as 'in relationships', to compare against those 'not in a relationship' or 'no longer in a relationship' (in longitudinal studies) will be returned to later on in this chapter.

Of course, the application of this 'relationship' definition is also partly governed by the range of data and research evidence that this report will include. For example, some studies will follow a similar broad definition, while others will look to distinguish solely between outcomes for those who are married compared to those who are divorced. Indeed, the legal status of being married makes people easy to identify in large-scale surveys, for example, rather than those who cohabit. Therefore, most of the research reviewed in this report will assess marital rather than relationship breakdown. Nonetheless, we consider that the married/divorced comparison does not encompass the variety of couple relationships that are evident within the UK.

When a relationship breaks down, this means that the once romantically connected couple are no longer together. For the majority of couples (married and cohabiting), this will mean that they are no longer living together once divorce proceedings or separation has occurred, although they may well be in a new couple relationship. It is acknowledged in Chapter 5 that divorce, separation and relationship breakdown is a 'process' rather than an event. Therefore, those 'not in a relationship' may well encapsulate people at different stages of this separation process (e.g. from those recently living apart to those legally separated through divorce).

1.3 Reviewing the evidence

The approach adopted in this review will be to report the effects of relationship breakdown on couples and their children. This will be achieved by, wherever possible, comparing the average outcomes among people (couples and children) affected by relationship breakdown to those whose relationships remain intact. It is important to note that this approach is not equivalent to comparing those, for example, who are married to those never married, as the never married may not have experienced the stressful events of relationship breakdown, divorce or widowhood. Nonetheless, in many of the studies reviewed, comparisons are made between 'single' (never married) and married groups, particularly when outlining the benefits of marriage (see Chapter 7). As will be seen later in this chapter, the 'stress' of relationship breakdown is one of the main theories to advance our understanding of why negative impacts may result.

A range of indicators will be used to report the impact of relationship breakdown. These will include physical health (mortality and morbidity), psychological health, and the social and educational development of children. Key questions will be answered, such as what effect does relationship breakdown have on physical health? What are the issues to consider when estimating the economic costs associated with relationship breakdown? What are the impacts of relationship breakdown on a child's educational attainment? Some of these outcomes, of course, may also act as causes of relationship breakdown: a point raised in great detail later in this chapter.

A comparison of this type using population samples reports 'average' outcomes rather than outcomes for individuals. Although, arguably, the most feasible way to summarise the impacts of relationship breakdown, this approach does present some limitations. Reporting the 'average' outcomes may overlook instances of where relationship breakdown is favourable (for example, in cases of abusive or high conflict relationships) and, similarly, the findings may disguise instances where the outcomes are extremely poor or beneficial. As a further complexity, the outcomes may be influenced by how couples or children are able to manage the relationship breakdown and also how sustained or temporary these outcomes are (see later in this chapter for further detail). Indeed, Dunn (2008) makes the important point that these average effects may mask the within-family differences that play an important role in affecting the impacts of couple relationship breakdown on children.

In assessing the impact of relationship breakdown, we will review data from a variety of sources, including:

- UK census data (latest year being 2001);
- longitudinal survey data from Britain and the UK (e.g. Millennium Cohort Study data, National Development Child Survey, British Cohort Study, the Office for National Statistics (ONS) General Household Survey, and the ONS Social Trends series), and various longitudinal surveys undertaken in other westernised countries, predominantly the US;
- cross-sectional survey data among specific population subgroups.

These data will be used to illustrate the impact of couple relationship breakdown within the UK. However, as will become clear, there is an enormous evidence-base of high quality data available from the rest of Europe, the US and Australasia that will be cited in areas where the UK research is limited. Sourcing these studies has the advantage of widening the relevance of this report beyond the UK. However, the caption of these international data dilutes the exclusively UK relevance, especially when considering the divergent cultures reflected through these international studies. A cautionary approach, therefore, should be adopted when applying data derived from other European countries, the US and Australasia to depict the impact of relationship background in the UK.

Finally, rather than solely including data to compare the outcomes of those who have or have not been affected by relationship breakdown, this report will include detail in six further areas.

1. The review will outline evidence for why some of the reported variations in outcomes exist (between those within a relationship and those experiencing a relationship breakdown). Understanding these mechanisms is absolutely crucial in interpreting the extent to which the

various associations are indicative of a causal relationship, and also in identifying protective factors that can minimise harmful outcomes. This will include reviewing the evidence for explaining any negative impacts of relationship breakdown, as well as the evidence highlighting the benefits of being in a couple relationship.

2. The review will discuss the latest research outlining risk factors for an increased likelihood of relationships breaking down (or remaining intact).

3. To extend the review from reporting the 'average' effects of relationship breakdown, it will explore why some people are more at risk or resilient to the effects of this breakdown.

4. The review will present the evidence for effective relationship support programmes, as a means to prevent some of the potential impacts of relationship breakdown from occurring.

5. Rather than focus exclusively on the negative impacts of relationship breakdown, this report will adopt a balanced approach. This will be by noting the situations where the impacts of relationship breakdown are temporary rather than ongoing, and also where they are favourable.

6. The review will draw reference to evidence noting the close association between the couple relationship, effective parenting and the parent-infant and child relationship (especially in this chapter's policy context and in Chapter 5).

1.4 The current context of relationship breakdown

It is important to place this report into its current context in terms of research, policy and practice.

Research

In reference to research, this is not the first report of its kind to present an overview of the impacts associated with relationship breakdown. Four notable reports have been conducted since the mid-1990s. They are summarised below.

In 1995, Fiona McAllister (from One Plus One) presented evidence of the predominantly health consequences of marital breakdown within the context of the Government's 'The Health of the Nation' Green Paper (Department of Health, 1991). This report covered data on mortality and various indicators of morbidity including stress, somatic impact, behavioural response, and mental health relating to both adults and children. Unlike the McAllister (1995) report, the three remaining studies included more reference towards the economic and financial costs of relationship breakdown.

Indeed, in the 1998 Australian House of Representatives' Legal and Constitutional Affairs Committee report, the impact of marriage and family breakdown is estimated to cost the Australian nation at least three billion dollars a year (and possibly twice that once the indirect costs and personal and emotional trauma are added). The six billion dollars per annum equates to about 1% of Australia's GNP (House of Representatives' Legal and Constitutional Affairs Committee, 1998).

The third study of note was compiled by Sir Graham Hart in his report to the Lord Chancellor on The Funding of Marriage Support review (Hart, 1999). In this report he notes the impact of marital breakdown on couples, children and society in various ways. These included human misery, suicide, damage to children's education and subsequent criminal behaviour. Again, the reference to the economic burden of marital breakdown is noted in terms of costs for social security, legal aid, social services, tax allowances and National Health Service (NHS) treatment. The estimate from the Hart report was five billion pounds or around 0.5% of Great Britain's GNP (based on data from 1994).

The fourth and most recent review was conducted by Family Matters (Lindsay et al., 2000). This report was notable in drawing more detail to the varying relationship types. Encompassed in the 'Cost of Family Breakdown' were relationships where people were formerly married or cohabiting, as well as more specific reference to single parenthood. The impacts upon crime, education, and health are noted, alongside the socio-economic aspects. The authors note that "as a generalization, the likelihood of adverse outcomes for children from broken families is about twice that from intact families" (Lindsay et al., 2000, p.5). They also refer to the previous studies noted above as underestimating the direct economic cost of family breakdown within Great Britain, which they estimate as fifteen billion pounds per annum. Of additional relevance to the economic impact of couple relationship breakdown, the latest available figure has been cited by the Social Justice Policy Group (2007), who estimate that within the UK "family breakdown costs the taxpayer £20-£24 billion each year" (p. 24). This report forms the basis of policy recommendations to the Conservative Party (see later under Policy context).

Acknowledging the most notable reviews of marriage or family breakdown that have been conducted in recent years provides an important context for this review. With the last report conducted in 2000, this current publication will, first of all, present a much needed update. In similar fashion to the Lindsay et al. (2000) report, this review will also reflect the growing variety of relationship types beyond married and divorced. In addition, with the economic estimates changing most rapidly of all, this review will include a specific chapter on the issues to consider when estimating the economic costs of relationship breakdown.

Policy

The leading political parties of the UK have long been concerned about relationship breakdown, with particular interest on the links between family breakdown and poverty. This interest has been demonstrated through the launch of the Social Exclusion Unit within a few months of New Labour coming to power in 1997. The reference to family breakdown is explicitly made in the Government's definition of social exclusion as "what can happen when people or areas have a combination of linked problems, such as unemployment, discrimination, poor skills, low incomes, poor housing, high crime and family breakdown. These problems are linked and mutually reinforcing" (Cabinet Office, 2008). Partly supported by Government funds, the Centre for the Analysis of Social Exclusion (CASE), established in 1997, has prioritised research into how family structures and parenting contribute to social disadvantage. A significant part of this work has involved exploring the impacts of marital breakdown on social disadvantage, in the context of financial hardship, housing and education and employment opportunities. More recently, the Social Exclusion Taskforce (established in 2006) published the Think Family report (Social Exclusion Taskforce, 2008) emphasising the major role for services to 'think family' in order to break the cycle of inter-generational exclusion.

The importance of preventing family breakdown has also been referred to in a number of additional policy documents. These include the 'Every Child Matters' Green Paper (Department for Education and Skills, DfES, 2003) that set out a number of ways to support parents and carers in improving the lives of children. Following the consultation, the Government published 'Every Child Matters: the Next Steps' (DfES, 2004), and passed the Children Act 2004, providing the legislative framework for developing more effective and accessible services focused around the needs of children, young people and families.

In addition, the RESPECT drive is a cross-Governmental strategy to tackle anti-social behaviour. This agenda recognises the importance of early intervention in tackling the factors associated with anti-social behaviour (DfES, 2006). The importance of maintaining stable families where respect is learnt is seen as a crucial component, and illustrated through family intervention projects and parenting programmes. More recently, the Government White Paper 'Aiming, High For Children: Supporting Families' (DfES, 2007a), highlights the ongoing policy context of supporting stable family relationships in order to improve childhood outcomes:

"Children's outcomes are best when they grow up in a stable family structures with a positive relationship between parents. The quality of each parent's relationship with the other is vital. Government wants to support stable relationships between parents. However, where relationships break down, the Government also wants to provide the necessary support to ensure children get the best start." (DfES, 2007a, p.35).

Additionally, the 'Every Parent Matters' policy document (DfES, 2007b), the development of the new Department for Children Schools and Families (DCSF) in 2007, and the publication of the 'Children's Plan' (DCSF, 2007) again recognise the importance of providing support for families. A central component of this support is to help prevent family breakdown where possible. To illustrate, the Children's Plan states:

"An effective family policy must start with supporting strong couple relationships and stable, positive relationships with families. Good local services are important in helping families cope with the inevitable stresses and strains.....It is important that services can recognise and support people through these periods of instability. For example, health visitors through the One Plus One [authors of this review] programme are being trained to listen to parents, spot problems between them following the birth of a baby, and offer specific help to the couple as well as ensuring the healthy development of the child." (DCSF, 2007, p23-24).

More recently, the 'Child Health Promotion Programme' (DCSF, 2008a) reiterates the important policy connection between family and child well-being, noting the importance of "Supporting strong couple relationships and stable positive relationships within families...." (p.7). The DCSF continues its commitment to strengthening families in the 'Children's Plan: One Year On' (DCSF, 2008b) where one of the priorities for 2009 is as follows:

"Introduce new ways to support parents at times when their relationships come under strain, and give more support to children when family relationships break down." (DCSF, 2008b, p.7).

Finally, the significance of family support and stability is shared across the remaining leading political parties. Indeed, 'Family Values' was a recurrent theme in the Conservative Government of John Major, and the theme of the family has been revived by the current Conservative Party under David Cameron. In 2006, David Cameron launched the Social Justice Policy Group, aiming to find ways to empower people to move from poverty to wealth. The product of this group was the publication of 'Breakthrough Britain' (2007). Promoting family policy is a core component of this report, backed by claims that the financial cost of family breakdown are up to £24 billion per year and costs each tax payer alone £800 per year. Recommendations include Family Service Hubs with an enhanced role for health visitors, a new Marriage and Relationships Institute, relationships education in schools, and the removal of the 'couple penalty' or fiscal disincentives for couples staying together. Their report into family breakdown concludes as follows:

"We believe that the tide of family breakdown (dysfunction, dissolution and dad-lessness) can be turned.......We unashamedly support an institution that can be so beneficial, but acknowledge that there is much preparatory work to be done to improve the relational health of the nation, especially in communities subject to multiple disadvantage." (Social Justice Policy Group, 2007, p.12).

This report builds on evidence from the earlier Social Justice Policy Group's, 'Fractured Families' report (2006), that notes the imbalance between parenting and couple relationship support allegedly established by the current Labour Government.

Practice

The policy context noted above has driven the development of a wider family-centred approach for a diverse range of professionals including those working in health, education, social care, and the legal system. More specifically, strengthening family support staff is seen as an essential component of this practice. Sure Start Children's Centres (first established in 1999 as a result of the 1998 Comprehensive Spending Review) are seen as critical to this support, by integrating the services provided by midwives, nursery nurses, health visitors and a range of early years staff. One Plus One (authors of this review) are playing a leading role in providing this support. As an illustration, One Plus One has created the evidenced-based 'Brief Encounters'® training programme which aims to support frontline practitioners in listening to, and providing valuable support for, couples and families undergoing relationship tension and stress. Independent evaluations, including a Randomised Controlled Trial, have demonstrated the positive impacts of this training programme on frontline practitioners and parents (Corney, 1998; Simons et al., 2001; Simons et al., 2003).

Naturally, it is difficult to specify the number of failing couple relationships that can be effectively reconciled through innovations in practice. However, the expansion of marriage and relationship counselling services provides an indication of this extent alongside the development of relationship education programmes (see later in this review). Moreover, the Government commitment to saving the saveable marriages is shown through the 1996 Family Law Act (HM Government, 1996) which states that "the parties to a marriage which may have broken down are to be encouraged to take all practicable steps, whether by marriage counselling or otherwise, to save the marriage". The earlier cited review by Hart (1999), in addition to documenting the impacts of marital breakdown, also evidenced the case for effective marriage support and strengthening couple relationships. Hart argued that the interventions were typically sought too late, if at all, at a stage when the relationship could not be reconciled. Critically, through voluntary sector funding to support training, service provision and good practice, his report advocates the case for relationship support programmes that can make a difference in maintaining and improving couple relationships. From reviewing a number of studies, Hart concludes the case for relationship support as follows:

"A rational approach to the funding of marriage support must take into account what evidence there is about the benefits it confers: for example, how far is it effective in averting marriage breakdown or in minimising the damage when such breakdown has irretrievably occurred?..... The conclusions I draw from the evidence and from discussions with other researchers are as follows. A high proportion of people using marriage counselling consider that they have derived benefit from it. This may simply take the form of feeling better, for a time at least, about their difficulties; but in addition many people are helped to modify their relationships and, in a significant number of cases, to save their marriage." (Hart 1999, Points 29-31).

1.5 Complexities in reporting the evidence – relationship formation and dissolution

Documenting the impact of relationship breakdown is a complex task. There are two main areas of complexity that need be outlined and they provide an important context to how the data presented in this review should be understood. This section deals with issues surrounding relationship formation and dissolution, and includes points surrounding relationship comparisons and initiation of breakdown. The following section (1.6) will address the validity of the research data available. These two sections will close by highlighting the types of studies and data that have been prioritised in this review.

1.5.1 Relationship comparisons

In terms of relationship formation and dissolution, comparing the differences between those in relationships to those where relationships have broken down involves a number of problems that need to be acknowledged. For example, for the 'in relationship' group, are we including married, cohabiting, and 'visiting' as equivalent groups? Also, how do we consider those remarried and step-families, especially as some children find transition into the latter family form especially difficult (see Chapter 5)? Should they be better considered as different types of 'in relationship' groups? We have already introduced the diversity in relationship forms that are often grouped together as 'cohabiting' or 'closely involved', and discussed the different expectations about relationship stability that may present for different age groups or in different scenarios.

Likewise, for those where relationships have broken down, do we regard divorcing, divorced, separating, separated, divorced and since remarried, and widowed as equivalent groups? As noted earlier, several studies reviewed in later chapters recognise the importance of seeing divorce as a 'process' encompassing the divorcing and divorced transitions (Rodgers and Pryor, 1998; Clarke and Berrington, 1999; Amato, 2000; Booth and Amato, 2001). And what about those who are not in a relationship and who have never experienced a relationship breakdown, same-sex couples, couples with or without children, and those whose relationship has broken down after (for example) one, five, ten or twenty years? Also, when considering the impacts on children, is it possible to assess the impacts of couple relationship breakdown on children who may have up to five different parents – an egg donor, a sperm donor, a surrogate mother who hosts the pregnancy, and the two social parents whom the child knows as 'mum' and 'dad' (Golombok, 2006). Likewise, outcomes for children in stepfamilies may differ where, for example, the stepparent has children from a previous partnership compared to where all children in the family are related to the mother.

Also, where should the more tentative or casual romantic relationships be included in terms of the 'in relationship' / 'relationship breakdown' groups? These problems are heightened by some definitions of marital status which can be confusing, in the sense that non-married can include 'never married', 'single', 'divorced', 'separated' and 'widowed', all of whom could be in a couple (albeit non-married) relationship. Indeed the definition of 'single' is not always used to define a person not in a couple relationship, but may be used to include those who are in a non-married couple relationship (see later when presenting the introductory data).

1.5.2 Initiation of breakdown

In addition, should divorced or separated couples be categorised together irrespective of who initiated the separation? (For the majority of cases in the UK[2] and US this is women – Sakraida, 2008). Indeed, adults can experience different trajectories of stress from divorce according to this initiation. As an example, the effects of divorce may not be apparent until the legal separation is completed for a spouse who wanted the marriage to continue. Conversely, stress may be more apparent at an earlier stage for the initiating spouse who, by the time the divorce is legal, could be in a state of relief (Amato, 2000).

Fortunately, these arduous questions raised above do not require a definitive answer, as the nature of the comparison groups is likely to be chosen by those responsible for the research evidence being reviewed. However, the important point is to acknowledge these complexities and limitations, as well as recognise that the reviewed evidence will be unlikely to include the full range of 'in relationship' / 'relationship breakdown' groups outlined above.

1.6 Complexities in reporting the evidence – validity of the research data

The second area of difficulty concerns the quality and validity of the research data being reviewed. In comparing the differences between the 'in relationship' and 'relationship breakdown' groups, a crucial distinction needs to be made between whether the impacts are deemed to be associated with relationship breakdown or actually caused by relationship breakdown. This degree of interpretation is critical in understanding the true (more causal) impacts of couple relationship breakdown. There are three sets of interrelated factors that can affect this: the range of variables included, the study design, and distinguishing between association and causation (as follows).

1.6.1 Validity of data – variable inclusion ability to explain effects

The first concerns the range of different variables that are included in models to determine the relationship between couple relationship breakdown and outcome. To take an extreme example, one study could be reporting the differences in mental health outcomes between married and divorced couples with no other factors considered. If the divorced group reported more mental health difficulties it would be incorrect to assume that getting divorced caused this effect. To attribute causation, a whole host of additional variables would have to be considered and controlled for, such as whether the two groups were similar (aside to their marital status) according to income, housing, age, employment status, socio-economic group, their own family background, etc. Indeed, it may be plausible that the different employment status of the two groups was, in fact, the main cause of their mental health problems rather than the fact that their relationship had broken down. Without measuring these other factors in this example, the precise nature of this correlation would never be possible to conclude. Although large representative samples can work to offset these difficulties, the possibility still remains that a number of such findings are spurious due to the potential influence of many different confounding variables. Of the potential confounders, controlling for the effects of personality types, genetic composition and behaviours that can affect outcomes is especially difficult.

Similarly, there are likely to be numerous characteristics of couples where relationships are more prone to breakdown that may inadvertently be reported as a result of the breakdown. For example, low income has been associated with an increased likelihood of divorce (Burgess et al., 2003; Rogers and DeBoer, 2004). However,

2. During 2005, 68% of the total divorces in England and Wales were requested by women (ONS, 2008a). This does not necessarily concur with an assumption that women are more likely to initiate a divorce than men (for example, the requesting of a divorce by women may be the result of her husband's infidelity).

distinguishing between whether income acts as a trigger for, or a cause of, or as a result of relationship breakdown is problematic. Likewise, because less healthy people may be selected out of relationships or more prone to relationship breakdown, people's health and well-being status outside of a relationship may be a product of these predispositions rather than the breakdown of the relationship itself. The key question, using these examples, is does relationship breakdown cause low income or poor health status, or is it the case that poor and unhealthy people are more likely to have relationships that dissolve? (See section 1.6.3 later in this chapter).

Furthermore, an additional complexity concerns how a relationship breakdown may impact on certain outcomes (such as physical health) through its effects on other variables (such as increased alcohol consumption). These mediated effects are often difficult to disentangle and this makes it problematic to ascribe relative importance to different variables. Even if numerous additional variables are included in studies, the presentation of a direct linear association between predictors and outcomes (impact of relationship breakdown) is often too simplistic. The problem of multicollinearity[3] may also have an effect in such studies given the high degree of correlation between a number of variables. For example, there is a close correlation between being in a relationship and being a parent, both of which could impact upon certain outcomes with the independent effects difficult to discern.

1.6.2 Validity of data – study design

An additional factor affecting the validity of the conclusions is the study design. A sophisticated study design has the capability of reducing the role of confounding variables and can thus derive more valid conclusions towards the effect of relationship breakdown. An ideal approach, but purely theoretical in this context to illustrate the complexities, is to adopt an experimental design. This involves randomly assigning large numbers of couples into two groups: those that separate and those where relationships remain intact. Murphy (2007) makes this point in relation to child outcomes whereby he states:

"The ideal comparison would be between children in two groups of families which were identical in every respect except that one group had experienced disruption and the other had not, but this is clearly unlikely to be the case." (Murphy, 2007, p.58).

He adds that the only meaningful comparison is knowing the outcomes that would arise if relationship breakdown did not occur which, by definition, is unknown. The important point to observe is that a somewhat cautious approach must be assigned to many of the data reviewed in this report, due to the study design limitations inherent in measuring the impact of relationship breakdown. Murphy (2007) emphasises this point further and introduces the complexities faced in such a review that will be detailed later in this chapter:

"For example, families that dissolve may be more likely to have a history of parental arguments, family stress and other similar effects. Furthermore, the results may show an association between child health effects and family dissolution, but this does not mean that family dissolution is the cause." (Murphy, 2007, p.58).

In relation to Murphy's observations, these points were also raised in the work of Sampson and

3. Multicollinearity is where two or more predictor variables in a regression model used to predict outcomes are highly correlated. This affects the ability or power of the regression model in calculating the predictive power of these individual, highly correlated predictors.

colleagues (2006) in documenting their counterfactual life-course approach to address the issue of causal status (see Chapter 10):

"The association of marriage with a wider range of adult outcomes is well accepted but controversial. Whether crime, mortality, binge drinking, drug use, depression, employment status, or wages, the literature is replete with findings suggesting that marriage is linked to well being. The meaning of these associations is another matter altogether. Questions of selection and confounding are paramount. For example, we may observe that married men are less likely to commit crime or be unemployed than unmarried men, but problems with differential selection into marriage hamper causal conclusions. Yet unlike in some social experiments with housing vouchers of job training, we cannot randomly assign marriage partners. Research must thus rely on observational data that yield ambiguous results subject to alternative interpretations." (Sampson et al., 2006, p.466).

With such ideal (randomised) designs not possible, the most significant and available studies are the impressive longitudinal (often cohort) studies following large numbers of people through their life-course. The key strength of these studies is to have information about people both before and after their relationship breakdown. These studies are, consequently, able to observe how changes in relationship status may have impacted on them and others. Although by no means conclusive, studies of this nature provide the most convincing indication of a causal relationship between relationship status and well-being. This is because longitudinal designs allow sample members to serve as their own control group, with the impact of relationship breakdown observed by comparing outcomes before- and after this breakdown. Critically, longitudinal studies avoid the need to compare two groups that may differ in their background characteristics which may also influence the health and well-being outcomes post relationship breakdown (as in a selection effect – see later). Nonetheless, although an extremely useful design, evidence for morbidity and mortality differences are particularly difficult to track given that these outcomes may only be apparent many years after the breakdown (Wood et al., 2007). Unlike cross-sectional studies, longitudinal studies that track the same people should be acknowledged as the design that is most suitable (and feasible) in unravelling the different contributions of selection and cause (see next section) in explaining the impact of relationship breakdown. Nonetheless, although longitudinal studies have been referenced widely in this review, it is important to point out that there have been recent advances in multiple measures, designs and statistical approaches that have attempted to further our understanding over the precise link between relationship breakdown and outcomes (see Chapter 10).

1.6.3 Validity of data – association, causation and prioritising data

Closely related to the association / causation debate are the competing explanations for the impacts of relationship breakdown. Although dealt with in greater detail in Chapter 7, readers should be aware that there are three main theories behind this. Murphy (2007) presents a useful synopsis of these theories. The first is selection effects, whereby unhealthy people are less likely to marry or stay married since ill-health is said to interfere with establishing and maintaining relationships. The selection theory is unable to support a causal relationship between relationship breakdown and well-being. Selection theory argues that poorly functioning people (predisposed to score low on well-being after a relationship breakdown) are especially likely to divorce. This predisposition or pre-existing factors, rather than the divorce itself, causes a lowering of well-being (Amato, 2000). Likewise, when examining the impacts on children, selection theory implies that poor child outcomes post-divorce may be the product of poor parenting and family functioning prior to divorce, rather than the divorce itself. Nonetheless, selection theory can also produce a causal effect in the sense that such poorly functioning people may be the reason, or cause, of the relationship breaking down (Amato, 2000).

The second theory concerns the protective effects of marriage that can provide a buffer against stress. These benefits include social interaction, intimacy, companionship, support, financial reward and the fostering of more healthy lifestyles. The breakdown of a relationship removes these protective benefits. The third theory concerns the effects of stress that are faced due to a relationship breakdown or through the bereavement felt due to the death of a partner. The second and third theories, unlike the selection theory, are more indicative of a causal relationship between relationship breakdown and outcome. In relation, Amato (2000) contrasts his 'Divorce-Stress-Adjustment Perspective' to selection theory, with the former used to explain how marital disruption causes adjustment problems which lead to a lowering of well-being (Amato, 2000, see Chapter 7 for further detail).

These theories are by no means mutually exclusive. However, a key challenge faced by many of the studies reviewed in this report is to decipher the contribution made by each of them in accounting for the difference in outcomes associated with relationship breakdown. Based on the above note, unravelling these theories will go someway to explaining whether the impacts of relationship breakdown can be considered causal. Some leading researchers have drawn conclusions relevant to the debate. Murphy (2007) in reviewing census evidence from the UK reports that "There is clear evidence of the protective effect of marriage over and above the selection effects". (p.66). Reviewing evidence from the US, Waite and Gallagher (2000) observe how the benefits of marriage are still evident when selection and health status are taken into account. They provide support for the protective effects of marriage, by suggesting that "....something about marriage itself moves people toward a healthier way of life" (p.52). Amato (2000), from a review of studies during the entire 1990's, concludes that "In general, studies support the notion of divorce causation, but a degree of selection also might be operating" (p. 1,275).

Further detail covering issues such as the direct physiological pathways through which relationship status affects health, the role of stressors or mediating variables, the indirect associations through health compromising behaviours associated with relationship status, and relationship quality versus relationship status will be covered in Chapter 7. In addition, detail will be provided as to why the severity and duration of the outcomes varies from person to person according to the presence of moderating or protective factors (Amato, 2000).

The overriding point to make from this discussion is that with people being exposed to a variety of different influences, it is clearly difficult to state for absolute certainty that relationship breakdown is the primary cause of some of the outcomes reported. Indeed, there are likely to be many different causal pathways leading to a particular outcome, one of which could be the breakdown of a relationship. Nonetheless, the same conclusions derived from different studies, involving different samples, can go some way in providing a convincing argument towards a more causal effect. In this review, therefore, drawing on complementary and extensive evidence to illustrate a particular impact of relationship breakdown will be adopted where possible. Moreover, offering plausible explanations to the reported impacts of relationship breakdown also lends more weight to the possibility of causation.

The issue of the association / causal relationship is a theme running throughout this review and one that cannot be emphasised enough. The essential point is that although associations between relationship breakdown and outcomes are reasonably easy to draw from the data, inference of a causal relationship, or that relationship breakdown leads to such an outcome is fraught with difficulties. There are no studies in this review proving, with 100% certainty, that a relationship breakdown resulted in such an outcome. However, through the use of sophisticated study designs using representative population samples and advanced statistical techniques, there is a powerful argument that causal relationships may be apparent in some circumstances. Note the hesitancy and cautious approach in the prior statement. This is further compounded by the fact that all outcomes documented in this review can be a product of a whole host of different forces besides relationship breakdown. Poverty, socio-economic status, genetic predispositions, age and sex, to name just a few. This is also exacerbated by the fact that relationship breakdown is not randomly distributed throughout the population, with higher rates found among those experiencing greater material and social adversity (Hawthorne et al., 2003). So when comparing those divorced to those not divorced, one is not comparing equal populations (hence the importance of longitudinal designs where people serve as their own control group with events pre- and post-divorce compared). Nonetheless, the purpose of this review will be to alert the reader throughout where evidence may offer stronger support for a causal relationship, in contrast to more descriptive data whereby only associations can be derived. As far as an introduction to the review is concerned, this problem of assigning associations to causal effects is the most important point to observe. The reasons behind this are neatly summed by Rutter (2009) as follows:

"Such reasons include genetic mediation of the causal risk effect, social selection (allocation bias), and reverse causation......the main problem in moving from an observed association to a causal inference did not lie in the effect of known measured confounders, but rather in the effect of unknown, unmeasured confounders". Rutter (2009, p.3).

In appreciation of these complexities, priority in this review will be given to the most robust evidence derived from longitudinal cohort studies where several covariates have been controlled for (often called the net relationship). These will be prioritised, for example, over studies where potential confounders are excluded from the analysis or from cross-sectional studies (often called the gross relationship). Studies that acknowledge or control for the range of characteristics that may mitigate a causal relationship are deemed as more noteworthy. Alongside the validity of the conclusions drawn from these studies, it should also be reiterated that priority will be given to UK data given the aim of the study outlined previously. As a further basis to this review, the next chapter contextualises the reviewed research by outlining trends in relationship formation and dissolution. This will provide a graduation to further chapters and emphasise the timely production of this review.

1.7 Conclusion and key findings from Chapter 1

This first chapter has provided an introduction to the review, by outlining its aim and intended audience as well as highlighting some of the complexities and challenges encountered. The review is also contextualised in the current climate of practice, policy and research. As for all chapters in this review, a list of key points emerging from this introduction are now presented.

- The review will provide up-to-date evidence on the effects of couple relationship breakdown.

This review is innovative by including the breakdown of a range of couple relationship statuses (where possible), and also by including detail on variety of 'related issues' (such as mechanisms behind the impacts) and by providing a framework for assessing the economic costs.

- This report has been written for a broad audience. It will be of interest to researchers, students, policy-makers and practitioners working in the field of parenting and couple relationships. The review is intended for a UK-based audience. However, much of the reviewed research has been conducted overseas, in particular from the US.
- To assess the effects of relationship breakdown, the approach will be to compare, where possible, the average outcomes among people (couples and children) affected by relationship breakdown to their lives prior to separation and to those whose relationships remain intact. Although adopted in several of the reviewed studies, it is important to note that this approach is not equivalent to comparing those, for example, who are married to those never married, as the latter may not have experienced the stressful events of relationship breakdown, divorce or widowhood. The 'stress' of relationship breakdown is one of the main theories to advance our understanding of the impacts.
- Reporting the 'average' outcomes may overlook instances where relationship breakdown is favourable (for example, in cases of high conflict relationships) and, similarly, the findings may disguise instances where the outcomes are extremely poor.
- There is great diversity in relationship formation, which is likely to result in different impacts of relationship dissolution. Married, remarried, cohabiting and 'closely involved' are some examples. However, with married people being more easily identified than other relationship forms, most of the reviewed research focuses on the effects of marital breakdown.
- The review reflects the growing recognition towards strengthening couple relationships and how this is integral in affecting the well-being of infants, children and adults. Supporting the couple relationship is also essential in fostering effective parenting. In relation to this, developments in policy and practice have acknowledged the importance of preventing relationship breakdown and minimising the impacts where this relationship is irretrievable. There is convincing evidence that some relationships can be repaired, improved and prevented from breaking down.
- In documenting the impact of relationship breakdown, the validity of the data reviewed is key in deriving meaningful conclusions. The types and range of variables included in studies, and the design adopted, will influence the ability to distinguish causal relationships from descriptive associations. Although associations between relationship breakdown and outcomes are reasonably easy to draw from the data, inference of a causal relationship, or that relationship breakdown led to such an outcome, is fraught with difficulties. It is impossible to prove, with 100% certainty, that a relationship breakdown alone has resulted in such outcomes.
- The key to establishing whether the association between relationship breakdown and outcome is causal is to assess the extent to which 'selection' effects are occurring. Selection bias occurs when comparing samples (e.g. married and divorced) that differ in a number of ways (e.g. history of mental health problems) that makes the impact of relationship breakdown difficult to discern. Selection theory argues that poorly functioning or less healthy people

(predisposed to score low on well-being after a relationship breakdown) are especially likely to divorce or experience a relationship breakdown. This predisposition or pre-existing factors, rather than the breakdown itself, may cause a lowering of well-being, and thus a causal relationship cannot be inferred (see Chapter 7 for more detail). The possibility of reverse causation (e.g. alcohol use causing relationship breakdown rather than vice-versa) and the inability to rule out other influences (behaviour, genetics, personality, etc.) bring further complications.

- In appreciation of these complexities, priority in this review will be given to evidence derived from substantial prospective longitudinal cohort studies where several covariates have been controlled. Longitudinal designs allow sample members to serve as their own control group, with the impact of relationship breakdown observed by comparing outcomes before- and after-breakdown. Critically, longitudinal studies avoid the need to compare two groups that may differ in their background characteristics which may also influence the health and well-being outcomes post relationship breakdown (as in a selection, non-causal effect). Of all the data reviewed, those derived from these designs will have a greater potential to infer a causal relationship between relationship breakdown and outcome.

Chapter 2
Data on couple relationship formation and dissolution

2.1 Introduction

This chapter introduces the reader to the latest British, UK, and England and Wales data on relationship formation and dissolution. There have been some striking trends observed over the last 40 years or so which have affected the family environment experienced by adults and their children. They serve to place a very important context to the research literature that will be presented later in this review. Data will be presented on marriage and divorce, civil partnerships and cohabitation and children and family formation. A summary of key findings will be presented at the end of the chapter.

2.2 Marriages and divorces

Family life and relationship formation in the UK has changed a great deal since the 1950s. Figure 1 (ONS, 2009) shows trends in the annual number of marriages (weddings) in the UK since 1950 to the most recent available data of 2007. This Figure shows the peak in new married relationships at around 480,000 in 1972 (attributed to the post-Second World War baby boom), and the subsequent decline in marriages to 2001. Since then, the number of marriages increased slightly and has since reverted to the downward trend with around 270,000 weddings reported in 2007 (2.7% lower than in 2006). For England and Wales, the latest available figure (data collected from 2007)

Figure 1 – Trends in the annual number of marriages in the UK: 1951 to 2007 (ONS, 2009)

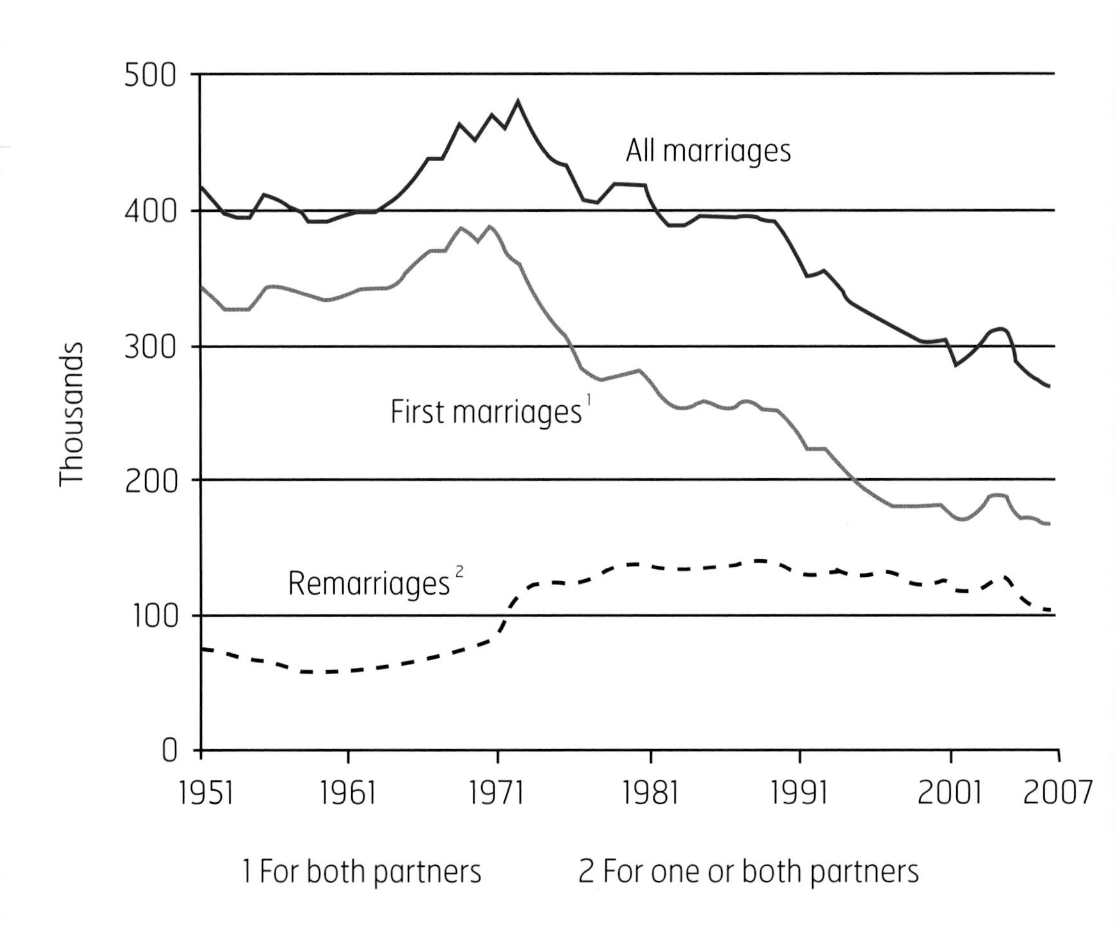

of 231,450 new marriages is the lowest number since 1862. In 2007, remarriages for one or both parties accounted for 38% of all marriages.

These trends are also reflected in the marriage rate which accounts for the changing population structure of those people in the marriageable age group. In 2006, the 'first marriage rate' (discounting the 'remarriage rate') for men was 22.8 men marrying per 1,000 unmarried men aged 16 and over and was down from 24.5 in 2005. The 'first marriage rate' for women in 2006 was 20.5 women marrying per 1,000 unmarried women aged 16 and over and again was down from 21.9 in 2005. These 2006 marriage rates, for England and Wales, are the lowest on record (ONS, 2008b). At the same time, however, marriage remains the most prevalent form of partnership between men and women. In 2006 there were 17.1 million families of all types in the UK (including married or cohabiting couples with and without children, and single parents); around 7 in 10 were headed by a married couple (ONS, 2007a).

The annual number of divorces in the UK has increased since the 1950s, with numbers doubling between 1958 and 1968, and doubling once again by 1972 to around 120,000. The marked increase between 1968 and 1972 was largely a consequence of the Divorce Reform Act 1969 (HM Government, 1969, coming into effect in 1971 for England and Wales).[4] Since then, the number of divorces has remained relatively stable until reducing over recent years. Between 2006 and 2007, the number of divorces granted in the UK fell by 2.6% from 148,141 to 144,220 decrees made absolute.[5] This is the third consecutive drop in the number of UK divorces and the lowest number since 1977. The figure is 18% lower than the highest number of divorces, which peaked in 1993 (180,018) (ONS, 2007b). This reduction in divorce since 1993 partly reflects a lower potential for divorce given the decline in the numbers of people getting married alongside the increasing numbers forming cohabiting relationships (see later). Indeed, it is argued that the married population is growing ever more homogenous, given that the 'riskier marriages' may now be developed in the form of these cohabiting partnerships. Hawthorne et al. (2003) make this point commenting that marriage is now "increasingly confined to those sections of the population most committed to enduring unions and who are less likely to experience divorce." (p1-2). Note, in terms of outcomes, that 51% of divorced couples in 2007, in England and Wales, had one or more child under the age of 16 (ONS, 2008c). These trends over the last 50 years, and relatively recent decline in the number of divorces, is mirrored in the divorce rate (Figure 2), which fell for a third consecutive year in 2007 and by 10% compared with 2006 (in England and Wales). The current rate of 11.9 divorcing people per 1,000 married population is now at its lowest level since 1981 (ONS, 2008c). Prior to these recent reductions, the divorce rate was relatively stable between 1994 and 2004, ranging from 12.7 to 14.1 per 1,000 married population.

4. A selection of legislative changes relevant for this review are attached at Appendix 1.
5. A decree absolute marks the legal end of the marriage. This can be obtained once agreement between parties has been reached and six weeks and one day after the decree nisi.

Figure 2 – Divorce rate in England and Wales, 1981-2006 (ONS, 2008c)

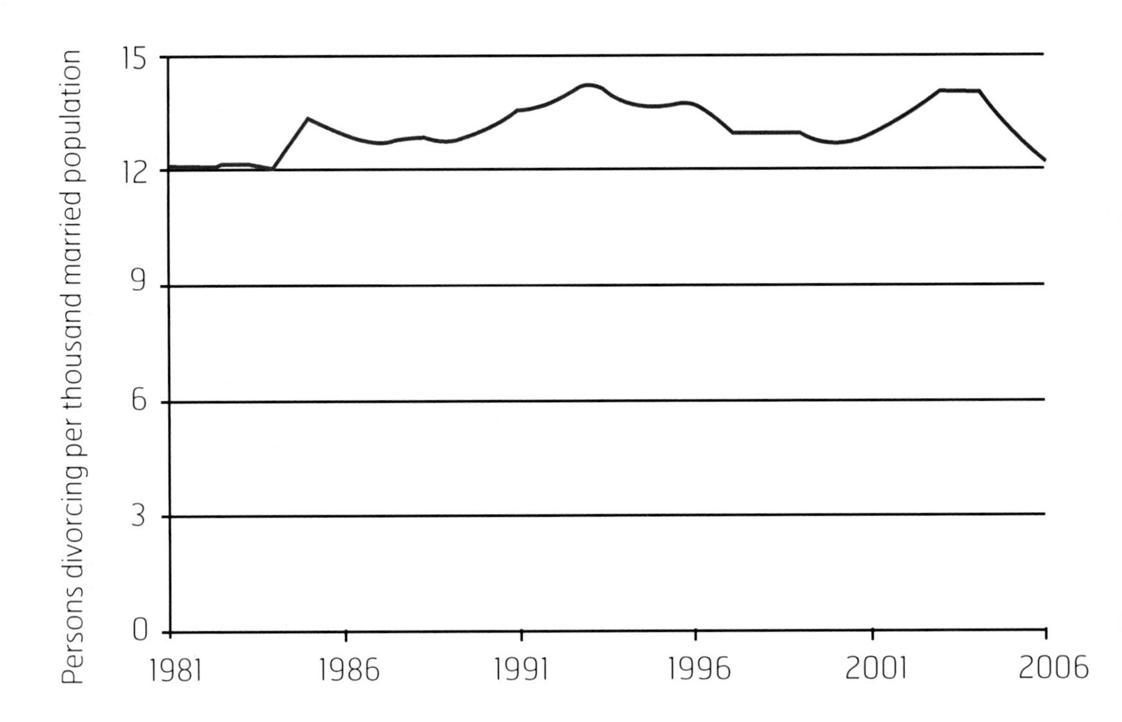

Repeat divorces are also more common, with one in five men and women divorcing in 2006 having a previous marriage ending in divorce – the proportion doubling over the last 25 years (ONS, 2008c). These trends in marriage and divorce are also reflected in the number of remarriages (Figure 1). For information, although the UK has one of the highest divorce rates in Europe (apart from some Scandinavian countries), it is significantly lower than the US.

A well publicised indicator of relationship breakdown is to estimate the proportion of marriages that will end in divorce. Although it is difficult to calculate a reliable figure, estimates have been placed at around 40% of marriages in England and Wales (Haskey, 1996). A more recent study (ONS, 2008d, using 2005 data) has provided an update on this figure, for England and Wales, to approximately 45% (an increase on the 1993/94 estimates). Taking into account complex mitigating factors such as migration and mortality, the 45% figure specifically refers to the proportion of marriages that will end in divorce prior to the 60th wedding anniversary, assuming 2005 divorce (and death) rates. Ten percent of these will survive to mark this celebration, while the remaining 45% of marriages will end due to death of one or both spouses.

The variations in this divorce proportion (using England and Wales data) are equally interesting with the likelihood of divorce varying according to both age at marriage and previous marital status. Among those marrying for the first time, there is an increased risk of divorce for those who marry at a relatively young age. For example, among previously unmarried bachelors who married in 2000, and who were under the age of 20 at this time, 28% were divorced within five years, compared with 10% of those aged 30 to 34 year-olds who married in the same year. For previously unmarried spinsters aged under 20 at the time of marriage, 27% were divorced within five years, compared to 9% of 30-34 years olds who married in the same year (2000). The likelihood of divorce also increases among those who have been divorced previously. For example (and again using data from marriages in 2000), 14% of marriages among previously married men aged 30-34 ended in divorce within 5 years compared with 10% of previously unmarried men of the same age. The likelihood of divorce also varies by duration of marriage. For example, just over one-fifth of divorces occur within the first five years of marriage, and around half of all divorces occur within the first 10 years. Once marriages survive for a decade, under 31% would end in divorce, and if marriage continued for 20 years this figure would decrease to 15% (ONS, 2008d).

A major feature of this report's context is that these divorce statistics illustrate how couple relationships have become increasingly fragile over the last 40 years or so. Coupled with this trend has been the increased diversity of relationship and family forms that will now be presented.

2.3 Civil partnerships and cohabitation

An additional legislative landmark to the Divorce Reform Act was the Civil Partnership Act 2004 (HM Government, 2004, which came into effect in the UK in December 2005) and permitted same-sex relationships to have equivalent rights and responsibilities to civil marriage across a range of areas. Between December 2005 and September 2006, boosted by the change in legislation, 15,700 same-sex civil partnerships were formed in the UK, a figure that declined to 8,728 during 2007 (ONS, 2008e).

A further significant trend in couple relationships has been the increased number of people cohabiting (unmarried couples living together) since the 1980s, partly related to an increasing age at marriage and the decline in the marriage rate. In 1986 (the first-year data are available on a consistent basis) 11% of unmarried[6] men aged 16-59, and 13% of unmarried women aged 16-59, cohabited in Great Britain. By 2006 these proportions had roughly doubled in Great Britain to 24% (ONS, 2008f). Table 1 (survey data from 2006) shows that cohabitation is most likely among divorced men (34% compared to 22% of single men and 2% of widowed men). Among women, the greatest proportion cohabiting are those described as being single (27%, compared to 8% of widowed and 24% of divorced women). Note this evidence is confined to survey data as there is no formal registration of cohabitation (or relationship breakdown of former cohabiting partners).

6. 'Unmarried' is defined as either single, widowed, divorced or separated and either cohabiting or not cohabiting.

Table 1 – People cohabiting: by marital status, 2006[1]

Great Britain				Percentages
	Single	**Widowed**	**Divorced**	**Separated**
Men				
Cohabiting[2]	22	2	34	23
Not cohabiting	78	98	66	77
All men	100	100	100	100
Women				
Cohabiting[2]	27	8	24	9
Not cohabiting	73	92	76	91
All women	100	100	100	100

[1] Aged 16 to 59. Includes those who describe themselves as separated but were, in a legal sense, still married.
[2] Includes a small number of same sex cohabiting.
Source: General Household Survey (Longitudinal), Office for National Statistics (ONS, 2008f)

It is understood that many cohabiting couples, accepting of pre-marital sexual activity, are living together as a prelude to, or as an alternative to, marriage (termed 'nubile' cohabitation). The exception here may be young cohabiting couples where expectations of a long-term relationship may be minimal, and, therefore, may be similar in some ways to the 'closely involved' category discussed below. However, because cohabiting couples can translate into marriage, dissolve or continue, the impact of cohabiting couples breaking down is more complex and generally less understood than marriage (Clarke and Berrington, 1999). Therefore, the impact of marital breakdown tends to dominate most of the studies that will be reviewed in this report.

Alongside the increase in cohabiting couples, the recognition of those termed 'closely involved' has been a relatively recent phenomenon. These couples are distinct from married, cohabiting, separated/divorced and those not in a relationship. They are particularly interesting in that they include couples who are not able to be defined in the traditional marital status categories. They are, therefore, likely to include those with marriage-like responsibilities as well as those dating or 'seeing each other', or those with few expectations of the long-term nature of their relationship. Evidence from the UK 'Millennium Cohort Study' (MCS) reports that 6% of parents at the time of the birth of their child (the child born at the turn of the millennium) described themselves as 'closely involved' (Benson, 2006). The MCS, cited elsewhere in this review, is a longitudinal study of 18,819 children aged around 9 months in 2001-2002. Although an emerging group, research has identified the 'closely involved' as being at the highest risk of relationship breakdown (some 13.3 times more likely than married couples – Benson, 2006). There has also been unsubstantiated speculation that a proportion of these 'closely involved' couples may be living apart 'together' as a means to claim additional welfare support.

2.4 Children and family formation

Coinciding with these trends reported above has been the increase in the number and proportion of children who have experienced the effects of the relationship breakdown of their parents. Reporting the impacts of relationship breakdown on children is a key part of this review. As noted earlier, 51% of the total number of divorces in 2007, in England and Wales, involved children aged under 16. From this figure, it is estimated that 117,000 aged under 16 years in 2007 experienced the divorce of their parents. Twenty per cent of these children were under five and 63% were under eleven (ONS, 2008c). These numbers illustrate a rapid increase on the estimated 71,000 of those aged under 16 years experiencing the divorce of their parents in 1970 (ONS, 2006).

In illustration of the complexity of family forms, the children of divorced parents can live in a variety of situations, including single-parent families, stepfamilies (either cohabiting or remarried), grandparents, other relatives, and foster families. Over the last 15 years stepfamily composition has remained similar, except the proportion of stepfamilies that include the father from the previous marriage (increased from 6% to 10%). Those including the mother from the previous marriage comprise 84% of stepfamilies. This composition is shown in Table 2.

Table 2 – Stepfamilies[1] with dependent children[2] (Great Britain)

					%
	1991/92	1996/97	2000/01	2001/02	2006[3]
Child(ren) from the woman's previous marriage/cohabitation	86	84	88	83	84
Child(ren) from the man's previous marriage/cohabitation	6	12	9	9	10
Child(ren) from both partners' previous marriage/cohabitation	6	4	3	8	6
Lone parent with child(ren) from a previous partner's marriage/cohabitation	1	-	-	-	-
All stepfamilies	100	100	100	100	100

[1] Family head aged 16 to 59.

[2] Dependent children are persons aged under 16, or aged from 16 to 18 and in full-time education, in the family unit, and living in the household.

[3] In 2005 GHS data collection changed from financial to calendar year.

Source: General Household Survey (Longitudinal), Office for National Statistics (ONS, 2008f)

The increase in cohabitation has also seen more children born outside of marriage (Figure 3). The percentage of births outside of marriage in the UK has increased from 12% in 1980 to 44% in 2006 (ONS, 2008f). With most of these births jointly registered by both parents, this indicates an increase in the proportion of parents who are cohabiting at the time of birth. This is based on the fact that three out of four parents, when registering the birth, lived at the same address (ONS, 2007c). These trends also relate to the changing sequence of family formation with marriage, for increased proportions in today's society compared to previous generations, occurring after the transition to parenthood.

Figure 3 – Percentage of births outside of marriage 1988 to 2006 in the UK (ONS, 2008f)

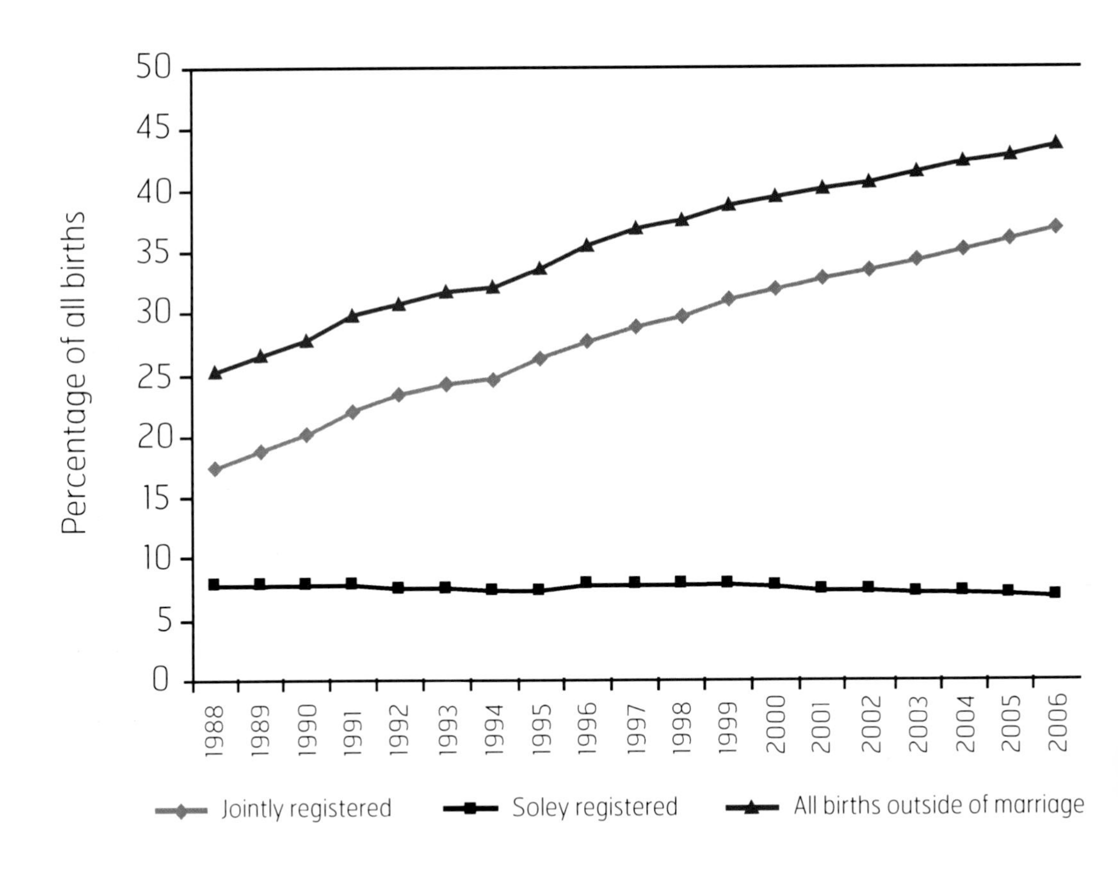

These changes in marriage, divorce, and cohabitation are reflected in the proportion of households having the 'traditional' composition of a couple with dependent children: in Great Britain this has fallen from around a third (35%) of all households in 1971 to just over a fifth (21%) in 2007 (ONS, 2008f), and also reflects the ageing population structure. Data from the 'Millennium Cohort Study' further illustrates these trends. Kiernan and Mensah (forthcoming) note that by the time the children were aged 5 years, 75% were living with both their parents compared to 90% of children born in 1970. Also, 41% of the MCS children were born to unmarried parents compared with 8% of those born in 1970 (although note that the MCS survey is disproportionately stratified to areas of high child poverty).

In relation, it is worth noting that following the first baby born to IVF in 1978, trends in child conception and development have shown further diversity in recent years. Indeed, it is now possible for children to have up to five parents: an egg donor, a sperm donor, a surrogate mother who hosts the pregnancy, and the two social parents whom the child knows as 'mum' and 'dad' (Golombok, 2006). Furthermore, an increasing number of lesbian parents and single heterosexual women are seeking assisted reproduction to conceive and raise children (Golombok, 2000).

2.5 Conclusion and key findings from Chapter 2

Many of these trends showing the increased fragility of couple relationships and diversity in family forms are mirrored in other westernised nations, such as the US. Cherlin (2004) highlights the 'Deinstitutionalization of American Marriage', noting a significant shift in the 1960s and 1970s from the 'companionate' marriage to the 'individualized' marriage. This shift is associated with a greater emphasis on personal choice, characterised by many of the trends seen in the UK (over the last 40-50 years) such as older age at marriage, more cohabiting relationships, increased divorce and relationship breakdown, and an increased proportion of children born outside of marriage.

These trends have shown the diversity in relationship formation and extent of relationship breakdown that is now apparent in the UK. Interestingly, with the emergence of cohabiting and 'closely involved' couples, together with rising divorce rates and the decline in marriage since the 1970s, it may well be that the married proportion of the population are now more homogenous than ever. With less people getting married, and the unstable marriages ending in divorce, the distinction between the advantageous state of marriage relative to those dissolved may be more pronounced than ever. Indeed, the stability of the relationship appears to be a critical issue, with more children born today into more unstable relationship forms. Evidence from the 'Millennium Cohort Study' has shown that the risk of relationship breakdown within the first three years after birth is 5.5 times greater for all unmarried couples (compared to married couples), 3.5 times for cohabiting couples and 13.3 times for the least stable 'closely involved' (Benson, 2006). It appears, therefore, that the variety of relationship forms is closely associated with the increasing proportion of adults and children that experience the effects of relationship breakdown. However, although marriage is seen as the most stable of relationship forms, there will always be many stable relationships outside of marriage that encompass the variety in contemporary family forms just described.

These introductory data include demographic indicators that are used to outline where relationship breakdown may be more likely (for example, more so among cohabiting couples than those married). This will be covered in greater detail in Chapter 8. However, it is worth emphasising at the outset that although this broad level of explanation is offered, there is still a dearth of research into the details of why relationships breakdown and why this is more apparent in today's society. There may be psychological, structural and societal forces at work that make relationship breakdown more evident, but the precise mechanisms within individual relationships are clearly complex and highly varied from one situation to another. Finally, it is hoped that by presenting these data justifies, arguably more so than ever, the need to develop an evidence base for the impact that relationship breakdown can have on couples, children and society. This evidence will be presented in the forthcoming chapters.

A summary of key findings from Chapter 2 are now presented.

- The annual number of marriages in the UK has shown a steady decline since the 1970s, although this has been interrupted by a rise in marriages in 2001. For England and Wales, the latest available figure of 231,450 new marriages in 2007 is the lowest number since 1862.
- The first marriage rate, 22.8 men marrying per 1,000 single (never married) men aged 16 and over and equivalent rate for women of 20.5, is the lowest on record for England and Wales.
- Nonetheless, marriage remains the most prevalent form of partnership between men and women. In 2006 there were 17.1 million families of all types in the UK (including married or cohabiting couples with and without children, and single parents); around 7 in 10 were headed by a married couple.
- The annual number of divorces in the UK has increased since the 1950s, with numbers doubling between 1958 and 1968, and doubling once again by 1972 to around 120,000. Since then, the number of divorces has remained relatively stable, until the last two years where the numbers have fallen. These changes in divorce statistics are set within the context of declining marriage rates since the early 1970s.
- The divorce rate fell for a third consecutive year in 2007 and by 10% compared with 2006 (in England and Wales). The current rate of 11.9 divorcing people per 1,000 married population is now at its lowest level since 1981.
- Based on 2005 data, it is estimated that 45% of marriages in England and Wales will end in divorce prior to the 60th wedding anniversary. Ten percent will survive to mark this celebration, while the remaining 45% of marriages will end due to death.
- Among those marrying for the first time, there is an increased risk of divorce for those who marry at a relatively young age. For example, among previously unmarried bachelors who married in 2000 in England and Wales, and who were under the age of 20 at this time, 28% were divorced within five years, compared with 10% of those aged 30-34 years who married in the same year. For previously unmarried spinsters aged under 20 at marriage, 27% were divorced within five years, compared to 9% of 30 to 34-year-olds who married in the same year (2000).
- The likelihood of divorce also increases among those who have been divorced previously. For example (using English and Welsh data from marriages in 2000), 14% of marriages among previously married men aged from 30 to 34 ended in divorce within five years compared with 10% of previously unmarried men of the same age.
- The likelihood of divorce also varies by duration of marriage. For example, just over one-fifth of divorces occur within the first five years of marriage, and around half of all divorces occur within the first 10 years (England and Wales).
- The Civil Partnership Act 2004 (which came into effect in the UK in December 2005) has permitted same-sex couples rights and

responsibilities identical to civil marriage. Between December 2005 and September 2006, 15,700 same-sex civil partnerships were formed in the UK, a figure that declined to 8728 during 2007.

- The proportion of people cohabiting within Great Britain in 2006, derived as a percentage of all unmarried (defined as either single, widowed, divorced or separated and either cohabiting or not cohabiting) men and women under the age of 60 has roughly doubled since 1986 to around 24%.
- There has been a recent recognition of couples described as 'closely involved'. They include those with marriage-like commitment and responsibilities as well as those dating or 'seeing each other', and those with few expectations of the long-term nature of their relationship. They are distinct to married, single, cohabiting, separated or divorced. Evidence from the UK 'Millennium Cohort Study' reports that 6% of parents at the time of the birth of their child described themselves as 'closely involved'.
- Around one-half of the total number of divorces in 2007, in England and Wales, involved children aged under 16. This proportion and associated numbers has increased since the 1970s, although it has remained relatively stable over the last couple of years, to a current annual figure of around 117,000 children aged under 16. Twenty per cent of these children were aged under five and 63% were under eleven.
- The percentage of births outside of marriage in the UK has increased from 12% in 1980 to 44% in 2006. The increase in cohabiting partnerships is indicated by three out of four parents living at the same address when registering the birth.
- These changes in marriage, divorce, and cohabitation are reflected in the proportion of households having the 'traditional' composition of a couple with dependent children: in Great Britain this has fallen from around a third (35%) of all households in 1971 to just over a fifth (21%) in 2007 and also reflects the ageing population.

Chapter 3
Impact of couple relationship breakdown on adults: Physical health

3.1 Introduction

This chapter will outline the impact that couple relationship breakdown has on the physical health of adults. By adults, we mean the adult members of a couple relationship that may have since broken down. In terms of physical health, this chapter will cover the following areas.

- Mortality.
- Morbidity (general and specific health issues).
- Health-related behaviours (e.g. drug and alcohol use).

Where possible, gender differences will be outlined and some of the explanations for differential rates of mortality and morbidity will be introduced (although more detail on this will be provided in Chapter 7). As for all forthcoming chapters, a conclusion and brief summary of findings will be presented.

3.2 Mortality

Data reporting the association between couple relationship breakdown and mortality are understandably of great interest. Since being first reported as far back as 1858 by William Farr, the association between relationship breakdown and higher mortality is unequivocal. However, as outlined in Chapter 1, this is derived from reviewing the 'average' effects of a relationship breakdown (i.e. this association does not apply to all people). Also, the mechanisms behind this association are extremely complex and it is difficult to ascertain the extent to which relationship breakdown has contributed to the differences in mortality. The evidence is derived from a mixture of nationally collated statistics and longitudinal survey data that frequently include additional measures that are controlled for (such as social class).

Statistics for England and Wales (ONS, 2007d) show elevated mortality rates for non-married males and females for all age groups between 25 and 64 years (Table 3 and 4). In these tables, 'single' is defined as never married, but may include those people who are in a non-married couple relationship as well as those that are not. Also, the 'single' category here and elsewhere in this chapter may include those who have never been in a relationship as well as those whose non-married relationship may have broken down. In this manner the marital status definitions do not allow a precise distinction between those in, or not in, a couple relationship at the time of death. Although the data are presented in a manner that does not take into account any potential confounding variables, the comparisons between married and non-married are stark. These figures show that the greatest difference is seen between widowed and married groups up to, and including, the ages of 40-44 among men and 45-49 among women. Thereafter (defined when referred to later as 'from middle age') the difference is greatest between the married and single groups. Those experiencing a breakdown of a married relationship (divorced) also show elevated mortality rates relative to the married group with the differences increasing from middle age to the age of 60 to 64. For interest, although the single groups show the highest mortality for ages between 60 and 64, further data from the Office for National Statistics (ONS) show that the difference between single, widowed and divorced diminishes in older age. In those aged 75 and over, single groups show slightly lower mortality rates compared to the previously married, although rates still exceed the married groups (Murphy et al., 1997; Murphy, 2007).

Overall, the elevation of mortality rates among unmarried groups is greatest among men of all ages. For example, comparing ages 45-49, the death rate for married men is 1.90 per 1000 population compared to 4.97 of those men classified as single and 4.09 divorced. The equivalent data for women are 1.50 (married), 2.77 (single) and 2.35 (divorced). Using Office for National Statistics data from England and Wales, Murphy (2007) notes that between the ages of 30 and 50, single men have death rates about three times that of married men, and single women have rates about double those of married women.

Table 3 – Death rates per 1,000 population by age group and marital status – males.

Age	Married	Single	Widowed	Divorced
25-29	0.49	0.75	1.12	0.86
30-34	0.51	1.15	1.71	1.08
35-39	0.72	1.86	2.48	1.69
40-44	1.05	3.08	3.13	2.56
45-49	1.90	4.97	4.89	4.09
50-54	3.18	7.81	6.55	6.73
55-59	5.29	12.30	9.51	10.10
60-64	9.08	20.79	17.45	17.69

Source: Mortality statistics: Series DH1 no.38, London, ONS, HMSO, 2007d.

Table 4 – Death rates per 1,000 population by age group and marital status – females.

Age	Married	Single	Widowed	Divorced
25-29	0.28	0.35	0.47	0.37
30-34	0.35	0.56	0.79	0.50
35-39	0.49	0.94	1.68	0.86
40-44	0.88	1.80	2.54	1.27
45-49	1.50	2.77	3.35	2.35
50-54	2.53	4.77	4.07	3.51
55-59	3.83	7.61	6.03	5.67
60-64	5.99	10.64	9.48	8.78

Source: Mortality statistics: Series DH1 no.38, London, ONS, HMSO, 2007d.

Projections undertaken by the Government Actuary's Department using national data for England and Wales indicate that higher mortality rates, across the life-course for single, divorced and widowed people (relative to those married), are set to continue (Government Actuary's Department, 2005). Interestingly, Murphy (2007) also shows how the difference in mortality rates by marital status, in England and Wales, has actually increased since divorce has become more common. This is contrary to theorists who argue that as divorce and relationship breakdown becomes more accepted in society, the mortality advantage of being married would diminish through time (see Chapter 7). As noted in the previous chapter, these mortality differentials may reflect the recent declines in marriages and the increased homogeneity of married partnerships (with those more predisposed to divorce and being less healthy selected out of marriage).

These differences in mortality according to marital status (not equivalent to relationship status) are apparent in other European countries. Datasets analysed in Hungary (Hadju et al., 1995), Netherlands (Van Poppel and Joung, 2001) and Finland (Martikainen et al., 2005) show comparable differences with lower mortality levels among married adults. A notable and recent study by Murphy and colleagues (2007) investigated mortality differentials by marital status among those aged 40 and over across seven European countries. Mortality differentials were examined over the period 1990-1999. The data included information on 19.3 million deaths and just under one billion person years of exposure (Murphy et al., 2007). The data show lower rates of mortality, or "mortality advantage" (p. 290), among married people compared to those single, widowed and divorced. In relative terms, the age-adjusted mortality rates for the married were typically 10-15% lower than the overall rate.

Drawing from such a huge dataset, the Murphy et al. (2007) results are extremely convincing and support the evidence noted earlier. Likewise, the seven European nations showed that the differentials in mortality are greater for men than women and increase steadily with age. Significantly, the differentials in mortality according to marital status are similar in magnitude across the seven countries. Also, for most countries and age groups, trends over the 1990s indicate an increase in relative mortality difference between married and non-married people, especially among the older age groups. This reported increase over time is evident among men and women (although the magnitude of the "mortality advantage" is greater among men).

From these various datasets, and arguably most convincing from the Murphy et al. (2007) study, the overriding conclusion is that not being married, or having a marriage that has broken down, is associated with an increased risk of death. However, of critical importance in interpreting the evidence, Murphy et al. (2007) notes the limitations which apply to all the reviewed studies above. That is, these datasets are most useful in identifying mortality differentials rather than explaining precisely why these differentials exist. Evidence from longitudinal studies, to be detailed next, may help to unravel some of these reasons.

Evidence drawn from longitudinal studies, although dealing with smaller numbers compared to national datasets, offer greater detail to the mortality/relationship status association by controlling for possible confounders. Studies of this nature have a greater potential indicate a causal relationship between relationship status and well-being. This is because longitudinal designs allow sample members to serve as their own control group, and this avoids the need to compare two groups that may differ in their background characteristics (that may produce a selection effect – see below). Nonetheless, evidence for morbidity and mortality differences are particularly difficult to track given that these outcomes may only be apparent many years after the relationship breakdown (Wood et al., 2007).

From a longitudinal study among British women for seven years, being single (defined as never married but not exclusively including those experiencing a relationship breakdown) has been shown to be associated with higher mortality compared to being married (Cheung, 2000). This study is particularly significant as the effect of marital selection is controlled for. As noted in Chapter 1, marital selection is considered as one possible reason for the differences in mortality between married and unmarried people, in that health can determine marital status (with those of poorer health less likely to marry or stay married). The alternative, 'protection hypothesis' suggests that marital status has a causal impact on mortality. By controlling for these marital selection effects, it is therefore possible to assess the case for a more causal association between marital status and mortality. The study used health and lifestyle data from 3,497 randomly selected women aged 35 or over in England, Wales and Scotland. Marital selection effects were controlled through five variables, including self-reported health status, smoking and alcohol consumption. The study showed that after adjustment to these selection factors, excess mortality (relative to married women) was seen among single women (Hazard Ratio or HR[7]=1.45) but not among those who were widowed and divorced (HR=1.09). There was also some evidence that unmarried status has different psychosomatic and behavioural implications. Being single and widowed were more associated with non-Cardiovascular Disease (CVD) and non-cancer deaths, and being divorced was more associated with cancer deaths. The author concludes that there are indications of a causal relationship between being single and excess mortality, aided by controlling for marital selection effects, although she also recognises the need for much longer-term studies to provide confirmation of this.

A more recently published longitudinal study assessing the impact of marital breakdown on the mortality of Danish males has been reported by Lund et al. (2004). This study was innovative by recording changes in marriage across the life-course among a relatively young population. Most other studies of a similar nature have been among older people with marital status recorded only at baseline. With over 10,891 participants in the study, all born in 1953, the outcome measure was the 401 deaths occurring from 1993 to 2002. Marital status was recorded on four occasions prior to 1993, and included the duration of years married and divorced. Therefore, the study was able to assess the impact of marital status at different ages on mortality, as well as the cumulative effects of the number of years married and divorced. Multivariate regression analyses included the following covariates (that were controlled for): mother's marital status, father's social class at time of birth, birthweight, psychiatric admission and having a biological child. The study found a strong protective effect of being married, compared with not being married or divorced, at every age, with a stronger association among middle-aged men. Therefore, middle-aged men had a higher mortality risk when divorced compared to younger men who divorced. Their study supported a model of cumulative effects, with the strength of these associations

7. The Hazard Ratio is the effect of an explanatory variable, in this case marital status, on the hazard or risk of an event. A higher Hazard Ratio in this context indicates a greater risk of mortality.
8. Multicollinearity is where two or more predictor variables in a regression model (used to predict outcomes) are highly correlated. This affects the ability or power of the regression model in calculating the predictive power of these individual, highly correlated predictors.

increasing by numbers of years married and divorced. Having experienced more than one marital break-up was also associated with higher mortality. Although the authors acknowledge the problems around multicollinearity[8] and inability to control for a range of additional variables such as behaviour, income and personality, this study clearly shows that being divorced was a strong predictor of mortality in young men, independent of the covariates included. Of additional interest, and acknowledging the small sample size, the mortality cases were mainly suicides and cirrhosis-related.

From the US, Kaplan and Kronick (2006) used the 1989 National Health Interview Survey merged with the 1997 US National Death Index (n8=67,000), to investigate the relationship between marital status and mortality. Using logistic regression analyses, the study controlled for a number of demographic and socio-economic characteristics such as age, sex, ethnicity, education, income, and perceived health. Compared to the married population, those divorced or separated had a 27% greater risk of mortality and those widowed had a 39% greater risk. The greatest risk was seen among the never married who had a 58% increased likelihood of mortality. These findings for the never married concur with the earlier studies and national data showing that single people, from middle age, fare worst of all among those who were unmarried (rather than divorced, separated and widowed). Kaplan and Kronick (2006) also reported that never being married was a greater risk factor (compared to divorced, separated and widowed) for death from 'all causes' (as a combined measure), and particularly in terms of infections (Kaplan and Kronick describe as "presumably HIV", p.760). Deaths from cancer and pulmonary disease were more likely among the divorced, separated and widowed.

Although Kaplin and Kronick (2006) recognise that causal effects of marital status are difficult to assess, the study does pose some interesting explanations for the reported associations. For the "never married penalty" (p.764), they highlight that those who are never married are more socially isolated, including those reporting more illness (those being ill make less suitable marriage partners through the marital selection hypothesis), and engage in higher risk behaviours that impact upon their health (see Section 3.4, Health-related behaviours). With the difficulties in accounting for these mortality differences, this paper provides insights into plausible explanations.

Additional data sets from the US, including the National Longitudinal Mortality Study (n[9]= 281,460 men and women aged 45 years and over) further confirm the association between marital status and mortality (Robles and Kiecolt-Glaser, 2003). Across all causes of mortality, non-married individuals (never married, divorced/separated and widowed) had higher rates of mortality compared to married individuals. Authors Robles and Kiecolt-Glaser (2003) conclude the evidence as follows:

"The relationship between marital status and mortality exhibits a generally consistent pattern in longitudinal studies, with marital status affording greater protection from mortality for men compared to women (50% higher among women, 250% higher among men)." (Robles and Kiecolt-Glaser, 2003, p.409).

These greater gains by men from marriage are confirmed by data from three nationally representative longitudinal studies (two from Britain and one from the US) reviewed by Grundy et al. (2005). Among men, the data showed that a lower percentage of time married and having

9. n=sample size.

experienced multiple marriages or divorce were associated with higher mortality rates at older ages.

With interest in life annuity policies, Spreeuw and Wang (2008) used data from 11,454 Canadian insurance contracts (from couples) to specifically assess the impacts of widowhood on mortality rates. The study used data over a five-year period, and compared the mortality of widows and widowers to mortality experienced by married couples. Using a mathematical model, the study concludes that the mortality of widow(er)s is significantly higher than those whose partner is still alive. In more detail, they report that the impact of death of the partner is stronger at higher ages, where relationships have lasted longer. This contrasts to those widowed at younger ages where a more extensive social network may help people to recover from bereavement. This study, therefore, illustrates that the impact of being widowed increases mortality (relative to those married), and more so among the older age groups.

Longitudinal studies showing similar impacts of marital changes across the life-course on mortality are reported by Lillard and Waite (1995); Ebrahim et al. (1995); and Tucker et al. (1996). Tucker et al. (1996) found that being inconsistently married (i.e. having experienced a marital break-up) was significantly associated with an almost doubled mortality compared with those consistently married. Lund et al. (2006) also documented evidence of divorced men having a doubled risk of mortality by the age of 39.

Although occasionally noted in the work reviewed above, a number of studies have explored the relationship between marital status and specific causes of death in greater detail. In the UK, data from 1983-2004 shows that despite an overall reduction in suicide rates since the early 1980s, there has been no overall narrowing of the gap in suicide rates between those who are married and those who are single (never married) or divorced (ONS, 2008g). Across this time period, suicide rates for those single and divorced men, and divorced women, were generally around three times higher than for married men and women. Using trend data, there was some evidence of the widening of the differentials among women (suicide rates increased from two to nearly three times more likely among single women across the time period) offset by a slight narrowing of the differentials among men (ONS, 2008g). From the US, data from the 'National Longitudinal Mortality Study' (Kposowa, 2000) also explored the association between marital status and suicide. Although from a subset of the sample, this vast longitudinal project consists of approximately 3 million records with over 250,000 identified mortality cases. After controlling for age, sex, race, education, family income and residential location, the study found that the risk of suicide among divorced men was over twice that of married men (RR=2.38, CI 1.77-3.20).[10]

Again from the US, Eaker et al. (2007) explored the relationship between marriage and death from Coronary Heart Disease (CHD). The study involved 3,682 participants who were followed up for 10 years. Significantly, after controlling for a number of risk factors for CHD such as age, systolic blood pressure, body mass index, cigarette smoking, diabetes, and total cholesterol/high density cholesterol, the married men compared with unmarried men were almost half as likely to die during follow-up (RR=0.54, CI=0.34-0.83). However, among those that were married, poor resolution of conflict (through self-silence) and work distress also increased the risk of dying from CHD.

10.RR = Risk Ratio or presentation of the probability of risk and CI = Confidence Intervals set at 95% i.e. there is a 95% likelihood that Relative Risk of suicide in this instance falls between these two values.

In reference to survival rates from breast cancer in the US, Weihs et al. (2007) found that there were two aspects of relationships that were protective against breast cancer progression among 90 women. Decreased mortality was predicted by a 'confiding' marriage (RR=0.31, CI =0.10-0.99), and number of dependable, non-household supports (RR=0.41, CI=0.21-0.80). A composite measure of 'close relationships' had a strong protective effect against mortality from breast cancer (RR=0.30, CI=0.13-0.69). The latter studies illustrating the protective effect of marriage provide some further insights into explaining these mortality differentials.

3.3 Physical morbidity

Studies reporting associations between relationship status and physical morbidity also offer some explanation behind the differential mortality rates noted above. Psychological morbidity is covered in Chapter 4. In this section we look at the associations between marital and relationship status with health in general. The following section (3.4) looks at the associations between relationship status and specific health-related behaviours that can have an impact on health status. In general, the morbidity data are consistent with the mortality differences noted above, with married people showing less ill-health compared to single and previously married groups. Further detail of this evidence is now outlined.

3.3.1 Physical morbidity – general health status

The negative impact of living alone on health has been evidenced among young men participating in a longitudinal study in England and Wales (Donkin, 2001). This study assessed the relationship between living alone (not necessarily indicative of relationship status) and risk of death or long-term illness. The longitudinal study is a 1% representative sample of the 1971, 1981 and 1991 England and Wales census. This study found an association between living alone and elevated mortality rates. To illustrate, those men aged between 45 and 64 who were living alone in 1971 and 1981 had a 50% greater likelihood of death than those of similar age who lived with others. In terms of morbidity, or long-term illness, those men aged between 45 and 64 who were living alone in 1981 were significantly more likely to report such illness, after controlling for age. Thirty per cent of those living alone in 1981 reported a long-term illness in 1991 compared to 21% of those living with others (in 1981). Using multivariate logistic regression analysis, the likelihood of long-term illness was independently and significantly associated with increased age, lower social class and becoming divorced or remaining single. Donkin (2001) notes how her research concurs with other studies that have reported a 'bereavement effect' on health during the transition from marriage to widowhood, and negative impacts upon those who were divorced or separated. Through her longitudinal design, Donkin (2001) notes how these effects on health are likely to persist for many years after the event.

Using data from the nationally representative British 'General Household Survey' for three consecutive years, Benzeval (1998) assessed the health differences between single and married parents. From this substantial sample of 16,736 parents, the study was significant in controlling for the socio-economic differences between single and couple parents that may have an impact on health status. From reviewing 15 studies that had compared the health of single and couple parents in Britain, Benzeval (1998) notes that her research was innovative by possessing a sufficient sample size to derive meaningful conclusions. As a limitation, however, not all single parents had experienced a relationship breakdown, with 36%

reporting that they were not widowed, divorced or separated from their partner. Five health variables were used as outcome measures and included subjective assessments of 'good', 'fairly good' and 'not good' health status. Other outcomes included longstanding illness and disability. In the multivariate regression analysis, demographic (e.g. age, gender) and socio-economic factors (e.g. employment status, household goods) were controlled for. Prior to controlling for these potential confounders, single parents reported worse outcomes than couple parents. However, when the demographic and socio-economic factors were controlled for, the differences in health were reduced but still remained statistically significant for four out of the five health measures: 'fairly good or not good health', 'not good health', 'longstanding illness' and 'recent limiting illness'. This suggests that rather than the health differences being a product of differences in socio-economic status, Benzeval (1998) concludes that there is something distinctly health-damaging about being a single parent per se.

More recently, using data on family structure and health statistics, Murphy (2007) notes the association between health status and marital status in two domains – psychological well-being and limiting long-standing illness. The data, derived from the 2001 Health Survey for England (n=14,838 adults aged 20 and over), also include cohabiting couples and are presented below in Table 5:

Table 5 – Relative risk of health problem by marital status (married=1.00), by sex (2001 data).

Psychological morbidity	Men aged 20-64	Women aged 20-64
Single	1.14*	1.22*
Separated	1.50*	1.58*
Divorced	1.32*	1.26*
Widowed	1.02	1.30*
Cohabiting	1.10	1.14*

Limiting long-standing illness	Men aged 20-64	Women aged 20-64
Single	1.15*	1.24*
Separated	1.11	1.34*
Divorced	1.26*	1.27*
Widowed	0.96	1.18*
Cohabiting	1.12	1.07

*statistically significant at the 5% level.

Source: Focus on Families (Murphy, 2007)

In general, the data confirm the marriage advantage, with poorer health seen in the non-married groups, especially the divorced and separated. The Table also shows how marital breakdown appears to have a more detrimental impact on the general physical and psychological health of women relative to men. Note how the greater marriage advantage among men reflected in the earlier reported mortality data is not mirrored by these two self-report measures. Also, the greater disadvantage seen among the separated and divorced is not entirely in tune with the earlier reported mortality data which showed the highest rates of mortality among single people (albeit from middle age which is not discernable from these data). Further reference to psychological morbidity is outlined in Chapter 4.

Interestingly, Murphy (2007) also notes that the health differences may not be so apparent for the more extreme age groups, with young married or cohabiting adults often being more disadvantaged than single people in terms of employment and education. Also, those single people aged 80 or over actually report better health than married groups, possibly because those single people reporting more ill-health may have died by this age (Murphy, 2007).

Also in terms of general morbidity, Prior and Hayes (2003) report data on the relationship between marital status and bed occupancy within health and social care in Britain between 1921 and 1991. Using census data, the study population was defined as the total population of individuals who, on the night of the census, occupied beds in communal establishments designated as general health or social care facilities. Prior and Hayes (2003) note how married individuals demonstrated much higher levels of physical health than the non-married (widowed, divorced and single), with this relationship holding strong throughout all the census years (1921-1991). In further illustration, in 1991, 90% of the beds occupied were by non-married people (compared to 10% occupied by those who were married) – described by the authors as a "large marriage gap" (p.132). Given the study time frame, the data are also able to show significant trends such as an increase in this marriage gap throughout more recent times. Furthermore, more recent data show an increase in bed occupancy among widowed individuals rather than the never married or single that predominated in the earlier parts of the last century. The Prior and Hayes (2003) paper is also noteworthy by presenting a brief review of the international evidence surrounding marital status and health. Their study provides "ample evidence" (p.146) for marriage to offer protection against institutionalised treatment that has also been reported elsewhere. This evidence is neatly summed in their own words:

"Despite the increasing rejection of the centrality of marriage within modern life, the health benefits of marriage have been consistently confirmed in both national and international research. This is particularly the case in the United States, where the majority of studies, or the most comprehensive investigation of the issue, has taken place. In other words, irrespective of whether the association between martial status and mortality, marital status and morbidity, or, to a lesser extent marital status and health service use is considered, all the evidence points to a positive relationship between marital status and health". (Prior and Hayes, 2003, p.126).

Based on their measure of bed occupancy, Prior and Hayes (2003) also highlight how their research concurs with some more recent findings reporting that marriage has more beneficial health effects for women (e.g. the earlier reported morbidity data undertaken by Murphy, 2007). The authors highlight the inconsistency in the international literature about these gender differences, by citing research in the 1980s that reported more beneficial effects of marriage for men compared to women. This is clearly an area in need of further investigation.

Further evidence showing that married people tend to have less ill-health than those unmarried has also been reported by Macintyre (1992); Wyke and Ford (1992); Joung et al. (1997); Murphy et al. (1997); Aldous and Ganey (1999);and Amato (2000). The Amato (2000) review, examining studies published in the 1990s, states that "...the general conclusion that emerges from studies published in the 1990s – that the divorced are worse off than married in multiple ways – is consistent with research conducted in the 1980s..." (p.1,274).

More recently, three further studies add weight to these conclusions. Firstly, Ashby and Step (2004) found that 52% of widowed, divorced or separated people in the UK had been an NHS hospital patient[11] within the last two years, compared to 36% of single people. This study also found that 43% of married or cohabiting respondents had been an NHS hospital patient over the same time period (Ashby and Step, 2004). Secondly, and from the US, Meadows (2007) uses data from the 'Fragile Families and Child Well-Being Study' (n=4,331) to demonstrate further health differences (see Chapter 5). The study found that one year after the birth of a child, continuously married fathers were in better mental and physical health than unmarried fathers, although the disparity did not increase over time. Thirdly, a review of evidence on the health benefits of marriage by Wood and colleagues (2007) in the US reports robust evidence for the association between marriage and fewer doctors' visits, shorter hospital stays and reduced risk of nursing home admission. For these examples in the Wood et al. study (2007), the role of a partner deputising for professional health care seems intuitive.

Further research from the US is also particularly prominent in assessing the link between couple relationships and health. Using data from the National Health Interview Surveys (1999-2002), Schoenborn (2004) reports prevalence estimates by marital status among a total of 127,545 adults aged over 18. From this vast dataset, married adults were generally found to be healthier than adults in other marital status categories (widowed, divorced or separated, never married and cohabiting). Regardless of sex, race, income, or education, the percentage of adults reporting 'fair' or 'poor health' and those who had an 'activity limitation' was lowest among married people across three main age groups (18-44 years, 45-64 years and 65 years and over). Interestingly, and after adjusting for age, married and never married adults were less likely to report low back pain and severe headaches compared to those divorced, widowed and cohabiting (Schoenborn, 2004). Schoenborn (2004) concludes that "for the most part, data presented and discussed in this report offer further evidence that married adults are healthier than those in other marital status groups" (p.10). Further evidence from the US 'National Longitudinal Mortality Study' (Johnson et al., 2000) supports the evidence that married adults have lower rates of morbidity and mortality compared to unmarried adults.

3.3.2 Physical morbidity – specific health conditions

Further evidence of the association between relationship status and morbidity has been observed through specific health conditions. Nilsson et al. (2007) used data from 2,533 non-disabled men and women enrolled in the Danish 'Intervention Study on Preventive Home Visits' programme. After being followed up 4.5 years later, the study found that living alone, relative to those not living alone, significantly increased the

11. NHS hospital patient defined as outpatient, day patient, Accident and Emergency department or inpatient.

risk of onset of disability (RR=1.74, CI=1.22-2.47) and the risk of sustained poor functional ability (RR=2.35, CI=1.44-3.84) among men. However, and most interestingly, these effects were not observed among single-living women.

A significant study undertaken among 9,011 British civil servants observed the relationship between the quality of 'close relationships' and Coronary Heart Disease (De Vogli et al., 2007). This prospective cohort study followed people for an average of 12.2 years and questionnaires were completed about their close relationships on two occasions. The study was impressive in its control for a range of additional variables including socio-demographic characteristics (age, sex, marital status and employment), biological factors (obesity, hypertension, diabetes and cholesterol) and health behaviours (smoking, alcohol, exercise and diet). After controlling for these factors, they found that people who experienced a high level of negativity in their relationship were 1.34 times more likely to have a CHD event compared to those with more positive relationships. Their study showed the particular importance of negative relationships having a damaging impact on CHD. Their concluding comment makes this point concisely:

"In conclusion, a person's heart condition seems to be influenced by negative intimate relationships. In this prospective cohort study, we showed that negative aspects of close relationships, not confiding/emotional support and practical support, are associated with CHD." (De Vogli et al., 2007, p.1,956)

Note also how this final point introduces us to some of the mechanisms behind the relationship between marital status and physical morbidity, in terms of emotional and practical support and good relationship quality, that will be examined further in Chapter 7. In addition, De Vogli et al. (2007) cites several studies where the relationship between poor marital quality and elevated CHD has been evidenced (for example, Orth-Gomer et al., 2000; Lakka et al., 2002; Hanson et al., 2002 and Troxel et al., 2005). Therefore, although being married may be a protective factor against physical morbidity (as reported by studies in this section), it appears that this may only be apparent in satisfying relationships. Indeed, the quality of the marital relationship may be more of a significant predictor of CHD than marital status in this instance. Evidence reported by Coyne et al. (2001) also shows the relationship between marital quality and congestive heart failure. Their analyses showed that marital quality had a statistically significant relationship with patient mortality from congestive heart failure, independent of the prediction based on illness severity (Coyne et al., 2001). Further reference to the quality of the relationship has been evidenced by Gallo et al. (2003) and Grewen et al. (2005) who found that those in high quality relationships had better outcomes than those in low quality relationships and those who were single.

A recent study conducted in the US by Holt-Lunstad and colleagues (2008) explored in greater detail the impacts of marital status, relationship quality and network support on blood pressure. Although derived from a relatively small (n=303) and cross-sectional sample, they conclude that the quality of the marital relationship was of primary importance. By comparing measures of relationship satisfaction to blood pressure, they conclude, "Therefore, marriage must be of a high quality to be advantageous. In other words, one is better off single than unhappily married". (p.5). The study also found that the spousal relationship (in high quality marriages) is more influential than other social relationships in lowering blood pressure. Therefore, a supportive social network among single people is not able to compensate for the beneficial health effects of being in a high quality marriage.

A study by Gallo et al. (2003) explored cardiovascular risk factors among middle-aged women, and assessed the influence of marital quality and marital status. Their longitudinal study, among 493 women from the University of Pittsburgh's 'Healthy Women Study', assessed variables on more than five occasions and across 13 years on average. The study also examined outcomes in terms of cardiovascular risk factors (e.g. blood pressure and cholesterol) and risk factor trajectories during a period of increasing risk for women (middle age and the menopausal transition). This study confirmed the importance of marital quality and satisfaction, with the former showing a health advantage when compared with participants in low satisfaction marriages and with those unmarried (single, widowed or divorced). Those in satisfying marriages, relative to the others, showed less cardiovascular risk factors and, in some cases, showed a lower risk trajectory on possible risk factors. The authors conclude that "marriage appears to confer health benefits for women, but only when marital satisfaction in high." (p.1).

Further conclusive evidence is drawn from a paper by Robles and Kiecolt-Glaser (2003) who cite evidence from several different longitudinal studies in the US linking marital quality, or greater 'marital strain', to elevated general illness, mortality (in terms of recovery from illness) and cardiovascular disease. From their own laboratory study of 90 newly-wed couples, followed up after 10 years, they describe how marital strain affects health through three primary physiological pathways that mediate the relationship between stress, social relationships and health: cardiovascular function, neuroendocrine function and immune function (see Chapter 7 for more detail on these mechanisms).

The notion of marital or relationship quality is most significant. When examining the impact of couple relationship breakdown, it should not be assumed that all relationships are satisfying. Based on the evidence introduced above, it appears that the quality of the relationship is of primary importance. Stressing the importance of relationship quality has important ramifications for policy and interventions. Thus, it is not just a case of preventing marriages or relationships from breaking down that is key, but also to maintain and improve the quality of those relationships that do exist even if they remain intact and do not dissolve (see Chapter 7).

Although the above evidence appears conclusive, there were occasions where marital status was not associated with specific morbidity. For example, Jatoi (2007) reported data from 5,898 non-small cell lung cancer patients and found that there were no differences in survival or quality of life based on marital status at the time of diagnosis.

3.4 Health-related behaviours

The impacts of relationship breakdown on physical health have also been shown to operate indirectly, by increasing the incidence of risky health behaviours which, in turn, can have a negative impact on health. One of the most widely observed health related behaviours in this context has been alcohol misuse, with heavier levels of drinking reported among divorced and single people compared to those married. For both single and divorced people, unravelling the nature of this association is extremely complex. For example, elevated rates of drinking among single people could be due to selection, in that heavier drinkers are less likely to marry. Also people may be more likely to divorce due to their heavy drinking behaviour (in a reverse causation manner). However, the relationship breakdown association could also be causal, with minimal social or emotional support from a former partner, for example, leading to heavier drinking.

One of the leading studies that has sought to clarify this complex relationship was undertaken by Power and colleagues (1999) using data from the 23- and 33-year follow-ups of the 1958 'British Birth Cohort Study'. At age 23, 12,537 people were interviewed and this decreased to 11,405 at age 33. Using this longitudinal design, and with the associated sample sizes, the results and conclusions drawn are clearly robust. The study assigned heavy drinkers based on a weekly consumption in excess of 35 units for men and 20 for women. At both ages, the divorced adults had the highest consumption levels with married reporting the lowest. Although high rates of drinking persisted among never married people, the impacts of the relationship breakdown on drinking levels was most evident. Although average levels of drinking declined between ages 23 and 33, increases were most apparent among those divorced compared to those married (OR[12]=2.05, CI=1.49-2.83 [men] and OR=2.61, CI=1.67-4.09 [women]). These differences were even more noticeable among those recently divorced (for example, OR=4.97, CI=2.86-8.57 [men]). In real terms, more than a third of recently (within the last two years) divorced men reported drinking more than 35 units in the week preceding interview. Significantly, the advanced analyses used in this paper demonstrate that these differences in alcohol misuse were not entirely due to selection, but were more causally associated with divorce and (to some extent) leading to relationship breakdown.

A study referred to earlier in this chapter also draws out the link between relationship status and health compromising behaviour. Using data from the US National Health Interview Surveys (1999-2002, n=127,545), the Schoenborn (2004) study explored the relationship between marital status and leisure-time physical inactivity, cigarette smoking, alcohol use and obesity. After adjusting for age, she found that married adults were the least likely to be physically inactive, with widowed adults the most likely. Cigarette smoking differed notably, with about 1 in 5 married adults smoking, compared to double, or 2 in 5, who were living with a partner or who were divorced. Women were marginally less likely to smoke, although the ratio of smoking among married versus non-married women was comparable to men. Alcohol consumption, measured in terms of 'heavier drinking', showed greater gender difference with the married groups again showing healthier behaviour. To illustrate, the rates were highest among men who were widowed, divorced or separated or living with a partner (all around 9%) and lowest for those men who were married (4.1%).

Table 6 – Relative risk of cigarette smoker by marital status (married=1), by sex, 2001.

Cigarette smoker	Men aged 20-64	Women aged 20-64
Single	1.32*	1.75*
Separated	1.43*	1.66*
Divorced	1.79*	1.99*
Widowed	1.27	1.67*
Cohabiting	1.44*	1.66*

*statistically significant at the 5% level.
Source: 'Focus on Families' (Murphy, 2007)

12. OR = Odds Ratio or the relative odds, in this case, of increasing consumption of alcohol. This is not the same as the Risk Ratio reported earlier which compares the probability of risk.

Among women, the highest prevalence of heavier drinking was seen among those living with a partner (7.3%), with all other marital status groups being similar at around 3-4%. However, the Schoenborn (2004) study found that never married adults were less likely than adults in any other marital status category to be obese regardless of ethnicity, education or poverty.

Evidence from an additional study referred to earlier is also of interest. From the 'Health Survey for England' (n=14,838 adults aged 20 and over), Murphy (2007) shows the relative risk of cigarette smoking by marital status. His data are summarised below and the elevated rates of smoking among the non-married are stark, and are similar to the US evidence on cigarette smoking above. Note however, within England, the married / non-married differences in smoking were greatest among women (Table 6).

Interestingly, a recent paper (Heinz et al., in press) demonstrated further effects of the couple relationship on health-related behaviour. They found that being married and having a close relationship with your partner reduced the likelihood of drugs misuse, over the course of 35 weeks, among adults enrolled in an addiction treatment programme. Other reported associations between substance misuse and relationship breakdown have been reported from a literature review by Leonard and Rothbard (1999) and a qualitative study in the US by Kissman (2001), and additional evidence is outlined in Chapter 7 when discussing the benefits of being in a relationship.

Finally, this section has detailed the negative health behaviours associated with relationship breakdown. For an alternative perspective, it has also been recognised that being in a relationship or married can promote less healthy behaviours. A recent synthesis of research evidence by Wood and colleagues (2007) in the US mentions that "Marriage has mixed effects on health behaviours....." (p.1). In line with the research evidence above, they highlight the association between marriage and a reduction in alcohol consumption and drug use. However, they review a number of rigorous studies that report associations between marriage and a more sedentary lifestyle, with marriage leading to modest weight increases for both men and women and a decline in levels of physical activity. This review adds that marriage, however, is generally associated with more positive health behaviours, including the use of preventative care such as cancer screenings.

Interestingly, the Wood et al. review (2007) pays much attention to the complexities of drawing out causal relationships between marriage and health that were discussed at some length in Chapter 1. With this in mind, it seems appropriate to cite this evidence as a final finding for this chapter. Wood et al. (2007) make the critical point that the existing evidence surrounding marriage and health are based on descriptive methods that often fail to fully control for a range of other variables that may select healthier people into marriage (and less healthy people out of marriage). This is further complicated by studies focusing on health indicators pre- and immediately post-divorce. This raises real questions over whether premature mortality or morbidity, perhaps occurring decades after the relationship breakdown, can be attributed directly to that event. Only longitudinal studies offering data throughout the life-course could draw such firm conclusions. Based on this convincing argument, Wood et al. (2007) conclude that "...rigorous research evidence concerning the effect of marriage on specific physical health outcomes is limited, and few solid conclusions can be drawn." (p.5).

3.5 Conclusion and key findings from Chapter 3

This chapter has explored some of the physical

health impacts of couple relationship breakdown. The association between marital status and couple relationship breakdown to premature mortality is stark. A causal effect is naturally difficult to prove. However, evidence demonstrating the association between relationship breakdown and morbidity, and health-compromising behaviours, suggests that relationship breakdown may play an important role in contributing to such an outcome. Moreover, as documented by Murphy (2007), the protective effects of marriage such as social interaction, intimacy, companionship and support, that are assumed to decrease morbidity and mortality, indicates further the plausibility of a causal association. Although selection (non-causal) effects are present, it is argued that the protective effect of marriage is operating over and above this (Murphy, 2007): a critical conclusion to draw from the research evidence. This chapter concludes by listing key findings.

- The association between a couple relationship breakdown and higher mortality is unequivocal, although a causal effect is difficult to deduce.
- Mortality statistics for England and Wales (in 2007) show elevated mortality rates for non-married (single, widowed and divorced) males and females for all age groups between 25 and 64 years.
- National data (England and Wales) also show that the greatest difference in mortality is seen between the widowed and married up to and including the ages of 40-44 among men and 45-49 among women. For older age groups, the difference is greatest between the single (never married) and married groups.
- Overall, the elevation of mortality rates among unmarried (single, widowed and divorced) groups compared to those married is greatest among men of all ages. Likewise, marital status affords greater protection from mortality for men compared to women. Office for National Statistics data from England and Wales shows that, between the ages of 30 and 50, single men have death rates about three times that of married men, and single women have rates about double those of married women. However, and although there is some inconsistency in findings, separation and widowhood appear to have a greater negative impact upon the general physical and mental health of women compared to men.
- These differences in mortality according to marital status are apparent in other European countries. For most countries and age groups, trends over the 1990s indicate a relative increase in the mortality difference between married and non-married people, especially among the older age groups.
- Evidence from longitudinal studies that are able to control for potential confounders (such as marital selection and health differences, father's social class at time of birth, birth weight and psychiatric admission) supports the plausibility of a causal relationship between marital status and mortality.
- Studies indicate that the protective effect of marriage may be predominant in explaining health differences, rather than the effect of people being selected out of marriage, or being more predisposed to relationship breakdown due to their poor health status. However, throughout these studies, it must be acknowledged that the absolute certainty of a causal effect is hampered by not controlling for a range of additional but likely influential variables such as behaviour, income, genetics and personality.
- There is evidence of an 'accumulative' effect, with the strength of mortality associations increasing by the number of years non-married. More than one marital break-up is also associated with higher mortality.
- Specific estimations of the mortality risk from

the UK have included that, between the ages of 30 and 50, single (never married) men have death rates about three times that of married men, and single women have rates about double those of married women. Evidence from the US suggests that marriage provides a protective effect against mortality at the 50% level for women, and 250% among men. Other studies show that, compared to the married population, those divorced or separated had a 27% greater risk of mortality, those widowed had a 39% greater risk, and those never married had a 58% increased likelihood of mortality.

- Associations between marital status and morbidity are also evident. This applies to general health status and specific health conditions such as Coronary Heart Disease and blood pressure. Longitudinal studies, the controlling of potential confounders, and reviews of reviews point to a positive relationship between marriage and health.
- The likelihood of psychological morbidity and limiting long-standing illness is greatest among the divorced and separated, which contrasts to the differences in mortality which was greatest among single people from middle age.
- Significantly, for the few studies that have assessed relationship quality and health, the marriage must be of a high quality to be advantageous. Indeed, evidence suggests that the health outcomes for single people are more positive than those reporting unhappy marriages.
- The impact of relationship breakdown on physical health has been shown to operate indirectly, by increasing the incidence of risky health behaviours (such as alcohol and drug use) which, in turn, can have a negative impact on health. However, some studies have also shown that marriage is associated with more sedentary behaviours, lack of physical activity and weight gain.

Chapter 4
Impact of couple relationship breakdown on adults: Psychological health

4.1 Introduction

This chapter will extend the evidence presented in this review by examining the impact of relationship breakdown on the psychological health of adults. Included under this topic will be a range of outcomes including 'psychological well-being', as well as general mental health, depression and anxiety. The scope of the outcomes included in this chapter are broad, as illustrated by The World Health Organisation definition of mental health as follows:

"A state of complete physical, mental and social well-being, and not merely the absence of disease" (World Health Organisation, 2008).

Research evidence presented here will look at the impact of couple relationship breakdown on mental health outcomes in a variety of domains (such as those measured by general mental health questionnaires) and specific mental health outcomes (e.g. depression). Reference to how the impacts differ by gender will be added where possible. In addition, to help explain the reported associations, factors that can minimise or provide protection from the impacts will be outlined as well as a note about the causal pathways involved. Finally, this chapter will close by considering the role of selection and reverse causation in some of the observed psychological impacts and, as for previous chapters, conclude by summarising the key findings. Please note that health-related behaviours, including drug and alcohol use which are sometimes considered to be an aspect of mental health, were covered within Chapter 3.

4.2 Relationship breakdown and general measures of psychological health

A wide range of evidence has indicated an association between couple relationship breakdown and elevated levels of mental health problems. The majority are vast longitudinal studies which have been shown, in Chapter 1, to offer robust evidence of such claims.

An important study demonstrating this association has been presented by Gardner and Oswald (2006) who used the 'British Household Panel Survey' (BHPS) to examine the years before and after divorce. The BHPS is a nationally representative survey which follows the same individuals over a number of years, and has been in operation since 1991. The survey interviews all adults within a household, and where adults split off into other households they continue to participate along with the other adults within their new household. Over 10,000 people have been interviewed for the BHPS, with 430 experiencing a divorce, and 278 experiencing a transition to widowhood over the study period. Divorce was defined as either a legal divorce or marital separation. The time period studied by Gardner and Oswald, covered 1992 until 2001. As Gardner and Oswald (2006) discuss, the numbers of divorces appear initially quite low, however, the study population is narrowed by only including those in the analysis who were married at the first wave studied, and who subsequently experienced divorce within the study period. Pre-existing divorces were not included. The sample covers both those who have been married for a considerable amount of time, and newly-weds. As divorce rates are highest in the first few years after marriage (see Chapter 2), many of the marriages within the survey (recorded at the first wave) are likely to be more resilient and less likely to divorce, again reducing the number of divorces in the study. The twelve item 'General Health Questionnaire' (GHQ-12, Goldberg, 1992), a widely used measure across medical research and psychiatry, was used to indicate 'psychological strain'. Each statement is scored on a four-point scale, from 0 to 3, with items including "Have you recently been able to concentrate on whatever you are doing?" and "Have you recently lost much sleep over worry?" Items are recoded so that a maximum score of 36 would indicate the worst possible score of mental well-being; healthy scores would generally lie around 10 to 13 on the scale. In order to examine the effects of divorce on mental strain, relative to remaining married and experiencing widowhood, the authors use a five-year time period, examining the two years prior to the event (divorce or widowhood), the year of the event, and a further two years after the event.

Gardner and Oswald (2006) found that those who remain married over time have a small but statistically significant rise in mental strain (with GHQ scores rising from 10.92 to 11.08 over the five-year time period). Widowed and divorced people reported greater increases in psychological strain. Those who were widowed reported an acute and sudden rise in psychological strain in the year of the bereavement, with GHQ scores rising from 11.69 two years before their partners death to 17.20 the year of the event, before falling back two years later to a stress level only marginally higher than the time two years before their partner's death. Divorced people showed elevated levels of stress in the two years prior to divorce, peaking during the year of divorce, and falling in the two years following divorce. Two years after divorce, stress levels had dropped below the original level of stress before the divorce (scores on the GHQ on average rose from 12.98 two years before divorce, to a peak of 14.85 in the year of divorce, before falling back to 11.98 two years post divorce). This finding indicates a relief from stress over the longer-term (and ties in with the positive effects of relationship breakdown in Chapter 8). This supports the short-term/crisis model (as opposed to the long-term/chronic strain model) as outlined in the 'Divorce-Stress-Adjustment Perspective' (Amato 2000, see Chapter 7). For this divorced group, it may be suggested that the rise in psychological strain pre-divorce is likely to be related to poor relationship quality and increased conflict affecting mental health, as well as the legal proceedings that may be under way.

The improvement in mental strain two years post-divorce may be attributed to an improvement in these situations – decreased conflict due to not living with the former partner, and a potential end to legal proceedings. This changing pattern of mental health illustrates the importance of viewing divorce as a 'process' rather than a single event.

Of relevance to child health, Gardner and Oswald's (2006) research also suggests that those couples with children experience greater levels of stress from one year prior to, and two years post-divorce compared to those separating without children. Other research has indicated that depressed parents are more likely to have children who also have emotional and behavioural problems (Jacob and Johnson, 2001; Shiner and Marmorstein, 1998; Phares et al., 2002; all cited in Spector, 2006), indicating a process of transmission for the negative effects on children (see Chapters 5 and 6).

The finding of poorer mental health following separation has been supported in other countries including Germany and the US. In more detail, Lucas (2005) examined this in a German longitudinal household panel survey of 30,000 people, followed up for 18 years. Lucas used a single item measure, which asked individuals to say on a scale of one to ten how satisfied they were with their lives. A higher score indicated a higher level of life satisfaction. This item was presented annually, allowing a comparison over time. In the year of divorce the drop in life satisfaction was 0.50 on this ten-point scale. The research found that in the two years following divorce, satisfaction did not return to baseline, but remained at between 0.22 and 0.34 points below the baseline level. Interestingly, (and in support of the selection effect, see Chapters 1 and 7), those who later divorced actually showed lower life satisfaction in the years prior to marriage.

The lower level of life satisfaction following

divorce, indicative of a more long-term impact, appears to be inconsistent with results from Gardner and Oswald's (2006) 'short-term/crisis' finding. However, there may be some methodology effects, with Lucas's study using 'life satisfaction,' as opposed to mental health measures, and this being recorded in a single item question compared the questionnaire that indicates the GHQ. It is important, therefore, to also examine other methods of measuring mental well-being, which may be more sensitive and able to pick up statistically significant changes in impact.

Research evidence from the US has further shown that previous marital history can have an impact upon mental health. Using a sample of 2,000 people aged over 30, with data collected longitudinally between 1982 and 1983 in North Carolina, US, Barrett (2000) examined the effect of multiple relationship transitions on depression, anxiety, and substance use and dependence. The data collected allow for a complete marital and psychiatric history, and symptom counts for the mental illnesses listed above. The Diagnostic Interview Schedule or DIS (Robins et al., 1981, cited in Bennett, 2000) was used as a method of investigating the symptom count of the three disorders, based upon DSM-III categories ('Diagnostic and Statistical Manual of Mental Disorders', American Psychiatric Association, 1980).

Barrett (2000) found that multiple marital transitions were significantly associated with all three of these indicators of mental health. Interestingly, in some instances, the more marital transitions the poorer the symptoms. For example, for substance use and depression, those in their third marriage had more symptoms than in their second marriage, and those divorced twice reported more symptoms of depression compared to those divorced once. In anxiety, the only significant pattern was shown where those who had been remarried had more symptoms than those who had been continuously married. The effect of previous marital history was shown to be moderated by the length of time in the current marital status. With previous research showing that marriage is a predictor of better mental health (see Chapter 7), this research explores some of the moderators of this association, with weaker health benefits shown for those with a greater number of marriage events.

It is clear from these studies that there is an observed association between relationship breakdown and mental health. The general consensus is that the mental health impacts are short-lived with most research reporting improvements in health two to three years after this breakdown (although the ways in which mental health is measured may contribute to this some of the inconsistencies in the findings).

4.3 Relationship breakdown and specific psychiatric conditions

Much of the research cited above uses a method of assessing psychological well-being via recognised scales or counting symptoms to establish changes in mental health over time. Whilst this is extremely valuable, some may consider that specific psychiatric diagnoses present the most convincing evidence of worsening mental health following relationship breakdown. Using the longitudinal 'National Study of Health and Development in the UK', Richards et al. (1997) examined the effects of divorce specifically on anxiety and depression, with a wide range of variables controlled for, including parental divorce, education, and age at first marriage. This sample was chosen at random from a larger sample of babies born in one week in 1946. Medical examinations were made throughout the study period. By 1989, when the cohort were aged 43 and the study population comprised 3,262, 3,018 had been married, of whom 2,179 had remained married to the same individual and 779 had divorced at least once. The study compares the outcomes for these latter two groups. Anxiety and depression were measured using the Psychiatric Symptom Frequency scale (PSF, Rodgers, 1994) when participants were aged 43 years. There were 18 items on the scale, and questions included, "I would like to get some idea about how you have been feeling about things over the last year. How often have you felt on edge or keyed up or mentally tense?"; and "How often have you been in low spirits or felt miserable?". Answers were coded into a 5-point scale, from 0 (not in the last year) to 5 (every day), with a total score calculated. The risk of alcohol abuse was also measured using the CAGE (Ewing, 1984), which asks whether the respondent feels that they should Cut down their drinking, if others have been Annoyed by their drinking, if they have felt Guilty about their drinking, and whether they have ever had a drink in the morning to get over a hangover (Eye opener)? The four items in italics form the letters that make up the CAGE (Cut down, Annoyed, Guilty, and Eye opener). Other aspects measured included: current stressors, financial hardship, availability of a confidante, and frequency of social contact with friends and family; socio-demographic indicators, including level of educational attainment, occupation of fathers, and age of first marriage; early vulnerability in terms of parental divorce before reaching 15 years of age, and a measure of personality administered at 13 years of age.

When those ever divorced were compared to those who had remained married, Richards et al (1997) found that divorce was associated with increased depression and anxiety, and greater risk of alcohol abuse. This association remained significant when other factors were controlled for, such as financial hardship, age at first marriage, educational attainment and the absence of a confidante. Importantly, the study found that there was no association between the mental health outcomes and time since divorce, indicating that these effects may be long-term with a new relationship unable to "eliminate the detrimental effects of previous divorce" (p.1,127).

It is interesting to contrast this Richards et al. (1997) study with the findings in the previous section on general measures of psychological health. With general measures it is indicated that mental health tends to improve after around two to three years after divorce. However, this Richards et al. (1997) paper found that although alcohol abuse had eventually reduced during the time since the divorce, the impacts on anxiety and depression continued, especially among women. This detail is likely to be missed in more general measures of psychological health.

Also within the UK, Kiernan and Mensah (forthcoming) used the 'Millennium Cohort Study' to examine depression in mothers over time (see Chapter 1 for details of the MCS). They used data from the fourth sweep, when the children were five years of age. Using the Kessler 6-item scale of depression (Kessler et al., 2002), mothers married when their child was five years old were least likely to be depressed, and this was independent of their marital status at the time of the birth of their child. By contrast, single mothers following the break-up of a cohabiting or married relationship reported high levels of depression, with the highest being those who had previously lived with a partner, potentially indicating the impact of multiple relationship transitions. This research is in line with the findings of Barrett (2000) in the previous section, who indicated that a greater number of marital transitions was associated with poorer mental health outcomes on a range of areas, thus reducing the protective effect of marriage.

From overseas, Rotermann (2007) reported findings from a longitudinal health study with a substantial sample of over 24,000 Canadian individuals married or cohabiting at baseline. The study used a two-year interview cycle, with individuals aged 20 to 64 years of age at the baseline, who were living with their partner, and were without depression at the first time point. Data used in the study were collected over six waves. 'The Diagnostic and Statistical Manual of Mental Disorders – Revised' (DSM-III-R American Psychiatric Association, 1987), and presence of a Major Depressive Episode in the 'Composite International Diagnostic Interview' (CIDI) were used to record depression (Statistics Canada, 2009). When a number of variables were controlled for (including changes in income, social support, presence of children, employment status, history of depression, education and age) a statistically significant relationship between depression and relationship dissolution was maintained. Men were three times more likely, and women two and a half times more likely, to experience an episode of depression than those who remained in their relationships (see later in this chapter for gender differences). However, this research also indicated that depression may be short-lived: more than three-quarters of those who had had a depressive episode when the relationship had ended did not report another episode of depression at the next follow-up (two years later). This study appears to be less sensitive to less serious episodes of depression than others reported here, as a result of depression being coded dichotomously (either depressed or not depressed), compared to other studies which use scale measures to record a spectrum of mental health and symptom counts (i.e. better or worse). This may partly explain the reduced long-term effect reported above.

Afifi et al. (2006) looked at the lifetime psychiatric diagnoses of never married, married, and separated / divorced mothers using a nationally representative, cross-sectional study in the US, with a sample of over 1,500 people. After controlling for various socio-demographic and stressor variables, the authors found that, compared to married mothers, those who were separated and divorced had a significantly higher lifetime prevalence of psychiatric diagnoses, including: depression, dysthymia, Generalised Anxiety Disorder (GAD), Post-Traumatic Stress Disorder, and anti-social personality disorder. Compared to never-married mothers, the separated and divorced were more likely to have diagnoses of GAD, depression and anxious-misery disorders. This research indicates that the increase in symptoms of poor mental health following relationship breakdown is translated into raised numbers of psychiatric diagnoses. Interestingly, this research also demonstrates some elements of the protective effect of marriage on mental health. When compared to the married, the never married experienced a statistically greater likelihood of Post Traumatic Stress Disorder and drug abuse. There was a trend, albeit to a non-significant level, for the never married to have greater likelihood of poorer mental health than the married across the broader range of mental health problems, but not to the same extent as those experiencing the strains of separation or divorce. The authors described never married mothers as being in,

"... a somewhat intermittent position between married and separated / divorced mothers with regard to psychopathology." (Afifi et al., 2006, p.126).

However, due to the cross-sectional nature of this study, clarifying the direction of this association is not possible. Interpretations of this study include poor mental health as a result of relationship breakdown, as well as mental health as a causal factor for relationship breakdown (see later in this chapter).

4.4 Gender differences in psychological impact

The gender differences in the psychological effect of relationship breakdown have been widely studied. Note that further reference to variations in the health impacts of couple relationship breakdown is detailed in Chapter 7. In research examining mental strain in the two years prior to, until two years post-divorce, Gardner and Oswald (2006) observe that the shape of the mental health pattern is broadly similar, with no statistically significant differences found between men and women's scores on the GHQ (for further details on this research see earlier in this chapter). However, Lucas (2005),using a single item measure, demonstrated that men's report of life satisfaction falls significantly faster and quicker than women's in the period leading up to divorce.

In further illustration using Canadian data, Rotermann (2007) demonstrated that men experiencing the break-up of a marriage were more likely to experience depression than women. This is in contrast with research which shows that women are more vulnerable to depression, and men more vulnerable to alcoholism as methods of showing distress (Simon, 2002). This increased depression has been supported by Kendler et al. (2001) in the US, who also show that fathers are more sensitive than mothers to depression post-separation, and that non-resident fathers are likely to experience feelings of guilt and severe anhedonia (loss of ability to feel pleasure). In a literature review examining the presence, risks for, and familial effects of depression in fathers, Spector (2006) concludes that where there have been marital difficulties clinicians should look for signs of depression,

"Marital difficulties may be the most common trigger for first-time depression in husbands just as divorce amplifies depressive episodes especially when children are involved. Fathers experiencing marital conflict and its aftermath must be evaluated for symptoms of depression." (Spector, 2006, p.876-877).

Examining patterns of suicide also shows elements of gender variation. In the UK, trends over the last 25 years have shown that men who have been divorced between the ages of 25 and 44 have the highest rates of suicide, whereas for women the rate of suicide is roughly equal for those who are single and those who divorce (ONS, 2008g). For both sexes, married people have the lowest rates of suicide. In an older population group, aged 45 to 74, both men and women who were single were more likely to commit suicide than those who were married; however, there is less distinction between single, divorced and widowed for this population. For those aged over 75, data are not consistent across individuals categories; however, the earlier pattern of lower suicide rates of married people when compared to unmarried persists (ONS, 2008g). These findings are consistent in the US, where Kposowa (1999) reported that for divorced men there is a more than doubled risk for suicide compared to married men, using the National Longitudinal Mortality Study (see Chapter 3). Divorced women had only a marginal increase in their risk of suicide.

It must be recognised that these gender differences in psychological health may be associated with the larger number of women who petition for the divorce – in 2005 68% of divorces and dissolutions were granted to wives (ONS, 2008a). Nonetheless, evidence is not conclusive and further research is needed. As an additional point, research has also shown that those entering into marriage demonstrate a decrease in symptoms of depression, especially among those who are depressed before marriage, and those who have the highest levels of marital happiness (Frech and Williams, 2007). This would indicate that a bi-directional effect exists, acting to improve symptoms of depression when people move into marriage, alongside the research above which identifies worsening symptoms of depression as they move out of long-term relationships. Finally, in a review paper discussing the role of psychological norms following divorce, Brinig and Nock (2003) suggest that it may not be the divorce per se that leads to an elevated risk of psychological ill-health for fathers, but rather the effect of non-custodial parenthood, for which fathers have an increased likelihood relative to mothers.

4.5 Moderating factors

In relation to the gender differences noted above, a range of psychological and situational factors have been found to moderate (exacerbate or reduce) the impact of separation on mental health. Note that further detail on moderating factors is provided in Chapters 6 (for children) and 7. Using a nationally representative household panel survey in Australia, Crosier et al. (2006) examined the mental health of single and partnered mothers. In line with other research presented in this chapter, they found a higher rate of mental disability (defined in this paper with mental health problems causing limited daily living and functioning) among single mothers compared to those who were partnered. Their study found that financial hardship (indicated by going without meals, or being unable to heat home as a result of financial difficulties) and a perceived lack of social support accounted for most of the difference in mental disability between these two groups. Single mothers had a doubled risk for perceiving low levels of social support and were six times more likely to report instances of financial hardship compared to partnered mothers. This paper did not control for the time since separation, and so it is unclear whether these moderating factors have different impacts over time, as would be suggested by the 'Divorce-Stress-Adjustment Perspective' (Amato, 2000 – see Chapter 7). Furthermore, this study was derived from a single wave of a panel survey (i.e. a cross-sectional rather than a longitudinal approach) and, therefore, the direction of the association between mental disability, financial hardship and social support cannot be clarified.

In a meta-analysis[13] of 21 studies conducted in a range of Western countries (published between 1978 and 2004), Krumrei et al. (2007) examined the role of social support in protecting well-being in the post-divorce period. Different forms of social relationships were found to be associated with positive post-divorce adjustment. Studies showed that network relationships (support through groups for example) were associated with higher levels of well-being ($z=0.21$, $p<.05$), and greater positive effects after divorce ($z=.36$, $p<.05$), with the authors suggesting that this form of support may give emotional support, encouragement and help to meet a range of needs. Social, one-on-one relationships, for example with a best friend or family member were also positively associated with psychological adjustment ($z=.13$, $p<.05$), indicating a protective effect. The authors hypothesise that these forms of relationships offer a means by which personal thoughts and feelings can be shared, providing a buffer against stress. These findings appear to show an interesting role of social support mediating the potentially negative mental health effects of separation. Interventions with individuals experiencing, or who have experienced, relationship breakdown may produce positive effects when they encourage the formation and strengthening of social relationships which provide emotional support and encouragement from other individuals.

As further illustration of moderating factors, Saffrey and Ehrenberg (2007) investigated the influence of attachment anxiety, rumination (thinking for long periods of time), and reflection on later psychological adjustment. They studied a sample of 231 young adults aged from 17 to 24, attending a Canadian university and who had been in a relationship for a minimum of three months before separating (mean = 14 months). Whilst

13. A meta-analysis is a form of research which combines the results from a number of studies which address similar research questions in order to get a clear understanding of the nature of a relationship.

unrepresentative of the broader population, this student sample was chosen partly as a result of trusting and meaningful relationships which may have ended in a particularly difficult manner, as those in the study may not have experienced a loss before. Using the 'Experiences in Close Relationships Questionnaire' (Brennan et al., 1998), including items such as "I worry a fair amount about losing my partner", romantic attachment anxiety was related to higher levels of preoccupation and relationship regret. Reflection was associated with positive adjustment, whereas rumination was more associated with negative adjustment. Whilst this study may not provide findings that can be generalised to the wider population, as a result of its focus on young adults, these initial findings that rumination is associated with the relationship between attachment anxiety and negative adjustment may provide some insight as to the varied outcomes for people emerging from relationships. Those who dwell for longer, and in less positive ways, experience poorer relationship outcomes that are also affected by their attachment anxiety levels. As the authors state,

"Thus, in day-to-day life, when not experiencing a relationship loss, rumination may maintain individuals' awareness of vulnerability to rejection and abandonment. Notably, when individuals high in attachment anxiety make negative attributions for partner-related behaviour (Collins et al., 2006), they may then ruminate on these instances further exacerbating negative adjustment." (Saffrey and Ehrenberg, 2007, p.364).

Forgiveness of the partner has been identified as potentially affecting the strength of the link between relationship dissolution and poorer mental health. Forgiveness has been seen to represent two distinct elements: an absence of negative, and a presence of positive feeling (Rye and Pargament, 2002). In a sample of 200 divorced people attending divorce recovery groups from the Midwest of the US, 94% of whom were either Catholic or Protestant, Rye et al. (2004) examined the association between forgiveness, religiosity and mental health. Forgiveness was assessed using the Forgiveness Scale (Rye et al., 2001), with two subscales: the absence of negative (including items such as "I can't stop thinking about how I was wronged by this person"), and the presence of positive (for example "I have compassion for the person who wronged me"). When demographic and background variables were controlled for, the presence of positive feeling towards the former partner was associated only with improved existential well-being (meaning and purpose in life related to the sacred). However, a more striking finding was that the absence of negative feeling was associated with lower levels of depression and anger, and higher levels of existential well-being and religious well-being. The authors propose that this association between forgiveness, depression and anger may be as a result of decreased rumination, giving the potential for new ways of thinking about events which are more beneficial for mental health. It is important to note that some reasons for separation may facilitate forgiveness to a greater extent than others, for example mutual agreement may be more forgivable than divorce as a result of an affair – and these reasons may have effects on mental health in addition to the forgiveness effects. This research identifies the need for support to help individuals be able to forgive former partners, especially to enable negative feelings to be overcome where possible, allowing improvements in their own mental health.

Stewart (2005) studied an Australian sample of 245 single parenting, maritally separated women in a cross-sectional study to examine the role of demographic, contextual and intrapsychic variables on life satisfaction. Intrapsychic variables included emotional attachment to the ex-partner, the sense of control that they believed they had, and their sense of coherence in which events have meaning, are manageable, and comprehensible. Using a predictive path model, greater sense of control, sense of coherence, depression and / or less grief over the loss of the relationship were found to have a strong predictive power for higher life satisfaction. There was an indication that social support and living standards helped to contribute towards a greater sense of control. Women who were more depressed had less sense of coherence and of control over their lives. Longer time since separation was also associated with higher life satisfaction, supporting Amato's (2000) 'Divorce-Stress-Adjustment Perspective' (see later in this chapter and also Chapter 7). Satisfaction with social support and changes to living standards were the two other contextual variables which impacted upon life satisfaction, supporting previous research identifying social support and financial position as important in mediating the impact of divorce. Finally, this research also indicated that time since separation has an influence upon grief, but not depression, indicating that grief may be more transitory, and depression a more pervasive outcome of separation. In conclusion, this research indicates that there are a range of processes which operate following marital separation. In women, life satisfaction may be affected by both contextual and intrapsychic variables; however, this research indicates that intrapsychic variables may be influenced in turn by these contextual variables. The authors suggest that the clear role of these intrapsychic variables may indicate that more emphasis should be placed on these to help with coping, rather than the less influential contextual factors:

"The research presents a shift in focus from the perception that women are 'victims' of their environmental context to a perception that they are in a potentially empowering position, one in which they can re-establish their lives with renewed sense of meaning." (Stewart, 2005, p.103).

Another potentially influencing variable on an individual's ability to cope following relationship breakdown may be the extent to which they decided upon the separation or divorce. Sakraida (2008) examined the experiences of 150 women from the US, aged 34-53 years, who had divorced within the two years prior to the research. This study used the Coping Response Inventory (Moos, 1993) to indicate perception of stress and eight types of coping responses, under the two broader categories of approach and avoidance strategies. Another scale, the Personal Profile Form was developed for the study and broached questions including whether it was the respondent, their former partner, or a mutual decision to divorce.

Sakraida (2008) found that compared to initiators and mutual deciders, non-initiators were less likely to consider the divorce as a challenge, and 85.7% were more likely to see the divorce as a threat. The non-initiators were also more likely (83.3%) to report that they did not know the divorce was going to happen, and that they did not have enough time to prepare. In the majority of divorce cases in the UK, women are the initiators of divorce (ONS, 2008a – see earlier), so further research with men examining the influence of initiator status and mental health outcomes would be of interest. Sakraida (2008) found that there was not a strong effect of the decider status on the coping response used. After controlling for multiple tests only one of the subscales, 'acceptance and resignation', was significant being used more by the non-initiator group than the mutual deciding group. This is a passive coping response. Overall, this coping response contributed only 4.3% of the variance. Viewed in the context of the research by Stewart (2005) reported above, this research by Sakraida identifies that those who were non-initiators of divorce may be more vulnerable and require further support around intrapsychic variables, in order to help them to re-appraise the divorce as a challenge, and to empower them, improving their life satisfaction.

4.6 Mechanisms of effect

In order to more fully understand the reasons for mental health difficulties around relationship dissolution, it is worthwhile examining the potential causal processes involved. Several mechanisms have been posited which may help to explain the rise in depressive symptoms following a divorce (Wheaton, 1990; Williams, 2003; Kalmijn and Mondon, 2006). Note how these mechanisms, although specific to mental health, relate to the additional mechanisms of effect that are detailed more comprehensively in Chapter 7. By their very nature, these explanations assess the plausibility of a causal relationship between couple relationship breakdown and psychological ill-health. There are four main points to note.

1. The 'crisis' effect (Raschke, 1987) – when there is a temporary increase in symptoms of stress, depression and anxiety as a result of the disturbing and emotional nature of divorce.

2. The 'Divorce-Stress-Adjustment Perspective' (Amato, 2000) – proposes that separating spouses initially experience estrangement from each other, which continues through the divorce. However, following the divorce there is a period of adjustment, influenced by a range of variables including social support and financial resources. High levels of acutely stressful events are linked to depressive symptoms and impacts on physical health (see Chapter 7).

3. The loss of a supportive partnership – the loss of resources that come from a relationship and are responsible for a longer-term increase in poor health. There is, however, mixed evidence to support this assertion, with some finding that those who repartner shortly after divorce experience a smaller rise in depression than those who do not (e.g. Kalmijn and Monden, 2006). This would suggest that some of the lost resources that result from the ending of a relationship can be provided by a new partner. However, despite repartnering, some research has shown a small increase in depression symptoms for women following separation, which would argue against this supportive partnership theory. To illustrate, Gardner and Oswald (2006) found that remarrying quickly following divorce does not appear to make a significant difference to well-being until two years after divorce. This may be a result of the different measures used. Whilst Kalmijn and Monden (2006) used symptoms of depression as an indicator (using the abbreviated version of the Depressive Symptom Scale), Gardner and Oswald (2006) used a broader measure derived from the General Health Questionnaire (see earlier in this chapter) which may be more sensitive to impact.

4. Finally, there may be an opposing system whereby there is relief from the relationship stresses that contributed to the divorce or relationship breakdown. Evidence for an 'escape' or 'relief' hypothesis has emerged in which people who had the poorest marital quality or lowest fairness in their relationship experienced the smallest rises in depression symptoms following divorce (Kalmijn and Monden, 2006). Moreover, some research has suggested that divorce may actually improve the mental health of those who were experiencing major depression at the time of marital dissolution (Cohen et al., 2007). It is not yet clear whether the effect of the escape

hypothesis is an active reduction in depressive symptoms or a comparatively smaller increase in them, and it is possible that this process acts in a different manner in clinical populations, with the clinically depressed potentially experiencing a different mechanism. However, Kalmijn and Monden (2006) also found that those coming from relationships in which there was physical or verbal aggression actually experienced a greater increase in depressive symptoms, in contrast to those where aggression is not indicated. Although this research detailing an escape hypothesis may be inconsistent, it does appear that for all mental health impacts, the nature of the relationship prior to breakdown will have a bearing on the effects. At the simplest of levels, it is intuitive to assume that for those escaping high-conflict destructive relationships, the impacts on mental health may not be as negative to those who did not want the relationship to end (see Chapter 8 for more detail on the positive effects of relationship breakdown).

4.7 Conclusion and key findings for Chapter 4

This chapter has detailed some of the psychological impacts of relationship breakdown. As in the previous chapter on physical health, the case for a causal relationship, in that relationship breakdown causes psychological problems, is difficult to assume. Rather than relationship breakdown causing psychological strain, reverse causation may apply with the relationship breakdown occurring as a result of psychological ill-health.

Indeed, the contribution of poor mental health leading to the dissolution of partnerships has been investigated from the 'British Household Panel Survey' data referred to earlier (Gardner and Oswald, 2006). Wade and Pevalin (2004) also find support for the suggestion that specific mental health characteristics may lead to a greater propensity for divorce in a reverse causation manner. Wade and Pevalin found that in the year immediately prior to divorce or separation, higher scores, indicating poorer psychological health on the 'General Health Questionnaire', were associated with a greater propensity for divorce or separation. Examining the four years prior to the time of divorce it was evident that divorce could be predicted by the presence of moderate and severe mental health problems. However, it is uncertain the extent to which a poor relationship contributed to this psychological ill-health. This, therefore, provides evidence supporting the selection of those with severe mental health problems into divorce, but also does not discount previous research which has identified that poorer mental health follows in the period after the relationship dissolution. Further evidence of poor mental health contributing to relationship breakdown has been reported by Pevalin and Ermish (2004) from a longitudinal study also using the 'British Household Panel Survey' data.

In light of these reservations over assigning causality, the key findings from this chapter are as follows.

- Relationship breakdown is associated with poorer mental health, two years prior to breakdown, with a peak at the time of divorce. This is a robust finding, measured through a range of measures including life satisfaction, symptoms of depression and the number of psychiatric conditions.
- The general consensus is that the mental health impacts are short-lived with improvements in health observed two to three years after this relationship breakdown (although the ways in which mental health is measured may contribute to some inconsistencies in the research findings).
- The number of marital transitions negatively impacts upon the level of mental health

outcomes. With increasing partnerships, the beneficial effects of relationships upon mental health are reduced. Some research indicates that the most depressed of mothers are those who were single parents at the time of research but who had formerly lived with a partner – indicating the effect of multiple transitions.

- Those with children experience more stress in the years before and shortly after divorce. This may have effects on the time and energy they are able to devote to parenting.
- In terms of mental health, the married are typically shown to have the most optimal mental health (across a range of indicators), followed by the never married, and then the divorced or separated.
- Making clear conclusions with regard to the mechanism of effect can be made more complicated by the wide range of measures used – some studies focus upon well-being or life satisfaction, others use measures relating to depression.
- There are a range of factors which may mediate the link between separation and worsening mental health, including existing mental health, the forgiveness of the partner, financial circumstances and the perceived sufficiency of social support. These mediating factors appear robust and are demonstrated across numerous studies.
- The direction of mental health problems and separation appears to be bi-directional, with mental health problems contributing to marital strain, and marital separation increasing the likelihood of poor mental health.

Chapter 5
Impact of couple relationship breakdown on children: Multiple impacts

5.1 Introduction

A great deal of research has examined the impact of couple relationship breakdown on children. The introductory statistics in Chapter 2 illustrate the number of children that experience the relationship breakdown of their parents in England and Wales. The numbers have increased dramatically with around 71,000 under-16-year-olds experiencing the divorce of their parents in 1970 (ONS, 2006) compared to 117,000 in 2007 (ONS, 2008c). Twenty per cent of these children in 2007 were aged under five and 63% were under eleven. It is estimated that 1 in 3 children will experience parental separation before the age of 16 (Maclean, 2004).

The impact of couple relationship breakdown on children is presented in two chapters. This, the first, will present the growing evidence from reviews and large longitudinal datasets that have shown multiple impacts. Relationship breakdown and its impact on more specific outcomes will be presented in Chapter 6, and will include reference to physical and psychological health, education and employment, and health-damaging behaviours. In introducing the scope of these two chapters, evidence is largely derived from marriages that have broken down rather than cohabiting relationships where there is relatively little information available (Amato, 2000). In addition, reference to single or 'lone' parents (not necessarily divorced or separated) will occasionally be made, and the impacts this can have on children.

Assessing the impact of couple relationship breakdown on children involves a number of complexities. Some, such as differentiating between association and causation, have been mentioned when reporting the impact on adults. Likewise, the variety in contemporary relationship types has already been discussed. For example, the dissolution of cohabiting, 'closely involved' or married relationships (which all may differ in their stability and commitment quality) are likely to have contrasting impacts on children. The impacts are also likely to differ according to the child's age (and ability to adjust to new situations), their economic resources, their relationship and contact with both parents after separation, and their family setting after the relationship breakdown (a single-parent family or involving a new stepparent, step-siblings, or new half-brothers or sisters, etc.). The impacts on children are further complicated by the life transitions that are commonly experienced by children and in particular that of adolescents. Separating out the changes experienced by young adults in terms of schooling, friendships, sexuality, identity, etc. makes the precise impact of parental separation difficult to specify. These points will be further detailed later in this chapter.

In addition, the actual process of relationship breakdown has an important part to play on child outcomes (Amato, 2000). For many, it may not be just the act of parental separation or divorce, but the likely parental conflict and management of this conflict that may have been apparent beforehand (and perhaps continuing after separation). From a review of over 250 international studies, Reynolds et al. (2001) found that children repeatedly exposed to marital conflict and discord are likely to develop emotional and behavioural problems. This conclusion has been well evidenced elsewhere (Grych and Fincham, 1990; Cherlin et al., 1991; Wallerstein,1991; Haveman and Wolfe, 1995; Seltzer, 1994; Davies and Cummings, 1998; Hart, 1999; Grych et al., 2000; Margolin et al., 2001; Cummings and Davis, 2002; Cummings et al., 2008; Mooney et al., 2009). Indeed, research has shown that the actual conflict between parents may be more significant in affecting child outcomes than the event of separation. From a review of research, McIntosh (2003) notes that "parental conflict is a more potent predictor of child adjustment than is divorce" (p.63).

This is particularly the case if this conflict is destructive characterised by verbal or physical aggression, non-verbal (the 'silent treatment') or intense quarrels, and arguments that are concerned with or involve the children. This is in contrast to constructive conflict, whereby children may learn from their parents how to effectively manage and resolve disagreements (Hart, 1999). Indeed, Cummings et al. (2008) note the importance of the type of conflict apparent between couples:

"A consistent finding is that it is not whether couples fight but how they fight that is most pertinent to the well-being of both adults and children." (Cummings et al., 2008, p.193).

In addition, Hawthorne et al. (2003) note that particular types of conflict are more detrimental to children:

"It is apparent from research on conflict that its most damaging aspects are when it is about children, is unresolved, and especially when children are directly involved as messengers between parents, or as recipients of negative information about one parent from the other." (Hawthorne et al., 2003, p.18).

In contrast to parents in conflict, children raised by parents reporting high relationship quality and satisfaction tend to have high levels of well-being (Cummings and Davies, 1994; Reynolds et al., 2001; Hetherington and Kelly, 2002; Hawthorne et al., 2003). When considering the various stresses faced by children after parental separation (see forthcoming section 5.2), there is an argument that all are mediated through the influence on the parent-child relationship. Therefore, good and effective parenting may be the most potent means of reducing any detrimental impacts on children (Hawthorne et al., 2003). Based on this evidence, it is also becoming increasingly acknowledged that couple relationships and parenting skills are inherently entwined. Poor quality parental relationships are associated with poor parenting and poor quality parent-child relationships (Reynolds, 2001; Strohschein, 2005). Likewise, improvements in co-parenting, or how parents support each other in their parenting style, has been shown to improve both couple and partner-infant relationships (Feinberg and Kan, 2008). This association is also summarised through the 'vicious' and 'virtuous cycles' of parenting whereby the degree of support for the mother affects levels of criticism of the father, which affects the father's satisfaction of relationship with mother, which in turn affects the father's involvement with the child, which affects the support for the mother, etc. (One Plus One, 2006). Effective parenting interventions to improve child outcomes need to acknowledge, therefore, the importance of the couple relationship.

A further point to place at the outset of this chapter is that, like the adults referred to in earlier chapters, it is not the case that relationship breakdown leads to sustained negative outcomes for all children. Indeed, quite the reverse is maybe true. Maclean (2004) makes the point that it is common for children of separated parents to go through a period of unhappiness, low self-esteem and behaviour problems (that may also be experienced through other life transitions common to children). However, with good relations between parents, the majority of children are able to settle back into a normal pattern of development (Maclean, 2004). The crucial point is that this return to the norm does not apply to all children, and that other factors may moderate or exacerbate the impact of the couple relationship breakdown. Rather than relationship breakdown per se, factors compounding the impact include poor parental communication and financial difficulties. Also, although reintegration into new families is common, repeated changes or 'multiple transitions' in family circumstances (new partners, step- and half-siblings, etc.) may prove to be more harmful to children than a stable family structure. In general, and as shown in more detail later in this chapter, it appears that younger children find these new family forms easier to adapt to compared to older children (Maclean, 2004).

As a final note to this introduction, this chapter will first of all present evidence from reviews and large longitudinal datasets. These sources are used to outline a range of different impacts on those children whose parents have experienced a relationship breakdown. This will be followed by evidence examining the impact of multiple transitions in family formation (beyond a single episode of relationship breakdown). As in previous chapters, a number of concluding points will be presented.

5.2 Impact of couple relationship breakdown on children – review and longitudinal dataset evidence

Within the UK, one of the most significant programmes of research into this area was supported by the Joseph Rowntree Foundation. They commissioned 12 research projects and reviews published between 1998 and 2003 detailing child and adult experiences of couple separation and divorce. A paper by Rodgers and Pryor (1998), that reviewed over 200 studies examining the impact of divorce and separation on children, is a fitting way to start this section.

The paper makes two important points. The first is that the separation process causes significant, albeit short-term, distress for most children, echoing Maclean's (2004) point made earlier in this chapter. They note that "The immediate distress surrounding parental separation usually fades with time and most children settle into a normal development" (p.4), and poor outcomes are far from inevitable. They note, however, that for a minority of children, negative outcomes are typically twice as prevalent compared to children from intact families. These outcomes, drawn from a range of studies in the review, include: poverty, behavioural problems including conduct disorder and antisocial behaviour, distress and unhappiness (operating independently of economic factors), educational achievement, future life transitions, and physical and emotional health problems.

To further illustrate these outcomes, Rodgers and Pryor (1998) note that the magnitude of the socio-economic disadvantage far exceeds all other outcomes listed, and may extend into adulthood. Relative to poverty, effect sizes for behavioural maladjustment were weaker. The links between anti-social behaviour, although widely documented, were found to be problematic given the extent to which underlying factors such as parental criminal behaviour were controlled for. In terms of poor educational outcomes, many of the reported associations in the UK were statistically insignificant once socio-economic status was controlled for, thus implying that poverty arising from the separation may be the primary concern. In terms of life transitions, the intergenerational transmission of parental and own partnership separation is well documented in the review (Rodgers and Pryor, 1998).

The second key point is that these outcomes are difficult to attribute directly or causally to the actual event of parental separation. Rather, separation should be seen as a 'process' with events pre-, during, and post-separation considered. The essential argument here is that a range of mediating factors are likely to influence the impact of the couple relationship breakdown on children. As an example, it is known that open and direct communication with children about the separation, and post-separation contact with the non-resident parent, is essential in improving the outcomes for children. Similarly, well documented ways to reduce the impact on children, as published by the Royal College of Psychiatrists

(2008), include making time to spend with your child, constant reassurance they will be loved by both parents, and making few additional changes to lifestyles and routines.

Additional mediating factors that determine whether children fall into the majority group who readjust well, or the minority who report sustained negative outcomes include: financial hardship before and after separation, family conflict (before and after separation), and parental psychological distress and readjustment. Evidence also suggests that multiple changes in family structure can cause more adverse outcomes for children (see Section 5.3). The Rodgers and Pryor (1998) report also found little evidence to support the notion that the age or gender of the children affects the degree of impact from relationship breakdown. The only significant age effect was that the risk of adverse outcomes for young people in stepfamilies, compared to those in single-parent families, appeared higher for older children with younger children faring better (Rodgers and Pryor, 1998). In a later review Hawthorne et al. (2003) note that the relationship between gender and outcomes is highly complex. They cite evidence suggesting that boys find parental separation more disturbing although girls show greater long-term impacts. Also, boys find adjustment to stepfamilies easier than girls, especially when girls are in early adolescence.

Finally, the Rodgers and Pryor (1998) review draws an interesting reference to those adult relationships that have broken down due to separation or death. Although linked by parental 'loss', the evidence suggests that bereaved children do not experience the same impacts in terms of educational achievement, later socio-economic disadvantage and mental health difficulties compared to those of separated parents. Nonetheless, impacts on substance misuse and life transitions are reported. There is also some interesting evidence suggesting that a parent re-partnering after the death of a parent may have more adverse consequences for the children than remaining with one parent, despite the frequent advantage in socio-economic terms (Rodgers and Pryor, 1998).

In extending their commitment to the family agenda, the Joseph Rowntree Foundation supported further review work to look at effective ways of supporting children through family change. The authors (Hawthorne et al., 2003) revisit the reviewed evidence on child impacts, and summarise as follows:

"It has become apparent from a considerable body of research that family change causes distress for most children. Some, too, experience negative consequences well beyond the time of change, with these sometimes persisting into adulthood." (Hawthorne et al., 2003, p.9).

Reflecting the expanding political interest in children and families (see Chapter 1), the Department for Children Schools and Families recently commissioned a review looking at the impact of 'family breakdown' on children (Mooney et al., 2009). Focusing on review-level evidence, their findings mirror those reported above. Although they acknowledge the effect sizes are "modest" (p.8), they do summarise that "the probability of poor outcomes occurring is nevertheless higher among children whose parents separate" (p.8). Their review makes a significant contribution to our understanding of how impacts on children may differ according to a number of risk and protective factors. Factors including parental conflict, parenting quality, maternal mental health, financial hardship and repeated transitions in family formation are likely to influence how much children are affected by family breakdown. As a consequence, the Mooney et al. (2009) review recognises that family functioning rather than family type may be more influential in explaining child outcomes from family breakdown. Mooney et al. (2009) illustrate this as follows:

Children from intact families can experience circumstances known to increase the risk of poor outcomes such as poverty, parental conflict, violence and poor parenting, whilst children whose parents separate may not experience these or can cope well, with the result that many children experiencing family breakdown will function as well as, or even better than, children from intact families." (Mooney et al., 2009, p.1).

This point on within-family processes acting as mediating factors for children exposed to parental separation is also evident through the work of Judy Dunn (2008). In the recent One Plus One biennial lecture, Dunn (2008) recognises the need to fully investigate the factors that may determine the differential impacts of parental separation on children (see Chapter 7 for more detail):

"Yet if we are to understand which children are most vulnerable [from changes in family life] and what provides effective support, we need to study both the broad and more intimate processes.... That is, we need to understand how the family processes may be mediating the effects of the broader social adversities on the children. Recent research has identified the central role of parent-child relationships in mediating these links, and highlights how important it is that we understand the influences and risks that affect individual differences in children's relationships with their parents in different family settings." (Dunn, 2008, p.7).

Dunn (2008), in examining research conducted directly among young children, also acknowledges the crucial way that grandparents, siblings and friends can help moderate the impacts of parental separation.

The impacts of parental separation on children have also been evidenced in the 'British National Child Development Study' (NCDS). Following the lives of around 17,000 people born in 1958, the 'Now we are 50' report (Elliot and Vaitilingam, 2008) looks at the effects of parental divorce on children. As in the Rodgers and Pryor (1998) review, divorce is very much seen as a process impacting on children, rather than a single event. For those children of divorced parents (relative to those from intact families), impacts include poorer reading and maths tests, and behaviour problems. The NCDS also shows the long-term nature of these impacts in terms of socio-economic attainment, mental well-being, health, and substance misuse. In addition, young women from divorced parents are also more likely to cohabit or marry at an earlier age, become teenage parents and conceive children outside of marriage. Both men and women from divorced families are also more likely to experience marital breakdown themselves. The important caveat added in interpreting these findings is that pre-existing factors, especially financial hardship, may be partly accountable for these outcomes rather than the divorce itself.

Professor Paul Amato has worked extensively in this area. His assessment of numerous studies carried out throughout the 1990s, published in 2000, is of clear significance to this review. The study covers the breakdown of marital relationships rather than other relationships forms. As in previous research, Amato (2000) sees the importance of viewing divorce as a process, with the negative impacts on children possibly occurring years before the final separation (for example, through parental conflict). In reviewing the evidence from the 1990s, Amato notes how children with divorced parents fare worse than those with married parents in terms of: academic success, conduct, psychological adjustment, social competence and long-term health. He notes the effect sizes have created a ".....small but consistent gap in well-being..." (p.1278). Amato's study published in

2000 clearly builds on his earlier meta-analysis of 92 studies, whereby children of divorced parents were found to be generally disadvantaged compared to those from married families (Amato and Keith, 1991).

Reviewing research adopting longitudinal designs, Amato (2000) also presents evidence that these child outcomes are more due to the effects of marital dissolution than marital selection (where parent or family problems may cause poor outcomes rather than the divorce). Even if pre-divorce family factors may predispose children to certain problems (as in selection), the divorce itself brings about new conditions that exacerbate these differences. Using his Divorce-Stress-Adjustment Perspective (see Chapter 7), Amato (2000) outlines the mediators or stressors of divorce and how they impact on child well-being. He summarises this evidence as follows:

"With regard to children, divorce can result in less effective parenting from the custodial parent, a decrease in involvement with the non-custodial parent, exposure to continuing interparental discord, a decline in economic resources, and other disruptive life events such as moving, changing schools, and additional parental marriages and divorces. These mediating factors represent the mechanisms through which divorce affects people's functioning and well-being." (p.1272).

In addition, to explain why some children fare better or worse than others, Amato (2000) reviews evidence demonstrating the role of buffers or moderating factors. These protective factors include effective coping skills enabling people to adjust to new situations, social support from friends, therapeutic interventions such as school-based support programmes, and an ability not to self-blame for the divorce. In relation, a positive parenting style has been shown to significantly reduce the detrimental effects of parental divorce on children (O'Connor and Jenkins, 2000).

The evidence presented in this paper (Amato, 2000) goes beyond a descriptive comparison of outcomes for children of divorced / married parents. Amato presents a list of possible age-effects experienced by children. For example, he notes that older children who see the distress of a failing marriage may be relieved at the divorce. Also, although younger children generally find adjustment easier that their older counterparts, for younger children who cannot recognise the distress, the removal of one parent may cause confusion and anxiety, and may lead to children blaming themselves for the breakdown (see Hawthorne et al., 2003). Amato also presents conflicting evidence demonstrating that the impacts of divorce on children can both decline and increase over time. For the latter, he suggests that economic hardship following divorce may discourage children to abandon their education and search for employment (albeit poorly paid) leading to lower occupational attainment and pay throughout adulthood. Likewise, marital problems in later life may be explained by poor models of parental relationships during childhood. From the alternative perspective, Amato also recognises the benefits, on both children and adults, where high-conflict marriages have divorced.

A further extensive study by Gruber (2004), using 40 years of US census data (1960, 1970, 1980 and 1990), assessed the impact of divorce on children in two unique ways. Firstly, he explored the implications of unilateral divorce or divorce that does not require the explicit consent of both partners. Secondly, he focused on the long-term impacts whereby the children of divorced parents were now adults. In his paper, Gruber reviews extensive evidence on the impacts of divorce on children. However, he also raises the recurring issue of whether these impacts are causal in nature or a product of effects operating through other determinants of child outcomes such as income and family size. He concludes the review of previous research in this area by stating that that "...the implications of divorce for child well-being are ambiguous" (p.806) and adds the point that a range of family background characteristics, which are yet unmeasured, may account for the differences between those children that do or do not experience parental divorce.

From the review of the US census data, Gruber (2004) finds that unilateral divorce regulations had increased the likelihood of divorce and thus increased the proportion of children who are more exposed to the impacts. He also presents powerful evidence on the impact of divorced marriages on these children when reaching adulthood. As adults, these children of divorced parents are less educated and have lower incomes. He speculates that these lower incomes could be due to their increased likelihood of being married at a young age, having more children and being less involved in the labour market. As is shown in Chapter 8, this early age of marriage is also associated with a greater risk of these marriages ending in divorce. However, Gruber concludes by noting that the reduced involvement in the labour market, and associated poverty, may be more an effect of poor welfare support rather than the breakdown of the marriage per se. As noted throughout this review of couple relationship breakdown, the important caveat is added that there may be a whole range of other (and yet unknown) variables, beyond parental divorce, that affect these child outcomes. Gruber (2004) calls for researchers to get inside the "black box" (p. 830) of intact marriages to unpick these causal pathways.

Connected to the Gruber (2004) research, a British study by Ely et al. (1999) examined the impact of rising divorce rates on the educational attainment of children. Although to be detailed in Chapter 6, the Ely et al. study also showed a lack of support for greater divorce rates leading to less damaging impacts for children. In tune with Gruber's (2004) conclusion, they report that higher divorce rates have meant that more children experience these negative outcomes. This does not support theorists who argue that as divorce rates increase and relationship breakdown is more common, the negative impacts on children should diminish in line with reduced stigma and more acceptance of relationship dissolution. Similar findings are reported by Sigle-Rushton et al. (2005) who conclude as follows:

"Using data from two British cohorts, we analyzed both shorter- and longer-term outcomes of children who experienced parental divorce and the extent to which the associations have changed over time. Estimating similar models for both cohorts, we found little evidence of any change in the size of the relationship as divorce became more commonplace." (Sigle-Rushton et al., 2005, p.427).

Murphy (2007), in relation to mortality data among adults (England and Wales), also shows how the difference in rates by marital status has actually increased since divorce has become more common (see Chapter 3).

Using data from over 2,000 married couples in the US and followed over 17 years (interviewed in 1980, 1983, 1988, 1992 and 1997), Booth and Amato (2001) further examine the impacts of divorce on children. The children, 691 in total, were aged 19 or over and were interviewed in 1992 and 1997. As in the previous study by Gruber (2004), this study also observed the effects on children into adulthood. Their study focused on the 85 couples who had experienced divorce between 1980 and 1997 and assessed how the pre-divorce relationships between the parents (low- or high-conflict) was predictive of the outcomes on children. The authors note two earlier studies by Amato et al. (1995) and Jekielek (1998) who also researched how the pre-divorce level of conflict was associated with child outcomes. Although both drawn from longitudinal studies, this current Booth and Amato (2001) study represents an extension to these by using a larger sample, a wider range of outcomes, and a more sophisticated method of analysis based on structural equation modelling. The outcome measures were: psychological well-being, support from kin (relatives other than parents), support from friends, intimate (married) relationships, quality of relationship with the parent, and educational attainment. When comparing results for children from divorced and non-divorced children, the outcomes for the children were clearly affected by the levels of conflict in the marriage prior to divorce. When high levels of marital conflict preceded the divorce, children reported improvements in well-being compared to those where there was low conflict. More specifically, the breakdown of relationships where there were low levels of conflict pre-divorce was associated with lower psychological well-being, fewer friend networks, fewer kinship networks and fewer intimate relationships or less satisfying intimate relationships. The difference in outcomes was related to the unexpected, unwelcome and unpredictable nature of the breakdown of low conflict marriages as perceived by the children. This study highlights that the impacts on children depend on the nature of the parental relationship pre-divorce and therefore reiterates the importance of viewing divorce as a 'process'. The study also relates to the mechanisms behind the different impacts of divorce, as well as some of the positive aspects of divorce, both of which will be discussed in greater depth in Chapters 7 and 8 respectively.

Although not necessarily the result of a relationship or marital breakdown, the characteristics of children born to single parents can also be viewed as relevant in this review. This is highlighted in the 'Fragile Families' initiative in the US which is tracking the lives of nearly 5,000 children born between 1998 and 2000, the majority of whom were born to unmarried parents. There are numerous publications derived from this programme that seek to improve the outcomes for parents bringing up children alone. The core study aims to address four main questions (1) What are the conditions and capabilities of unmarried parents, especially fathers? (2) What is the nature of the relationships between unmarried parents? (3) How do children born into these families fare? (4) How do policies and environmental conditions affect families and children? Funding has recently been secured to track the children up to nine years of age. The foundation to this entire programme is based on evidence that children brought up by a single parent, usually the mother and without the father, are likely to be disadvantaged as adults, although it is also acknowledged that finance and poverty are likely to play a greater role than couple relationship breakdown in affecting the extent of this disadvantage (for example, see 'Fragile Families Research Briefs', 2008).

5.3 Impact of couple relationship breakdown on children – multiple relationship transitions

A variation on the studies noted above includes those that have focused on the number of transitions in family structure, and resultant instability, rather than the experience of a single divorce or relationship breakdown event. Wu and Martinson (1993) were influential in assessing the 'instability hypothesis' or that the number of transitions in family structure has a greater influence on child outcomes compared to single parenting. Using pre-marital birth as an outcome of children experiencing family disruption, they found that this was more apparent among women experiencing a number of changes in family structure rather than the time spent in a single-parent family. They conclude that the changes in family structure (e.g. from marriage to divorce, to remarriage, involving step- and half-siblings, etc.) may be more disruptive to children than maintaining a stable family structure, including that of a single parent (also see Hawthorne et al., 2003). This research study subsequently questions the value of parents, after a relationship breakdown, remarrying or cohabiting as a means to improve the outcomes for their children. Note also that being divorced before increases the likelihood of future divorce (see Chapter 8) and thus greater likelihood of further transitions. Additionally, evidence suggests that the effect is accumulative, with increasing negative impacts according to an increased number of transitions experienced by children (Hawthorne et al., 2003). Similar observations have been found in the British NCDS (Elliot and Vaitilingam, 2008), whereby children in stepfamilies report more problems than those with continually married parents and about the same level as those with a single parent (despite the financial advantage of stepfamilies).

To build on this work, Formby and Cherlin (2007) assessed the importance of the 'instability hypothesis', against that of selection, in accounting for children's cognitive and behavioural outcomes following changes in family structure. They used longitudinal data from 1979 to 2000 from the US National Longitudinal Study of Youth and the 2000 'Mother-Child' supplement. Data were derived from 3,392 children and 1,965 mothers. Child outcomes included cognitive achievement and behavioural outcomes (externalizing behaviour scores indicated levels of conduct disorder, disobedience, hyperactivity, etc.), and predictor variables included family transitions (including two-parent family, mother-only family, and stepfamily forms). The descriptive analysis of the data revealed marked instability in family forms, with 64% of children living with both parents in 2000 (although 80% of the entire sample were born to married mothers). Nine percent lived with step-parents, and thus may have experienced the two transitions of relationship breakdown and remarriage. The authors also note that some children experienced up to nine transitions during the period of study. The two main findings from the multivariate analyses illustrate the complexities apparent throughout this review in disentangling the selection effect from the causal effect (in this case the instability hypothesis). Firstly, the mother's characteristics appeared to explain the association between the number of family transitions and decreased cognitive achievement, thus supporting a selection effect in this instance. Secondly, there was evidence of a more causal association between the number of family structure transitions and increased externalizing behaviour (aggression, delinquency, and hyperactivity) among the children. In conclusion, the number of family structure transitions led to an increase in the child's externalizing behaviour but, although also associated with depleted cognitive development, the latter was explained more by selection rather than a causal effect. The paper closes by hypothesising possible explanations for cognitive development not being equally influenced by family instability relative to externalizing behaviour. Explanations include the consistent school (unless the family structure involves changing schools) and fixed genetic factors having a stronger influence on cognitive development, whereby externalizing behaviour may be better explained through the child's social environment which is more closely tied to family disruption.

Further support for the stress of repeated family transitions experienced by children includes the work of Ahrons (2007). From US longitudinal data, this study reported findings from 20 years following a parental divorce. For the majority of those who had experienced a remarriage of their parent, this event was perceived to be more stressful than the divorce itself. Moreover, when both mothers and fathers had remarried, most (two-thirds) considered that the father's remarriage was more stressful than the mothers (Ahrons, 2007). From their longitudinal study of

411 South London men, Juby and Farrington (2001) also note the association between multiple parental transitions and elevated crime-related behaviour. To be reviewed in greater depth in Chapter 6, they note that comparing those experiencing one family transition to those experiencing two or more, the likelihood of criminal behaviour increased. This was observed through criminal convictions (OR=2.8, CI=1.0=7.8) and self-reported criminal activity (OR=2.7, CI=1.0-7.3).

Multiple transitions associated with the divorce process have also been explored in a qualitative manner, involving the perspectives of the young people themselves. Although there are issues concerning the generalisability of these findings, the study by Flowerdew and Neale (2003) makes an important contribution by unearthing some rich detail behind the impacts of multiple transitions on children. From a study of 117 English children living in post-divorce families, the Flowerdew and Neale (2003) study interviewed 60 of these after a three- to four-year-period. All children were aged 11-17 years. From the rich data, they explored why some of the difficulties existed in relation to stepfamily formation. Adapting to a new stepfamily as an adolescent was deemed to be particularly difficult (given the additional life transitions evident during this time of development), and was further complicated by new routines, coping with stepsiblings, and new ground rules. Note the supporting evidence from Hawthorne et al. (2003) and Wallerstein and Kelly (1980), in how children of different age may react differently to reintegration into stepfamilies. In relation, some of the interviewees also reported the loss of the single-parent stability when moving into a new stepfamily form (echoing earlier points made by Wu and Martinson, 1993, and Formby and Cherlin, 2007). A key finding from the Flowerdew and Neale (2003) study was that many interviewees did not report any long-term impact of their parental divorce. It appeared that the life transitions common to all children and adolescents were equally pressing in their lives (such as changing schools, search for identity, new friendships, sexuality, etc.). However, they also identified factors that would impact on their ability to navigate the changes and multiple transitions in family forms that were evident. The young people found it easier if one parent was re-partnering at any one time (rather than at the same time), and also that the pace of change was not too overwhelming for them allowing them a period of "emotional recovery" (p.153). In light of these findings, the authors conclude that,

"Children, like adults are likely to have experienced loss, change and transition in their personal relationships, particularly in the sphere of their friendships and a schooling, and these personal experiences are likely to assume as much, if not more, significance for them as the situations experienced directly by their parents." (Flowerdew and Neale, 2003, p.156).

It is for this reason, coupled by evidence that divorce was not perceived to be especially harmful for all their child interviewees, that Flowerdew and Neale (2003) make a case for "de-centring divorce" (p.155). Moreover, in contextualising their findings with previous research, they note the "shift in emphasis" (p.147) from the assumed negative impacts of divorce affecting all children (also see Chapter 7). Aside to the factors identified above, they highlight a range of additional factors that may affect the outcomes from parental divorce for children, including parental conflict, economic hardship, parental repartnership and stepfamily formation, with those experiencing multiple transitions of this nature reporting the most disadvantage. Therefore, separating out overall impacts of divorce to the impacts of multiple transitions has been useful in this chapter, with the latter generally shown to be more detrimental to the well-being of the children.

5.4 Conclusion and key findings from Chapter 5

This chapter has outlined some of the impacts of parental separation and divorce on children. The focus has been to outline a range of impacts derived from a number of review studies and longitudinal datasets. As when outlining the impacts on adults, the causal effect on child outcomes is difficult to conclude, with the ongoing challenge of controlling for a range of mediating variables (including those unmeasured). In conclusion, there are some grounds to suggest that the 'average' effects of relationship breakdown on children are more inconclusive compared to the more direct impacts on adults. Nonetheless, that is not to say that, for some children, the impacts are detrimental in the long-term. This chapter concludes by listing key findings.

- The impacts of couple relationship breakdown on children are particularly complex given the task of controlling for the effects of life transitions that are commonly experienced, especially through adolescence. Separating out the changes experienced by young adults in terms of schooling, friendships, sexuality, identity, etc. makes the precise impact of relationship breakdown difficult to specify. Disentangling the impacts of couple relationship breakdown on children is complicated further due to the potential selection effects operating through characteristics of themselves and through their parents. The increasing diversity of couple relationship types ('closely-involved', gay parents, surrogate parents, etc.) as illustrated in Chapter 2 presents a further complication when interpreting evidence.
- Evidence from extensive reviews of other studies and vast longitudinal datasets largely in the US and UK has reported associations between couple relationship breakdown and poor child outcomes. These include associations with poverty, behavioural problems including conduct disorder and anti-social behaviour, distress and unhappiness, educational achievement, substance misuse, and physical and emotional health problems.
- The impact of couple relationship breakdown on child health and behaviour has been shown to be long-term for some children through longitudinal, cohort studies. Long-term impacts on mental health, substance misuse, permissive attitudes to pre-marital sex and pre-marital childbirth have all been reported. Other long-term impacts include socio-economic disadvantage, cohabitation or marriage at an early age, teenage pregnancy, a child born outside of marriage, and increased risk of their own marital breakdown.
- These long-term effects are termed as a 'constancy hypothesis' which opposes the 'recency hypothesis' where effects of relationship breakdown would not be evident years after the event. Note also that in relation to problem drinking, a 'latency effect' has been shown whereby the impacts are delayed to manifest in more intensity many years after the divorce. There is, however, less evidence supporting the association between relationship breakdown and long-term consequences on cognitive ability, supporting the evidence of a selection effect (see later in these conclusions).
- Of these child outcomes, the impact on socio-economic disadvantage or poverty appears to be the most prominent and may potentially extend into adulthood.
- The negative associations reported, however, are not evident for all children of separated parents. Although a period of unhappiness may be apparent, most children are able to readjust perfectly well. A number of factors have been identified that may determine the effect on children, including parental conflict, parenting quality, financial hardship and multiple transitions. As a consequence, the way in which

the family functions has been considered to be more important than family type in shaping child outcomes. Poor outcomes for children are clearly far from inevitable, and some children may benefit by being removed from a harmful family environment.

- A range of factors are likely to determine whether negative outcomes are experienced by children of separated parents. Factors exacerbating negative outcomes include financial difficulties, poor parental communication and a continued high level of conflict, lack of post-separation contact, a lack of open communication between parent and child about the separation, and few supporting grandparent, sibling or friendship networks. Of all these factors, parenting and parent-child relationships (affected by the quality of the couple relationship) appear to be the most influential in affecting child outcomes. As many of these moderating factors are relevant both pre- and post-separation, the separation or divorce must be viewed as a 'process' rather than a single event. Also, these protective factors suggest that the separation of divorce, per se, is unlikely to be the major explanatory factor behind these impacts.
- Given these moderating factors, it is possible that many of the negative outcomes for children are attributed to a range of pre-existing factors rather than the break-up of relationships. However, research has also shown that divorce itself has the ability to exacerbate these outcomes, through an increased exposure to parental conflict, less effective parenting, and further disruptions such as new family formation and moving schools or location. The extent to which these selecting, pre-existing differences exist, relative to the impact of the divorce itself, remains unresolved (in similar fashion to the adult impacts). Experienced researchers in the field, consequently, highlight the ambiguous nature of the evidence and also call for more research.
- Divorce or separation where conflict between parents has been low or hidden has been associated with a lower level of child well-being compared to situations of high conflict. This is due to the event being more unexpected by children. Nonetheless, intense destructive conflict between parents has been shown to be more detrimental to children than the actual event of parental separation.
- There is little consensus over whether the impacts are affected by the gender of children. There is some evidence to suggest that boys find parental separation more disturbing although girls show greater long-term impacts. Also, boys find adjustment to stepfamilies easier than girls, especially when girls are in early adolescence. In terms of age, older children tend to report more adverse consequences of further transitions such as integration into stepfamilies (whereas younger children appear to find this easier to adapt to). However, younger children may not recognise the distress among parents and thus separation may result in greater confusion and anxiety, and may lead to them blaming themselves for the separation. Younger children experiencing the separation of their parents also have a greater potential to experience multiple transitions (due to their younger age) compared to older children.
- Even though divorce is more common nowadays, there is evidence to suggest that the detrimental outcomes for children associated with divorce are still equally apparent. This opposes the argument that increasing divorce rates diminish the negative impacts in line with reduced stigma and more acceptance of relationship breakdown.
- The instability associated with multiple changes in family structure, such as separation and remarriage, has been found to be more

detrimental to children compared to stable family forms, even if that stability is single parenthood. Other studies, however, have shown less of a divide between stepfamilies and single parenthood, with both being associated with lower child well-being compared to those from intact families (this is despite the financial advantage of many stepfamilies).

- Research has shown evidence of a causal relationship between multiple transitions and childhood externalizing behaviour (conduct disorder, disobedience, hyperactivity, etc.). However, the relationship between multiple transitions and decreased cognitive achievement may be better explained through a selection effect via the mother's characteristics. This may be due to multiple transitions having less impact on cognitive development where there may be stable schooling and fixed genetic factors, whereas externalizing behaviour may be better explained through the child's social environment which is more closely tied to the disruption of family structure.
- Long-term consequences of multiple transitions in family formation and dissolution have been documented. One longitudinal study showed that the majority of children found the remarriage of their parent more stressful than the divorce itself (that occurred over 20 years prior). The effects are also considered to be accumulative, with the increased number of transitions leading to greater consequences for children.
- Multiple transitions in family formation, in general, have been shown to be more detrimental to the child than the single event of parental divorce or separation. In view of this, some researchers have called for the 'de-centring' of divorce and a 'shift in emphasis' from the assumed negative impacts of divorce affecting all children. Overall, those experiencing multiple transitions report the most detrimental outcomes.
- Qualitative research has shown that children find multiple transitions easier if one parent is repartnering at any one time (rather than at the same time), and also if the pace of change is not too overwhelming for them.
- Although the majority of reviewed studies document negative outcomes, the breakdown of high conflict couple relationships can be seen as being beneficial to children (and adults).

Chapter 6
Impact of couple relationship breakdown on children: Specific outcomes

6.1 Introduction

This chapter continues to outline the impact of couple relationship breakdown on children. Differing to the previous chapter, this chapter reviews studies that have focussed on specific outcomes in terms of:

- physical health;
- psychological health;
- educational and employment;
- health-related behaviours; and
- wider aspects.

6.2 Impact of couple relationship breakdown on children – physical health

As an overall indication of the impact of relationship breakdown on the physical health of children, the 2001 census of Great Britain serves as a useful data source. Table 7 shows the relative risk of a 'limiting long-term illness' among children aged 0-15 years. Using children living with both natural parents as the benchmark (1.00), it is clear that children in all other family types have an elevated risk of having such illness. The highest by some margin are for those children not living in a family (1.87), followed by those living with a lone or single mother (1.66 – about two-thirds higher than those with both natural parents). As for all these comparative findings, they are unable to support a causal relationship. To illustrate, findings in Chapter 5 reporting detrimental outcomes for children of single parents support the importance of financial disadvantage (characteristic for many single parents) rather than single parenthood per se in contributing to such outcomes.

Table 7 – Relative risk of limiting long-term illness among children aged 0-15 by family type (with both natural parent = 1), by age and sex, 2001.

Family Type	Relative Risk	Number	Distribution (%)
Both natural parents	1.00	8,285,403	65.0
Natural mother and stepfather	1.30	464,577	3.6
Natural father and stepmother	1.11	58,043	0.5
Natural parents and stepfather	1.32	658,157	5.2
Natural parents and stepmother	1.27	113,388	0.9
Stepmother and stepfather	1.18	60,617	0.5
Natural parents and stepmother and stepfather	1.34	21,904	0.2
Lone mother	1.66	2,684,767	21.1
Lone father	1.29	255,918	2.0
Not in a family	1.87	135,155	1.1
Total		12,737,929	100

Source: Great Britain census, 2001, Murphy (2007)

* For definitions of family type see Appendix 1.

In providing further evidence, the impact of relationship breakdown on the physical health or development of children can be viewed as affecting various life stages. For example, research has assessed impacts on pre-natal and infant development, parental health behaviours with the infant child (e.g. breastfeeding), and pubertal development. These life stages will be reflected in the order of the material presented in this section. At the outset, descriptive evidence shows that low birth weight children are more likely to be born to mothers who are unmarried (Collingwood Bakeo and Clarke, 2006) or who have registered their children alone (ONS, 1988-2003) compared to mothers who are married. At this level of description, however, it is inaccurate to assume that such a link may be causal. As will be shown later in this chapter, recognising the different family trajectories provided by longitudinal studies will show greater insights into these apparent associations.

A significant international review of studies by Talge and colleagues (2007) presents convincing evidence that maternal stress (for which relationship conflict or breakdown may be one of several causes) during pregnancy can lead to detrimental outcomes for children. This includes a greater likelihood of emotional and cognitive problems, anxiety, language delay and an increased likelihood of Attention Deficit/Hyperactivity Disorder (ADHD). Importantly, these effects have been shown to be independent of post-natal depression and anxiety. From the review, Talge et al. estimate that the "...attributable load of emotional/behavioural problems due to antenatal stress and/or anxiety is approximately 15%" (p. 245). They highlight the physiological pathways that may be responsible for these outcomes, including the role of maternal cortisol levels. Although evidence of a link is substantiated in this study, the authors also note that the types of stress known to affect infant development still remains largely unanswered. Their concerns are shown as follows:

"There is still much to learn about the types of antenatal emotional disturbance or stress that is most harmful for foetal and child development and the contexts in which such effects may be attenuated. None of the published studies have employed clinical interviews, and it is not known whether specific sub-types of maternal psychopathology (e.g. phobia, generalized anxiety disorder, post-traumatic stress disorder (PTSD)) differentially predict postnatal outcomes." (Talge et al., 2007, p. 252).

Within the UK, Bergman et al. (2007) explored the impacts of maternal stress on infant cognitive ability and fearfulness. The study was conducted among mothers who underwent an amniocentesis at a hospital site in London. One hundred and twenty-three infants were assessed for cognitive development and 106 of these for fearfulness (as a precursor to anxiety problems). The study was particularly relevant to this review since maternal stress (during pregnancy and recorded postnatally) included specific reference to couple relationship strain alongside other stressors such as accidents, illness, financial, legal, employment and housing issues. Within the 'Stressful Life Events Questionnaire', relationship strain was assessed by measuring whether, when pregnant, they had become separated or divorced, had a serious argument with their partner, and whether their partner was 'emotionally cruel' to them. When 14 to 19 months old, the infant's cognitive development was assessed using the Bayley Scales of Infant Development, and the Laboratory Temperament Assessment Battery was used to assess fearfulness. The results showed that maternal stress affected the infant's cognitive development and fearfulness. For the former, a negative correlation was found (i.e. higher stress = lower cognitive development) and for the latter a positive correlation was observed (higher stress =

higher fearfulness). When undertaking a multiple regression, and controlling for maternal age, smoking and alcohol use in pregnancy, birth weight, and maternal education, the levels of maternal stress were still found to be a significant predictor of the infant's outcomes. More precisely, maternal stress was found to predict 17% of the variance in cognitive development scores, and 10% of the variance in fearfulness. Significantly for this review, the study also found that the three couple relationship strain items were the only ones associated with both outcomes. They accounted for 73.5% and 75.0% of the total variance of pre-natal stress events on cognitive and fearfulness scores respectively. In further discussion, the authors note that the cognitive and fearfulness outcomes were not correlated, implying that their associations with stress are mediated by different mechanisms. They also outline how factors such as genetic vulnerability may increase infant susceptibility to the possible effects of pre-natal stress but, understandably, are difficult to measure. This influential paper adds to earlier contributions in this field by controlling for possible covariates and also by identifying the specific types of maternal stress which may have the greatest influence (in this case, relationship stress).

The note about mediating variables identified by Bergman et al. (2007) can be used to link to this next study. In trying to understand more about how relationship status and quality can influence the health of the infant, Kiernan and Pickett (2006) explored the relationship between 'parent connectedness' and health behaviours of the mother that could be detrimental to infant health. Using data from the 'Millennium Cohort Study', which involved 18,819 children (born 2000-2001) who were aged about nine months during the first sweep during 2001-2002 (see Chapter 2), the study found that smoking in pregnancy, breastfeeding and maternal depression were significantly associated with parental (couple) connectedness, even when socio-demographic factors were controlled for. In more detail, smoking was more likely among mothers lacking an intimate relationship. For the damaging effects of smoking in pregnancy and its association with reduced birth weight and foetal growth, see Del Bono et al. (2008). Stronger parental bonds were associated with the initiation of breastfeeding, with a difference observed between cohabiting and solo mothers. Weaker parental bonds were associated with an increased risk of maternal depression. This study showed how the degree of parental connectedness, by affecting health-related behaviours, can affect the future health of the developing infant.

Moving into later life, the impact of couple relationship breakdown on age at puberty has been investigated by Ellis and Essex (2007). While puberty itself is a natural developmental phase, the timing of its onset has been shown to be associated with health. The Ellis and Essex (2007) paper draws reference to several studies that show that early pubertal maturation in girls is associated with a variety of negative health and psychosocial outcomes, including teenage pregnancy, mood disorders, substance abuse and cancers of the reproductive system. Using a longitudinal design, Ellis and Essex (2007) interviewed parents and children to assess the development of secondary sexual characteristics among 180 girls aged 11, and the presence of 'quality parental investment'. A subsample of 120 children (73 girls) were examined for the presence of adrenal hormones at the younger age of 7. In sum, the higher level of parental investment and the less reported marital conflict (reported by fathers) was found to forecast later pubertal development and be "...a central feature of the proximal family environment in relation to pubertal timing." (p. 1,799). The authors also note the additional factors that emerged as independently and significantly predicting later pubertal timing, including a mother's older age at menarche, higher socio-economic status, greater mother-based parental supportiveness and lower body-mass index. These findings are supported by a paper presented by Bellis et al. (2006). However, they are not supported by the secondary analysis of national sexual behaviour survey data (see later in this chapter) by Kiernan and Hobcraft (1997), who found "no strong evidence of a relationship between family disruption and age at menarche." (p.48).

To complete the life-course approach to this section, evidence on the physical development and health of children in later life would be an appropriate consideration. However, in comparison to the early years development, physical health characteristics in later life are more problematic given the range of additional factors that could affect this. In comparison to the earlier life events, there are simply too many variables to control for that would enable the effect of relationship breakdown to be determined, bar a descriptive comparison of outcomes. Nonetheless, of relevance, Herberth et al. (2008) present a very useful and recent paper on child health conducted in Germany. They note that stressful events, and specifically the divorce or separation of parents, is associated with an increase in the Vasoactive Intestinal Peptide (VIP) and high levels of the Th2 cytokine IL-4 in the blood. They hypothesise that the VIP levels may mediate the stressful life event and the Th2 response, which is associated with poor immune regulation. Although more detail on these mechanisms is provided in Chapter 7, the study clearly identifies a physiological response associated with parental separation that is detrimental to the physical health of children.

6.3 Impact of couple relationship breakdown on children – psychological health

Wilcox et al. (2005), in reviewing evidence from the social science literature, describes the relationship between divorce and the increased risks of "serious psychological and social problems for children" (p.4). In addition, a review of the prevalence of mental health problems among children in Great Britain, conducted by Darton (2005), provides further associations between parental relationship breakdown and child mental health. From a review of evidence, the Darton (2005) report makes three important points. Firstly, that the prevalence rates of child mental health are greater among single-parent families and stepfamilies compared to those where the parental relationship has not broken down. Secondly, the mental health state of the parents (especially the mother), plausibly linked to a relationship breakdown, may affect the mental health of their children. Thirdly, although there are always exceptions, it does appear that family conflict, alongside poverty, are the most important factors in increasing the risk of child mental health problems. This implies that the factors that precede and follow parental separation may be more important in shaping the impacts for children rather than the separation event itself (reiterating the importance of the divorce 'process' outlined in Chapter 5). The review also puts the importance of relationship breakdown into context, by recognising that a whole host of other factors impinge on a child's mental health such as parental imprisonment, physical and emotional abuse, and alcohol and drug use.

In more detail, much of the Darton (2005) review data are derived from an extensive survey carried out in 1999 by Meltzer et al. (2000) within Great Britain. From a total of 10,438 interviews with parents, teachers and children (interviews among children aged 11-15 within the total sample of 5-15 year olds), they reported that 10% of these children aged 5-15 had a mental disorder. Prevalence rates were also associated with various family forms. As examples, childhood mental disorders were more common among those raised by single parents (16% compared to 8% with two-parent families). Whether this single parent was widowed, divorced or separated had no bearing on the prevalence rates. However, there were interesting gender differences with nearly one in five boys of single parents having a mental disorder (mostly conduct disorder) compared to one in eight girls (equal proportions of conduct and emotional disorders). Heightened impacts of marital discord among boys relative to girls has been reported elsewhere by Earls and Jung (1987) and more recent research by Noller et al. (2000) outlined how boys and girls respond differently to conflict (e.g. by girls getting more involved in the conflict than boys).

The Meltzer et al. (2000) survey also found that mental disorders were more prevalent among children of reconstituted families where stepchildren were present (15%) compared to those without stepchildren (9%). The health or 'family functioning' of the family was also associated with child mental health. Using the McMaster Family Assessment Device (a number of statements rated by parents, for example, 'There are lots of bad feelings in the family'), children with a mental disorder were twice as likely to live within families defined by the Family Assessment Device as 'unhealthy' (35% compared with 17%). With the associations between couple relationship breakdown and poor mental health of parents (Chapter 4), and from the wealth of parenting literature, it is intuitive that these detrimental impacts on parental mental health are implicated among children. Nonetheless, throughout this Meltzer et al. (2000) survey, the relationship between family formation and childhood mental health are recognised as associations rather than causal relationships. Indeed, one of the most significant caveats noted by the authors is the substantial differences between socio-economic status and family formation (with married and cohabiting couples reporting a more favourable financial situation than single parents). The Meltzer at al. (2000) paper also cites evidence from Australia in support of these findings, whereby Zubrick et al. (1995) reported a 2:1 odds ratio or likelihood of childhood mental disorders among single parent families (compared to two-parent families).

Also within Great Britain, Chase-Lansdale et al. (1995) make a useful contribution to the literature. They report findings from The 'National Child Development Study' of a sample of children born in 1958. They explored the outcomes of parental divorce over the long-term, with these children followed up at ages 7 and 23. The value of such a longitudinal study is that it allows findings to be derived prospectively rather than examining the impacts of relationship breakdown through retrospective accounts. The sample was restricted to those children whose parents were married from birth to age 7 and who were successfully followed up at ages 7 and 16 (to note whether divorce had occurred in childhood). This culminated in a sample of 7,966 children, including 382 cases of where the child's parents were divorced or separated between ages 7 and 16. The mental health status of the children (now adults at 23 years of age) was derived using the Malaise Inventory (Rutter et al., 1970) and from information provided by parents, teachers, health service providers, and the young people themselves. Using regression and path analysis, the study found that the long-term effects of divorce in childhood had negative consequences in terms of adult emotional adjustment. The authors note that the impacts are "moderate" (p.1631) although a minority group will develop serious mental health problems as a result. They also found that divorce when children are adolescents tends to have a greater negative impact, possibly due to the life changes and degree of disturbance that they themselves are experiencing at the same time. Interestingly, they also found that divorce followed by remarriage did not significantly predict higher levels of mental health distress relative to those from intact families, which the authors note is a finding inconsistent with previous research.

Evidence from the UK 'Millennium Cohort Study' supports the association between parental separation and child outcomes. Kiernan and Mensah (forthcoming) found that relative to children of stable married families (between when the child was 9 months and aged 5), those children from single parent families, those of separated cohabiting parents and those from single mothers who had repartnered all showed more emotional problems. Interestingly, these differences in child emotional problems across these family trajectories became insignificant when poverty and maternal depression were taken into account. However, when observing behavioural problems, statistically significant differences were still observed across family trajectories when these two conditions were controlled for. The study showed that relative to continually married families, children born to cohabiting parents who separate and children of single mothers who cohabit with the natural father or partner another man are more likely to exhibit behaviour problems (Kiernan and Mensah, forthcoming).

The Chase-Lansdale et al. (1995) and Kiernan and Mensah (forthcoming) longitudinal studies show some consistency with the observations by Richards et al. (1997). Richards et al. (1997) also reported long-term emotional problems associated with parental divorce, and the growing consensus that emotional problems may be more pronounced than impacts on cognitive ability (see next section on educational attainment). Moreover, indications of a causal relationship between marital breakdown and emotional well-being among children was reported by O'Connor and Jenkins (2000) using Canadian longitudinal data from 2,598 children and 2,129 families. Nonetheless, a more recent study by D'Onofrio et al. (2007) failed to find evidence of a causal relationship between couple relationship breakdown and internalised behaviour, which was found to be an artefact of selection (via parents characteristics and genetic factors, etc.). The latter study shows consistency with the earlier-cited MCS findings reported by Kiernan and Mensah (forthcoming) whereby the associations between parental separation and emotional problems became insignificant when maternal depression and poverty were taken into account.

Further evidence of child mental health outcomes from divorce are reported by Strohschein (2005) using three cycles from a longitudinal data in Canada (1994, 1996 and 1998). The study tracked children aged 4-7 years living in two-parent families over a four-year period, comparing those children where parents did and did not divorce over this period. The study was able to control for the socio-economic (financial and human capital) and psychological resources (marital satisfaction, parental depression and family dysfunction) prior to divorce. As these factors have been shown to be independently associated with child mental health problems, controlling for them in this study could test whether the association between divorce and child mental health is spurious (where evidence of a causal relationship cannot be assumed). The age and gender of the parent and child were also controlled. The final sample size was 2,819 children, of whom 167 experienced a parental divorce. Child mental health was measured in terms of anxiety / depression and anti-social behaviour. Using a growth curve model[14] to control for the range of variables

14. A growth curve model is a sophisticated method of analysis that takes advantage of all the information provided by multiple waves of longitudinal data and explicitly models both individual and group patterns of change. Growth curve analysis is considered to characterise change over time more reliably and precisely than traditional statistical tests such as the analysis of variance (ANOVA) (Willett, 1994). Also see Chapter 10 for remarks on recent statistical advances.

specified, Strohschein (2005) found that children whose parents divorced during the study reported higher than average anxiety and depression prior to divorce, followed by an increase in these outcomes after the divorce. Conversely, although anti-social behaviour was similarly higher among children whose parents later divorce, this was not found to increase after the divorce event (unlike anxiety and depression). For interest, anxiety and depression was measured in terms of the extent the child was perceived by the parent to be happy, fearful, worried, miserable and nervous. These findings clearly show that there are divorce-specific increases in poor mental health (anxiety and depression) among children that cannot be accounted for by differences in socio-economic and psychosocial resources. The author closes by recognising the strength of the study, but also notes the importance of tracking child outcomes both pre- and for many years after the divorce to capture the impacts of the divorce 'process'.

In a later paper, Strohschein (2007), again using data from the 'National Longitudinal Survey of Children and Youth', compared methylphenidate use among children whose parents had been divorced between 1994 and 2000 to those who had not. Methylphenidate is a drug used to treat Attention-Deficit Hyperactivity Disorder. After controlling for age of the mother and age and sex of the children, she found that the use of methylphenidate was significantly higher among children whose parents had divorced compared to those who remained married (OR=1.85, CI=1.01-3.33). However, Strohschein notes that evidence of a causal link is subject to controlling for a range of further variables such as use of health care, genetic links and the selection effects of childhood ADHD leading to parental divorce.

Arguably the most dramatic outcome of poor psychological ill-health is suicide. Understandably, there are huge difficulties in exploring this area and therefore there is relatively little research exploring the precise influence of parental separation as a predictor of this event. A useful contribution from Smyth and Maclachlan (2004), as part of their study in developing their 12 item 'Trinity Inventory of Precursors to Suicide' derived from undergraduate student data, was their review of the available evidence in this field. They note the influence of family relationships alongside other factors as follows:

"A review of the current literature identified predisposing life events [of suicide] which generally fall into four broad themes; (a) interpersonal difficulty, (b) illness, (c) familial disruption and (d) loss." (Smyth and Maclachlan, 2004, p.85).

6.4 Impact of couple relationship breakdown on children – education and employment

One of the most comprehensive assessments of the impact of couple relationship breakdown on childhood educational attainment was reported by Ely et al. (1999). The study used data from three British birth cohorts (The Medical Research Council 'National Survey of Health and Development' – 1946, 'The National Child Development Study' – 1958, and the 'British Cohort Study' – 1970) comprising approximately 40,000 cases. Information about parental divorce was recorded at ages 15 or 16, and educational qualifications were recorded at ages 16, 23 and 26 (according to which birth cohort). As expected, average levels of educational attainment increased through time. To assess the impact of marital breakdown, they used the median[15] level of educational attainment as the outcome for each of the three birth cohorts. For those children experiencing parental divorce, the relative risk of achieving lower than the median level of educational attainment was 1.3 for the 1946

15. The median level represents the educational attainment of one-half of the population of cohort members.

cohort (CI=1.2-1.5), and 1.4 for the 1958 and 1970 cohorts (CI=1.3-1.5). Ely et al. (1999) acknowledge the lack of evidence to imply a causal relationship, with family income and socio-economic status known to be important mediating factors in this relationship. The authors conclude the significance of this association as follows:

"The risk [of lower educational attainment of children of divorced parents] is quite small compared to the effect of other factors on education such as socioeconomic status, but is one which is statistically significant based on the large cohort studies used here. Although the estimated relative risk is small, its social importance has increased as the proportion of children affected by this type of family change has increased in line with the increase in the divorce rate." (Ely et al., 1999, p.450).

Indeed, an important addition to the Ely et al. (1999) paper is its attention on how increasing divorce rates since the launch of these cohorts has impacted on educational attainment levels. Significantly, they note how these remarkably constant relative risks have not declined over the period of study, thus opposing a 'reduced effect hypothesis' (see Chapter 5). This counters evidence in previous studies cited in the paper, such as the meta-analysis conducted by Amato and Keith (1991) who noted the effect sizes on child well-being had reduced over time. The difference in findings may be due to the earlier time frame of the Amato and Keith (1991) study, as well as the increasing role of economic disparity rather than the more accepting attitudes to divorce that are associated with such a reduced effect hypothesis.

The impact of couple relationship breakdown on educational attainment can also be derived from studies that have explored the impacts of parental conflict, whether or not this acts as a precursor of later divorce. A recent longitudinal study by Harold et al. (2007) has explored precisely this, following up 230 school children in the UK during 1999, 2000 and 2001. The children were aged 11-13 years. The study recorded data on parent and child reports of inter-parental conflict, children's perceptions of negative parent-child relations, appraisals of self-blame for marital conflict, children's aggressive behaviour, and children's academic attainment on standardised tests. Although this review is more concerned with relationship breakdown rather than parental conflict, it is worth noting the two leading explanations for its documented negative impact on children, as outlined in the Harold et al. (2007) paper. These are due to the breakdown in the parent-child relationship and/or the negative emotions and representations of family relationships among those children exposed to this conflict (the latter including self-blame attributions). Using structured equation modelling, Harold et al. (2007) found that children experiencing high inter-parental conflict were at risk of lower educational attainment. However, an interesting element of this study was the greater explanation offered by the self-blame experienced by children in attributing their parents' arguments, rather then their perception of the parent-child relationship. Therefore, although interventions need to foster a continued parent-child relationship to alleviate the impact of parental conflict on children, they also need to consider ways in which children perceive and attribute conflict, especially in terms of the impact upon their educational attainment.

Although rarely considered by previous papers in this section, a further and perhaps more obvious impact of relationship breakdown on educational attainment could be the reduced time that parents have to dedicate interest in their child's educational development. A single parent may have competing interests and time pressures, whereas a two-parent family may have more time to convey their interest towards their child's educational attainment. This is particularly significant as Feinstein and Symons (1999), using data from 'The National Child Development Study', found that parental interest in education was more important in influencing a child's educational attainment compared to schooling variables such as teacher-pupil ratios.

The effects of relationship breakdown on educational attainment, like other outcomes, are clearly complex and evidence of a causal relationship is rarely supported. This point is made well by Sanz-De-Galdeano and Vuri (2007) who, whilst recognising the association between relationship breakdown and negative child outcomes, note that,

"...this large literature can hardly be interpreted causally because divorce is associated with socio-economic characteristics that also determine children's attainments.....therefore it is easy to overstate the detrimental impact of divorce." (Sanz-De-Galdeano and Vuri, 2007, p. 322)

Sanz-De-Galdeano and Vuri (2007) support this assertion through their own study using a representative sample from the US 'National Education Longitudinal Study', to examine the relationship between parental divorce and young people's performance on standardised educational tests. The longitudinal data used here were derived from 24,599 13 to 14-year-olds in 1988 who were followed up in 1990 (n=17,500) and 1992 (n=16,500). To unpick the association between parental divorce and educational attainment, they apply 'double and triple difference models' to their longitudinal data that are able to assess children from intact and divorced backgrounds both before and after the divorce takes place. This essentially allows them to control for "teenager-specific effects" (p.337) that would otherwise not allow them to differentiate between a causal and non-causal association. These effects (or factors that are controlled for in their analysis) include ethnicity, religion, parents' education and socio-economic status. In sum, and as the overriding conclusion, Sanz-De-Galdeano and Vuri (2007) find that parental divorce did not have a negative causal effect on teenager cognitive development. Also, they observed that teenagers from divorced families performed worse than their counterparts from intact families before the divorce occurred. This point is significant as it may account for a selection effect, whereby cross-sectional studies actually overestimate the negative impacts of divorce when attributing this educational attainment to the divorce event. Reasons postulated for this effect may include marital conflict and disinterest in the family which may both lead to divorce and worse outcomes for children.

Frequently linked to educational attainment is children's (of divorced parents) success in terms of employment and economic resources. A paper written by Gregg and Machin (1998) is particularly notable since it used data from the 'British National Child Development Survey' containing details on child development from age 0 (1958) through to age 33 (at the time of their writing). They essentially explored the relationship between a number of childhood disadvantage factors and compared them to economic success in later life. At the descriptive level, they found that poorer school attendance and performance was associated with single parenthood, as well as parents' financial difficulties and their educational level. Through their analytical modelling, they find that social disadvantages during childhood impact on economic success in later life. They report that educational attainment acts as an important 'transmission mechanism' in determining economic success, and they note that poor school attendance and childhood financial disadvantage are especially influential in affecting this education. For relevance to this review, Gregg and Machin (1998) note the association between single parenthood and poverty, thus explaining the link between single parenthood and economic success in later life described above. It is in this manner that poverty, rather than single parenthood per se, operates as one likely cause of economic success in later life among children raised by separated parents. Likewise, the role of poverty has been cited to explain many of the outcomes for children of single parents cited in Chapter 5 and the Table presented at the outset of this chapter on child limiting long-term illness. To illustrate, women in Britain have been found to be 40% more likely to enter poverty if they divorce than if they remain married (Aassve et al., 2006).

6.5 Impact of couple relationship breakdown on children – health-related behaviours

In terms of health-related behaviours, most research has examined the impact of relationship breakdown on substance misuse, sexual behaviour and crime. An interesting study by Ledoux et al. (2002) looked at the influence of family variables on substance misuse among 15 to 16-years-olds in the UK and France. Although their study found that parental knowledge about young people's whereabouts was the strongest predictor of substance misuse, they also showed that parental 'intactness' in the UK, and strong paternal relationships in France, were predictive of reduced substance misuse. In addition, and within the UK, Miller (1997) reported findings from a survey of 7,722 15 to16-year-olds and found that people living with both parents were significantly less likely to smoke and use illicit drugs compared to those where parents had separated. This association was more prominent among girls than boys. When controlling for psychological symptoms, social support and various other behaviours, the effects were reduced suggesting that these variables may mediate the relationship between family structure and substance misuse.

Using data from the British 1958 'National Child Development Study', Hope et al. (1998) outlined the relationship between parental separation in childhood and problem drinking in adulthood. Data were derived from 9,498 men and women who were interviewed at ages 23 and 33. Problem drinking was recorded via the CAGE measure ('Cut down', 'Annoy', 'Guilty', and 'Eye opener' – see Chapter 4) and heavy drinking was measured in terms of alcoholic units (more then 20 units for women and 35 or more for men over the course of a week). Parental separation in childhood was defined as when aged 0-16 years. The paper highlights two interesting findings. Firstly, those exposed to parental divorce in childhood experienced a significantly greater likelihood of problem or heavy drinking. Secondly, and of real added interest, for those exposed to childhood divorce, the effects on problem and heavy drinking were weaker at age 23 compared to age 33. At age 33, and when own marital status and socio-economic status had been controlled for, the odds ratios for problem and heavy drinking ranged from 1.29 to 1.90 relative to those not experiencing a parental separation (and exceeded the odds ratios for when aged 23). The authors describe this stronger effect at age 33 as "a degree of latency in relation to parental separation" (p.511) and cite other studies that have similarly observed a latency effect for psychological distress following parental separation. This study, therefore, shows further evidence for the long-term effects of childhood parental separation in later life (supporting the previously reviewed studies by Chase-Lansdale et al., 1995; Booth and Amato, 2001; and Gruber, 2004 that all reported long-term impacts of divorce).

The impact of parental relationship breakdown on sexual attitudes and risky sexual behaviour has also been documented. Data from the first British 'National Survey of Sexual Attitudes and Lifestyles' (NATSAL, Johnson et al., 1994), consisting of a nationally representative sample of

18,876 people aged from 16 to 59 years, has been used by Kiernan and Hobcraft (1997) to examine the relationship between parental divorce during childhood and three outcome measures. These outcome measures were early age at first intercourse, partnership, and parenthood. Their multivariate analysis found that early first intercourse (defined as age 16 or earlier) was more likely among children of divorced parents. Through further analysis, they examined whether this age at first intercourse had any bearing on the observed association between parental divorce and early teenage first partnership and teenage parenthood. They found that the association between parental divorce and teenage first partnership and parenthood is mediated through, or derived from, the early first sexual intercourse. In support of a more causal inference, they conclude:

"The analysis has shown that earlier sexual activity for men and women from disrupted families is an important proximate determinant of their earlier entry into partnership and parenthood, compared with those brought up with both natural parents." (Kiernan and Hobcraft, 1997, p.55).

The more recent NATSAL survey (Wellings et al., 2001), involving 11,161 16 to 44-year-olds also found an association between relationship breakdown and teenage parenthood. Girls from single parent (a proportion of whom may have experienced a relationship breakdown) households were 1.6 times more likely to become a parent before the age of 18 compared to those living with both parents.

From the US, Jeynes (2001) reported evidence from the 'National Educational Longitudinal Survey' for years 1988, 1990 and 1992 (n=18,726 17-18 year olds). The following results are derived from logistic regression where variables such as socio-economic status, race and gender were controlled. Jeynes (2001) notes how children of divorced parents had more permissive attitudes to pre-marital sex than children from intact families. He also notes that these impacts are long-term and are supportive of a 'constancy hypothesis'. This opposes the alternative 'recency hypothesis' which would assume that only children of those recently divorced (within the last four years) would have such attitudes. In terms of behaviour (a child born out of wedlock), the differences between children whose parents were divorced and together were again evident in later life (akin to the latency effect reported earlier in this section by Hope et al., 1998).

The impact of couple relationship breakdown has also been shown to affect criminal or 'delinquent' behaviour in children. Derived from the 'Cambridge Study in Delinquent Development', which was a longitudinal survey of 411 South London men, Juby and Farrington (2001) note the association between relationship breakdown and crime. First surveyed when aged 8 or 9 years (in 1961/62), they were contacted again seven times until the age of 46, alongside a series of repeated interviews with their parents. Crime outcomes were obtained from a combination of Criminal Record Office and self-reported behaviour. At the descriptive level, the associations between elevated crime involvement and relationship breakdown were clear in two domains. Firstly, family disruption (where the child was separated from the biological parent) was associated with an increase likelihood of convictions and self-reported 'delinquency' in childhood (OR=2.1, CI=1.2-3.7). Secondly, high family conflict also increased the likelihood of self-reported delinquency in childhood (OR=2.4, CI=1.3-4.4). Also at a descriptive level, they also found that loss or separation from the mother had more negative outcomes in terms of criminal behaviour, and conflict and disruption had a greater impact than parental death. Using multiple regression, they examined these factors more precisely by controlling for potential mediating variables, namely: family income, family size, convicted parent, parental supervision, attitude and discipline of parents, and the child's IQ, school attainment, hyperactivity, risk-taking and 'troublesomeness'. After controlling for these variables, parental disruption variables were found to be predictive of childhood convictions and self-reported criminal behaviour. However, rather than conclude the damaging impacts of parental separation, they also note that separation from the mother, multiple transitions into new families (see previous chapter) and high parental conflict are equally as influential in predicting crime. Likewise, where parental separation is followed by the boy living with the mother where there is no parental conflict or new family form, the likelihood of criminal involvement would be similar to those from harmonious two-parent families. The study details some of the theoretical evidence behind explaining these relationships, through a life-course perspective rather than trauma or selection hypotheses (see Chapter 7).

Farrington, in a earlier review published in 1996, also reported the association between parental conflict and parental separation with increased likelihood of youth crime. In this review, he also notes the increased role of parental separation and conflict over that of parental death, and also questions whether the separation or the conflict associated with the separation that has the greatest effect on youth crime. He also highlights that parental conflict and separation sits alongside "thousands of factors" (p.2) connected to youth crime and the problems associated in disentangling the many factors that coincide. A note of the other main factors, alongside parental conflict and separation, that increase the likelihood of crime illustrates this complex interaction of influences: low income, poor housing, deteriorated inner-city residence, impulsiveness and hyperactivity, low intelligence and school attainment, and poor parental supervision with harsh and erratic discipline.

Therefore, criminal behaviour appears to be associated both with the divorce or separation itself, as well as subsequent outcomes of the divorce that may include poor housing, poverty, poor parental supervision, etc. Returning to the substance misuse reviewed at the start of this section, the complexity raised by Farrington (1996) is also echoed in observing the link between behaviours and mental illness. For example, using a Swedish cohort of 47,033 conscripts followed up for 18 years, Hansagi et al. (2000) noted the relationship between parental divorce and both increased alcoholism and mental health problems. Clearly, it is particularly problematic to detect the causal pathway between alcoholism and mental health.

6.6 The impact of couple relationship breakdown on children – wider aspects

In terms of the wider impacts of relationship breakdown beyond other behaviours, the role of grandparents has also been researched. From the UK, Drew and Smith (1999) conducted a study that involved questionnaires completed by 86 grandparents of children aged from 4 to 15 years. The children's parents (sons and daughters of the grandparents) were divorced. The importance of this evidence stems from the knowledge that grandparents play an important part in the development and well-being of their grandchildren. These effects are either transmitted directly (leisure activities, cognitive development, emotional support, etc.) or indirectly (supporting parents financially, models of parenting, etc.). Factors affecting the significance of this support include age and mobility of grandparents, age of grandchildren (older children have more control on the grandparent-grandchild contact), and lineage (with most frequent contact through maternal grandmothers relative to paternal grandfathers). The study used questionnaires administered cross-sectionally to assess how the relationship between the grandparents and grandchildren had changed since the divorce of the child's parents.

Although a longitudinal design would have been preferred, and that the paper drew most reference to the effects on grandparents, there were some interesting aspects relating to the children. Drew and Smith (1999), using measures from a 5-point scale and two factor ANOVAs, found that parental separation had resulted in changes in proximity (distance lived from grandchild), contact (how often they are seen) and the emotional relationship. The effects on reduced contact and emotion were of greater statistical significance compared to proximity. To illustrate, following the divorce, proximity typically decreased from nearby to somewhere within the same town, whereas contact fell typically from weekly to monthly or yearly, and emotional bonds fell from 'very' or extremely close' to a 'little bit close' or 'close'.

Perhaps the widest of additional impacts on children is that identified by Amato and Cheadle (2005). Using the 'Marital Instability Over the Life Course' study (n=2033 married people), the divorce of grandparents was found to have negative impacts for the well-being of grandchildren. Given the range of evidence presented throughout this chapter, this indeed appears plausible, given the impacts on the second generation (grandparents' children) which are then passed on to the grandchildren. Disruptions to the grandchildren were identified as lower education, more marital conflict and poor quality relationships with their parents.

6.7 Conclusion and key findings from Chapter 6

To extend the findings from the previous chapter, this chapter has outlined some of the clear associations between relationship breakdown and child outcomes. The general consensus is that relationship breakdown among parents has been shown to be associated with physical and psychological ill-health, and further outcomes in terms of education and employment and health-damaging behaviours. Evidence to support causal relationships are hard to identify given the problematic issues presented throughout this review.

Although family and relationship breakdown is associated with negative outcomes among some children, and although mostly for a temporary period, there are many other social issues which have potentially a far greater impact. Wilcox et al. (2005) makes this point powerfully. They state that the influence of socio-economic status and poverty may be particularly powerful influences on child well-being, with the latter proving to be a better predictor of educational attainment, for example, over that of relationship breakdown. Some of the key findings from this chapter are outlined below and, as noted above and elsewhere, these are not assumed to apply to all children of separated parents, and are rarely proved to be causally related.

- Children in Great Britain aged 0-15 living with both natural parents had the least likelihood of reporting a 'limiting long-term illness'. The highest likelihood was evident among those children not living in a family (a relative risk of 1.87), followed by those living with a single mother (1.66 – about two-thirds higher than the reference group). As for all these comparative findings, they are unable to support a causal relationship.
- Antenatal maternal stress has been shown to impinge on the healthy development of the infant. More specifically, relationship strain has been shown to be associated with an infant's lower cognitive development and greater fearfulness, independent of maternal age, smoking and alcohol use in pregnancy, birth weight, and maternal education.
- Parental connectedness, by affecting health-related behaviours such as smoking and breastfeeding, has been shown to impact on the health of the developing infant. Parental

connectedness illustrates the important role of couple relationship quality in affecting health-related behaviours.

- Lower level of parental investment and marital conflict have been shown to be associated with the earlier onset of puberty, which itself has been associated with a variety of negative health and psychosocial outcomes, including teenage pregnancy, mood disorders, substance abuse and cancers of the reproductive system.
- Substantial review evidence supports the association between relationship conflict and the psychological ill-health of children. It has been stated that destructive conflict is more detrimental than the impact of parental separation.
- Mental disorders have been shown to be more prevalent among children of reconstituted families where stepchildren were present. Also, more boys than girls, from single-parent families, report a mental disorder.
- From the reviewed evidence, it is arguable that the relationship breakdown and mental health association may be more indicative of a causal relationship compared to the impacts on the physical health of children, although consistencies are apparent.
- Familial disruption, alongside other factors, has been shown to be associated with suicide.
- Substantial data derived from longitudinal cohort studies have shown a negative association between relationship breakdown and educational attainment among children. Some evidence has shown that these educational impacts have been consistent with rising divorce rates and have not diminished in line with more social acceptance of relationship breakdown (thus opposing a reduced effect hypothesis). Educational attainment has also been shown to act as an important 'transmission mechanism' in determining economic success.
- The association between parental conflict and lower educational attainment among children has been shown to be better explained by the children's attribution of the conflict, through self-blame, compared to the impact from the parent-child relationship. Therefore, although interventions need to foster a continued parent-child relationship to alleviate the impact of relationship conflict on children, they also need to consider ways in which children perceive and attribute conflict.
- Couple relationship breakdown has been shown to be associated with children's health-compromising behaviours, in terms of cigarette smoking, substance misuse (including alcohol) and early age of first sexual intercourse. Early age at first intercourse has been shown to act as a proximate determinant for earlier partnership and parenthood.
- Parental disruption variables are found to be predictive of childhood convictions and self-reported criminal behaviour. This association remains when controlling for potential mediating variables such as family income, family size, convicted parent, parental supervision, attitude and discipline of parents, and the child's IQ, school attainment, hyperactivity, risk-taking and troublesomeness. Nonetheless, the problems assigning this as a causal relationship is particularly complex given the numerous additional factors that may affect criminal behaviour.
- Parental separation has also been shown to affect the relationship between children and their grandparents which can be detrimental to their well-being. In similar fashion, the divorce of grandparents can prove to be detrimental to grandchildren.

Chapter 7
Couple relationship breakdown: Theoretical and empirical research explaining the impacts on adults and children

7.1 Introduction

This chapter presents information that contextualises the evidence outlined in previous chapters. To build on describing the impacts of couple relationship breakdown, this chapter will explain why and how these impacts arise and why some people fare better or worse than others. In this section, the main theoretical principles will be outlined as well as the physiological responses and specific mechanisms that apply to child impacts. These explanations are key in deciphering the precise contribution of causal relationships, a point that has been embedded throughout the review. In relation to this, the chapter closes by reviewing the benefits of being in a couple relationship, as a further means to identify the 'losses' when a relationship breaks down.

7.2 Why does relationship breakdown have a negative impact?

In this section, theories explaining the impact of couple relationship breakdown will be discussed, alongside physiological mechanisms and those specific to children.

7.2.1 Theories explaining the impacts of couple relationship breakdown

The introduction to this review (Chapter 1) provided a relatively brief description of the mechanisms behind the impacts of couple relationship breakdown. In sum, there are three main theories to discuss. The first is selection effects, whereby unhealthy people are less likely to marry or stay married since ill-health is thought to interfere with establishing and maintaining relationships. To illustrate, Murphy (2007) cites evidence from the 'British National Survey of Health and Development' cohort study to show that a significant proportion of people who were still single in their 30s had received special education as children (in this instance considered to be a reason for not marrying). Selection theory argues that poorly functioning people (predisposed to score low on well-being after a relationship breakdown) are especially likely to divorce. This predisposition, rather than the divorce itself, causes a lowering of well-being (Amato, 2000) and thus in this instance is unable to support a causal relationship between couple relationship breakdown and well-being. The second theory concerns the protective effects of marriage that can provide a buffer against stress and other changes in life. These benefits include social interaction, intimacy, companionship, support, financial reward and the fostering of more healthy lifestyles. Chapter 4, assessing the psychological impacts of couple relationship breakdown has shown how the loss of this protective effect can, for example, increase symptoms of depression (e.g. Richards et al., 1997; Gardner and Oswald, 2006; and Kiernan and Mensah, forthcoming). The third theory concerns the effects of stress that are faced due to a relationship breakdown or through the bereavement felt due to the death of a partner (e.g. the 'crisis' effect defined by Raschke, 1987, in Chapter 4).

The second and third theories, unlike selection theory, are more indicative of a causal relationship between relationship breakdown and well-being. Indeed, given that health and well-being may be both a cause (as in selection) and an effect of a couple relationship breakdown (as in a causal relationship), a real challenge for researchers is to adopt suitable methods, designs and statistical techniques to unravel the role of these theories. This is further complicated by these theories co-existing, for example, with the more advantaged or most healthy being more likely to marry (as in selection theory) and thus obtaining the protective effects of this relationship (Murphy, 2007). Understanding the relative contribution of these different (rather than competing) theories underpins the validity of this entire review, and the proposed interventions and innovative family policies that can result. Some of the most notable contributions to improving our understanding of this crucial area are outlined below.

Amato (2000) contrasts his 'Divorce-Stress-Adjustment Perspective' to selection theory, with the former used to explain how marital disruption causes adjustment problems which leads to a lowering of well-being (Amato, 2000). From an extensive review of literature published throughout the 1990's, Amato (2000) uses the Divorce-Stress-Adjustment Perspective to explain how divorce impacts on adults and children. Given the extent of his research, it is arguable that this particular paper is one of the most significant to be cited in this review. Amato's model (2000) represents a combination of various elements of other theories (including attachment theory, systems theory and general stress theory), and is comprehensively backed by the research evidence reviewed in his paper. There are four underlying components to this model which is presented in Figure 4, and it is an extremely useful illustration of how relationship breakdown can impact on parents and children. Consistent with the Divorce-Stress-Adjustment Perspective, Amato (2000) reviews evidence from longitudinal studies demonstrating how those people who divorce report increases in a variety of health problems including psychological distress and alcohol misuse.

Figure 4 – The Divorce-Stress-Adjustment Perspective (Amato, 2000)

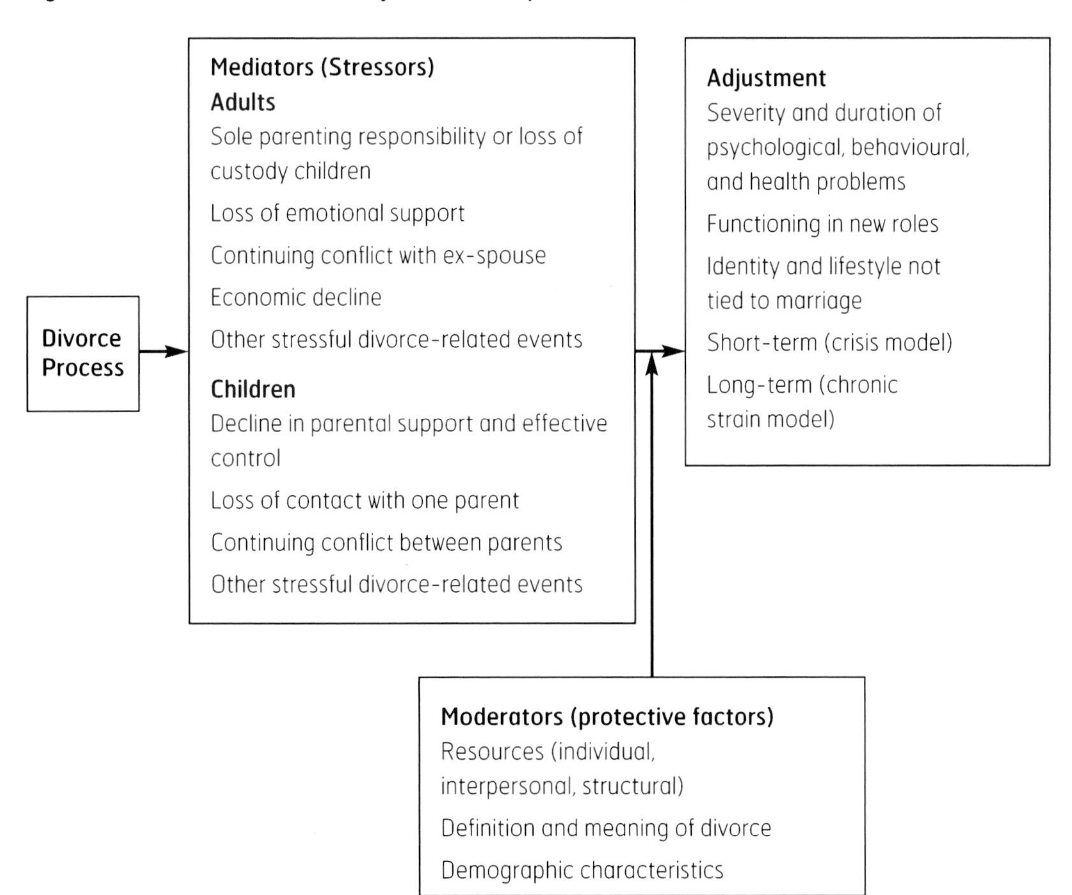

The principles of the Divorce-Stress-Adjustment Perspective are outlined as follows. Firstly, Amato's (2000) model highlights that divorce is considered a process rather than a single event (supporting statements outlined in Chapter 5). Therefore, events prior to divorce, such as parental conflict or lack of parental contact can have major impacts on children more so than the legal dissolution of the marriage. Secondly, a number of mediators or stressors brought on by the divorce are presented, including those pertinent to adults and children. Amato (2000) concludes from his review that the leading stressors associated with divorce are difficulties with solo parenting, continuing discord with the former spouse, decline in emotional support, economic hardship and additional stressful events. By noting these stressors, the benefits of marriage over divorce can also be identified through effective co-parenting, less conflict, more emotional support, economic status etc. akin to the protective theory outlined above.

Of all the stressors identified, previous research has shown that the associated poverty or economic hardship from couple relationship breakdown is a major influence on both adult and child outcomes. The interest in poverty has been particularly prolific in the US, and emphasised in the 'Fragile Families' initiative (unmarried parents and their children). From the numerous publications derived from this programme, it is reported that families headed by single females, for example, experience poverty rates nearly six times as great as families headed by married couples ('Fragile Families Research Brief', 2008). As to be outlined in Chapter 9, divorced women in Great Britain have a 40% increased likelihood to enter poverty if they divorce than if they remain married (Aassve et al., 2006). Equally, and related to the next paragraph, alleviation of poverty can act as a significant protective factor against some of the negative outcomes of relationship breakdown.

Thirdly, the way people respond to these stressors is likely to depend on a number of protective or moderating factors which explains why some people fare better or worse than others. These include educational attainment and employment status, supportive networks of friends (including support from a potentially new partner), maternal mental health, remarriage and the associated economic benefits that are likely, and the cognitive appraisal of the divorce and whether it is seen as a regrettable breakdown of a lifelong commitment. Other moderating factors would be in relation to the person who initiated the divorce, with the main driver of the divorce generally faring better (see more positive aspects of relationship breakdown in Chapter 8). Likewise, those reporting a great degree of distress within the marriage are likely to adjust quicker and report less negative impacts of the divorce. Specifically for children, the protective factors identified are active coping skills, family and friend support and access to therapeutic interventions (Amato, 2000).

From other research (cited earlier in Chapter 5), Flowerdew and Neale (2003) note a range of moderating factors that may affect child outcomes following divorce, such as pre-divorce and post-divorce parental conflict, economic hardship, parental re-partnership and stepfamily formation, with those experiencing multiple transitions of this nature reporting the most harmful outcomes. Flowerdew and Neale (2003) also noted that children found the transition to new family forms easier if one parent is re-partnering at any one time (rather than at the same time), and also that the pace of change was not too overwhelming for them allowing them a period of "emotional recovery" (p.153). Hawthorne et al. (2003) document a similar range of protective factors including economic resources, ongoing conflict, parenting and parent-child relationships, sharing information with children about the separation, age, support from grandparents and ensuring children's views are incorporated into effective ways of smoothing transitions. They state that when considering all the various stresses faced by children after separation that may influence the extent of their impacts, there is an argument that all are mediated through the influence on parent-child relationships. Therefore, good and effective parenting may be the most potent means of determining the impacts on children (Hawthorne et al., 2003). The importance of these risk and protective factors is also evidenced in a recent review by Mooney et al. (2009). Factors known to increase the severity of child outcomes were parental conflict, poor parenting quality, maternal mental ill-health, financial hardship and repeated transitions in family formation. In view of these risk and protective factors, the Mooney et al. (2009) review recognises that family functioning rather than family type may be more influential in explaining child outcomes from family breakdown. These views are also echoed by Dunn (2008) who, in researching the views of children, notes the important role that grandparents, siblings and friends play in moderating the impact of parental separation.

Recognition of these moderating factors is essential in understanding why divorce or relationship breakdown may have seemingly different effects for some people.

This illustrates that any review of the impact of relationship breakdown will offer average effects and that, in reality, outcomes for individuals are likely to differ. Likewise, recognition of these moderating factors may help to illustrate the type of support required to reduce the impacts of divorce and relationship breakdown on adults and children. However, of course, not all moderating factors are modifiable, with factors such as personality and genetic predispositions either difficult or impossible to change. A key conclusion to arise from this evidence is that financial support and parenting are both particularly significant in affecting outcomes.

As a fourth principle to this Divorce-Stress-Adjustment Perspective, the adjustment refers to the way people respond to the stressors in light of the protective factors. This essentially represents the impacts of the divorce, in terms of the "psychological, behavioural and health problems" (Amato, 2000, p.1,271) as described in Figure 4. These impacts are seen to be applicable both in the short- and long-term. The short-term or 'crisis model' assumes that divorce represents a stressful disturbance from which people are able to adjust and return to their pre-divorce level of functioning. The long-term or 'chronic strain' model implies that people are unable to adjust or return to their pre-divorce level of functioning. For the latter, this is likely to be a product of economic hardship, loneliness and the stress of sole parenting responsibilities (Amato, 2000). We have presented evidence in relation to psychological ill-health among adults (Chapter 4) and child impacts (Chapters 5 and 6) which show evidence of both temporary 'crisis' and, without the necessary protective factors, evidence of longer-term outcomes.

By presenting factors that show how divorce can lead to, or cause, adverse outcomes, Amato's (2000) Divorce-Stress-Adjustment Perspective opposes the selection theory whereby poorly adjusted people are selected out of marriage. Reviewing studies that used a fixed effects model to control for time-invariant individual variables (e.g. Johnson and Wu, 1996), Amato (2000) concludes that selection alone could not account for these effects of relationship breakdown: "In general, studies support the notion of divorce causation, but a degree of selection also might be operating" (Amato, 2000, p.1,275).

Indeed, returning to the causation and selection effects, the general consensus is that although selection effects are occurring, the causal or more protective effects outlined above are more prominent in our understanding of these impacts. Murphy (2007), in reviewing census evidence from the UK, reports that "There is clear evidence of the protective effect of marriage over and above the selection effects". (p.66). Reviewing evidence from the US, Waite and Gallagher (2000) observe how the benefits of marriage are still evident when selection and health status are taken in to account. They provide support for the protective effects of marriage, by suggesting that "....something about marriage itself moves people toward a healthier way of life" (p.52). Nonetheless, although this reference of causation is a key finding to emphasise in this review, attempts to quantify the relative contributions from these varying hypotheses remains unanswered.

Given the extent of the Amato (2000) review, it is justifiable to use his own words to provide a neat summation of the impacts of divorce and how they arise:

"First, we know that adults and children from divorced families, as a group, score lower than their counterparts in married-couple families on a variety of indicators of well-being. Second, although selection can account for some of these differences, the evidence is strong that divorce has an impact on well-being net of selection. Third, we have a good grasp of many of the mechanisms through which divorce affects individuals. These mediators include disruptions in parent-child relationships, continuing discord between former spouses, loss of emotional support, economic hardship, and an increase in the number of other negative life events, such as moving. Fourth, although some adults and children adjust relatively quickly to divorce (supporting a crisis model), others exhibit long-term deficits in functioning (supporting a chronic strain model). Fifth, a number of factors moderate the speed and extent of adjustment. For adults, protective factors include the use of active coping skills, support from family and friends, and having access to therapeutic interventions. For adults as well as children, the end of a highly conflicted marriage is likely to be followed by improvements, rather than declines, in well-being." (Amato 2000, p. 1,282).

Although in relation to criminal behaviour among children, Juby and Farrington (2001) outline three theories to explain the impacts of couple relationship breakdown on children. They have parallels with the above discussion, and are classified as 'trauma theory' (damaging impact due to break-up of the attachment bond between parent and child), 'selection theory' (as above, and the product of pre-existing conditions prior to the relationship breakdown such as poor income, mental health problems, etc. which can lead to a spurious relationship between relationship breakdown and outcome), and 'life-course theory'. In view of the discussion above, the trauma and life-course theories present some innovative explanations for the impacts of relationship breakdown. Although life-course and trauma theory note the impact can be more damaging at some ages than others, trauma theory argues that this is primarily at a young age when the attachment bonds are being formed between parent and child. Like the trauma theory, the life-course theory also argues that age is a factor, but this may extend beyond young childhood to include adolescence, for example, and other transitions in life. In addition, the life-course theory sees relationship breakdown very much as a process rather than a discrete event (as in the trauma theory), and thus recognises the impacts of pre-breakdown parental conflict as well as post-separation situations including relationships between post-separated parents and new family forms. In the Juby and Farrington (2001) study, outlined in Chapter 5 in more detail, they found that the association between relationship breakdown and criminal behaviour was explained mostly by life-course theory. The basis of this conclusion, over trauma and selection theory, was the significance of parental conflict and multiple transitions into new family forms as being particularly disruptive for children. Life-course theory, as they showed, has an ability to explain why the impact of relationship breakdown differs for some people, as other features of the life-course need to be taken into account. They conclude their study into youth crime as follows, and there are clear parallels to the family functioning rather then family type argument posted earlier by Mooney et al. (2009) and Dunn (2008).

"We conclude that some kinds of disrupted families are criminogenic (e.g. those where the boy does not remain with the mother), just as some kinds of intact families are criminogenic (e.g. those characterized by high parental conflict). Equally, some kinds of disrupted families (e.g. those where the boy remains with a lone mother) are no more criminogenic than intact harmonious families." (Juby and Farrington, 2001, p.37).

In relation to the selection versus causation debate, appropriate study designs that are sufficiently robust to disentangle the degree of association between divorce and outcomes are critically important. In regards to child mental health, this is especially significant as the outcomes may be a product of events prior to the relationship breakdown (such as parental depression and poor marital satisfaction that may prelude the divorce) rather than the separation itself. Strohschein (2005) makes this point clearly through her impressive three wave-analysis of Canadian longitudinal survey data using a growth curve model. She notes the differences in socio-economic and psychosocial resources in families that remain intact, compared to those who later divorce, that are already impacting on child mental health. Only when these pre-divorce differences are controlled for can the effects of divorce itself be ascertained. In this case, the study found significant increases in child anxiety and depression as a result of the divorce. This study also notes the importance of seeing divorce as a process, rather than an event, when disentangling the selection and causation effects. Indeed, when examining the impacts of relationship breakdown on children, the effect of selection becomes even more complex (than for the effect on parents) by operating in more than one dimension. This complexity is due to the potential selection effects operating through characteristics of the children themselves and through the influence of their parents (through genetic influences and that of the home environment). Therefore, when considering the effects on children, characteristics of the parents and the children themselves must be taken into account to determine the influence of selection and causation.

7.2.2 Physiological mechanisms

From a physiological perspective, the mechanisms behind the impact of relationship breakdown are described by Robles and Kiecolt-Glaser (2003). As to be shown, these impacts are inextricably linked to the stress and conflict that is likely to occur in most (but not all) instances when a relationship is breaking down. Robles and Kiecolt-Glaser (2003) outline how marital strain affects health (in a causal manner) through three primary physiological pathways that mediate the relationship between stress, social relationships and health: cardiovascular function, neuroendocrine function and immune function. They use evidence from observing couples, usually in a clinic or research setting, discussing areas of conflict for around 10 to 15 minutes. They found that both men and women reported cardiovascular responses, with greater (health-damaging) effects seen on women compared to men. In terms of endocrine function (including hormones that regulate cardiovascular, metabolic and immune functions), higher levels of conflict were associated with elevations in epinephrine, norepinephrine, adenocorticotropin hormone and growth hormone (indicating increased stress). Again, differences in hormone levels were more pronounced among women. Immunological change was also seen in situations of marital conflict, with declines in natural killer cells, again more pronounced among women than men.

In more detail, Robles and Kiecolt-Glaser (2003) describe four processes through which these physiological pathways can lead to poor health outcomes. These were 'repeated hits by novel stressors' (repeated instances of conflict), 'lack of adaptation to the same stressor' (lack of adaptation to the same area of conflict over time), 'failure to shut off physiological responses following exposure to a stressor' (a longer 'recovery' period following a stressor), and 'inadequate responses to stressors' (impairment of important physiological processes). The authors conclude that the physiological responses to marital conflict and stress have an accumulative and long-term effect on health, akin to the 'chronic strain' model detailed previously. Moreover, if regular conflict leads to more frequent endocrinological, immunological and cardiovascular changes, then those in higher conflict relationships could be at risk of more health problems over time. Although this study focuses on the strain from conflict, it is intuitive to conclude that equivalent physiological responses could be experienced due to a stressful transition from marriage to divorce or widowhood (as applicable to the stress theory outlined earlier).

7.2.3 Mechanisms specific to children

In similar fashion to this Robles and Kiecolt-Glaser (2003) paper, there is some important research examining the physiological pathways on how parental separation can lead to negative health effects in children. As part of a much larger study of immune regulation in children, Herberth et al. (2008) present findings from a cohort of children born in Leipzig between 1997 and 1999. The study involved the examination of blood from these 234 children at the time of their 6th birthday and questionnaire data from children and their parents during which life events were recorded retrospectively. Although the sample size is small, with around 10% of children experiencing parental separation or divorce, the paper does add insights in the mechanisms behind relationship breakdown and health status. They note that the divorce or separation of parents, is associated with an increase in the Vasoactive Intestinal Peptide (VIP) and high levels of the Th2 cytokine IL-4 in the blood. They hypothesise that the VIP levels may mediate the stressful life event and the Th2 response, which is associated with poor immune regulation in children. Of particular interest alongside showing the mechanisms, they note that in comparison to the severe disease or death of a family member is shown (through neuropeptide levels) to be less stressful than parental divorce or separation. Beyond providing technical details about the blood samples, the essential point is encapsulated in their conclusion as follows,

"Therefore, we conclude from these results that separation/divorce of the parents might be the most critical life event during childhood." (Herberth et al., 2008, p.6).

Evidence of the effects of marital conflict and discord have also been associated with emotional and behavioural problems in children (Hart, 1999, Grych et al., 2000, Margolin et al., 2001) – see Chapter 5. Cummings and Davies have published a number of key reviews in this area and present a useful update of the evidence that seeks to understand how these effects occur. In 2002, Cummings and Davies highlighted the importance of adopting a 'process-oriented approach' to understanding how parental conflict impacts on children. Such an approach recognises the role of specific contexts, histories and developmental periods that account for children's outcomes over time (Cummings and Davies, 2002). The paper reviews evidence in this area, and highlights the main advancements of their understanding of marital conflict effects on children, which include the following:

1. greater understanding of the effects of specific contexts characteristic of marital conflict;

2. identification of the psychological response processes in children (cognitive, emotional, social and physiological);

3. greater understanding of the role of child characteristics, family history and other contextual factors; and

4. advances in the conceptualisation of children's outcomes, including effects that are viewed as dynamic processes of functioning rather than clinical diagnoses.

Examining levels of pre-divorce conflict offers further insight to the mechanisms at work among children (see Chapter 5). An influential study in this area, by Booth and Amato (2001), noted how pre-divorce levels of low conflict meant children had little time to anticipate the separation, and thus had worse outcomes compared to those from high-conflict marriages. This study suggests that this lack of anticipation resulted in some children blaming themselves for the separation, formed from trying to make their own attributions for why the relationship broke down as it was not obvious given the low levels of conflict. Outcomes of self-blame include depression, externalising problems (aggression, delinquency, and hyperactivity) and low levels of self-competence. Likewise, Booth and Amato (2001) cite other studies where children reported a perceived lack of control after the break-up of low conflict marriages, making it more difficult for them to adjust to a new family setting. The Booth and Amato (2001) study is discussed in detail in Chapter 8, when exploring the risk factors for relationship breakdown among couples reporting low conflict.

7.3 Why does being in a couple relationship bring benefits?

A further perspective on the impact of relationship breakdown can be taken from literature highlighting the positive aspects of couple relationships. A couple relationship breakdown has the potential to eradicate these benefits. Murphy (2007) defines these benefits succinctly as follows:

"Evidence suggests that the benefits of marriage are emotional, financial and behavioural. The social support of marriage affects health and well-being by mediating stress." (Murphy, 2007, p.57).

A further concise note is provided by Halford et al. (2008):

"Evidence has been accumulating that a healthy, mutually satisfying relationship is a potent predictor of positive health and well-being for both adults and their children." (Halford et al., 2008, p.499).

From a review of longitudinal evidence in the UK and US, conducted mainly in the 1990s, Wilson and Oswald (2002) define three leading benefits from being married: improved economic well-being; emotional and instrumental support; and a 'guardian' effect, whereby married individuals tend to engage less in risky activities and more so in healthy ones. Wilson and Oswald (2002) conclude that marriage makes people live longer, healthier and also less likely to suffer psychological problems. Significantly, they also observed from their extensive review that, by comparing married and non-married cohabiters, that marriage itself seemed to make an important difference to physical and psychological health.

Similarly, from their 26 conclusions drawn from a review of the Social Science literature, Wilcox et al. (2005) group the favourable outcomes of marriage into four main areas: family; economics; physical health and longevity; and mental health

and emotional well-being. Some striking conclusions about the benefits of marriage include the following (Wilcox et al., 2005, p.1-2).

- "Marriage increases the likelihood that fathers and mothers have good relationships with their children" (Family).
- "Married couples seem to build more wealth on average than singles or cohabiting couples" (Economics).
- "Children who live with their own two married parents enjoy better physical health, on average, than do children in other family forms" (Physical health and longevity).
- "Marriage is associated with reduced rates of alcohol and substance abuse for both adults and teens" (Physical health and longevity).
- "Married people, especially married men, have longer life expectancies than do otherwise similar singles" (Physical health and longevity).
- "Marriage is associated with better health and lower rates of injury, illness and disability for both men and women" (Physical health and longevity).
- "Children whose parents divorce have higher rates of psychological distress and mental illness" (Mental health and emotional well-being).
- "Divorce appears to increase significantly the risk of suicide" (Mental health and emotional well-being).

From their 'fundamental conclusions', Wilcox et al. (2005) state that marriage is "..an important social good, associated with an impressively broad array of positive outcomes for children and adults alike" and, "...an important public good, associated with a range of economic, health, educational and safety benefits..." (p.5).

In specific reference to criminal behaviour, Sampson et al. (2006) offer a number of explanations to illustrate a reduction in crime when people are married. These include mutual support, changes in everyday routines, social restraint from spouses, and a sense of added responsibility.

As further evidence, in their synthesis of recent research evidence, Wood et al. (2007) report many beneficial effects of marriage on health. Alongside reduced morbidity, reduced depression and generally healthier behaviours associated with marriage, much of their review concerns the benefits of marriage on children. They note that children growing up with married parents (compared to those without) report healthier behaviours and improved physical health, higher educational attainment and increased longevity. In additional detail, Murphy (2007) states that the lower mortality rates among adults who are married, and who are parents, can be partially explained by an impact on health behaviours, in that,

".....marriage and parenthood both exert a 'deterrent effect on health-compromising behaviours' such as excessive drinking, drug use, risk-taking, and disorderly living. By providing a system of 'meaning, obligation, [and] constraint', family relationships markedly reduce the likelihood of unhealthy practices." (Murphy, 2007, p.58).

However, to add a note of caution to this section, a supportive social environment is not exclusive to married people, and may also be achieved by never-married people. Murphy (2007) cites evidence from the 2001 'Health Survey for England' where never-married women have been shown to report less detrimental health outcomes in terms of psychological health ('General Health Questionnaire') and the limitation of long-standing illness (compared to those who have experienced the stressful events of divorce or separation). This implies that the impacts of relationship breakdown extend beyond the loss of the benefits of being in a couple relationship, with the breakdown of the relationship bringing along further disadvantages (see end of this section).

However, it is also worth noting that these health effects are not in tune with the mortality data in Chapter 3, that showed greater mortality rates from middle age among single (never-married people) compared to those divorced or widowed (e.g. Cheung, 2000; Kaplan and Kronick, 2006; and Murphy, 2007).

As a further caveat, although the benefits of being married support the negative portrayal of when relationships breakdown, there is an assumption that all marriages or relationships are satisfying. This is an important assumption that warrants further discussion, with much research evidence highlighting that marriage or relationship quality is more significant than marriage or relationship status. This argument appears logical, in the sense that the protective effects of a relationship may indeed be replaced by the negative effects of conflict and marital discord in poor quality relationships. The important point to observe is that being in a couple relationship does not automatically bring the positive benefits noted above, even if this is the case for the majority of people. Convincing evidence from earlier chapters (e.g. Coyne, 2001; Gallo et al., 2003; De Vogli et al., 2007; Troxel et al., 2005; Wilcox et al., 2005; and Holt-Lunstad et al., 2008) have reported the importance of marital quality over marital status. Holt-Lunstad et al. (2008), in relation to adult blood pressure levels, conclude "Therefore, marriage must be of a high quality to be advantageous. In other words, one is better off single than unhappily married" (p.5).

From a policy and practice perspective, these findings demonstrate that it is not just a case of preventing marriages or relationships from breaking down that is key (where appropriate and achievable), but also to maintain and improve the quality of those relationships that do exist even if they remain intact and do not dissolve. Likewise, in recognition of relationship quality, it may be the case that the breakdown of a poor quality and unsatisfying relationship may prove to be beneficial to couples and children (see Chapter 8).

Finally, this and the previous section have identified reasons for the positive effects of being in a couple relationship and the negative outcomes that may result from relationships breaking down. These sections have shown that the dissolution of couple relationships results in a loss of the benefits from being in a partnership, as well as further strains associated with the process of separation. A further observation is that a wide range of different social and economic factors are at work in affecting the impact of relationship breakdown. An area that clearly remains unresolved is determining the different weights of these factors, and especially trying to ascertain whether the social (interaction, intimacy, support etc.) or economic aspects of marriage are playing the primary role behind the health benefits of marriage (Murphy, 2007). Therefore, as when assessing the impacts of relationship breakdown, the same complexities apply to determining whether the benefits of being in a marriage are actually caused by a 'marriage effect' or by other factors associated with marriage (Halford et al., 2008).

7.4 Conclusion and key findings from Chapter 7

This chapter provides additional detail to the predominantly descriptive evidence outlined in previous chapters. Theoretical and empirical research has provided plausible explanations as to why relationship breakdown may have the detrimental impacts that have been widely cited in this review. Examining the benefits of couple relationships also provides insights into the possible 'losses' that occur on relationship dissolution. Providing these plausible explanations for the reported impacts favours the case for a causal association between relationship breakdown and outcome. Key findings from this chapter are outlined below.

- There are three main theories to explain the association between relationship breakdown and its impacts – selection, protection and stress.
- The selection effect applies where unhealthy people (for example) are less likely to marry or stay married since ill-health is thought to interfere with establishing and maintaining relationships. Selection theory argues that poorly functioning people (predisposed to score low on well-being after a relationship breakdown) are especially likely to divorce. This predisposition, rather than the divorce itself, causes a lowering of well-being and, therefore, is not indicative of a causal relationship between relationship breakdown and well-being. The second theory concerns the protective effects of marriage that can provide a buffer against stress and other changes in life (through social interaction, intimacy, companionship, financial reward, etc.). The third concerns the effects of stress that are faced due to a relationship breakdown or through the bereavement felt due to the death of a partner. Theories two and three are more supportive of a causal relationship between relationship breakdown and impact.
- The effect of selection in children is particularly complex. This complexity is due to potential selection effects operating through characteristics of the children themselves and through the influence of their parents. Therefore, when considering the effects on children, characteristics of the parents and children must be taken into account to determine the influence of selection and causation.
- The Divorce-Stress-Adjustment Perspective (Amato, 2000) helps to explain some of the causal impacts of relationship breakdown. In this model, divorce is seen as a 'process' with events pre- and post-divorce affecting the outcome. The adjustment (or outcome of the relationship breakdown) is subject to a number of mediators (or stressors such as loss of emotional support) and moderators or protective factors (such as individual resources). The interaction between these factors determines why some people may fare better or worse following a relationship breakdown.
- Of all the stressors identified from divorce, economic hardship is particularly salient. The financial consequences of divorce may determine how people fare after relationship breakdown. Nonetheless, in observing the health benefits of marriage, there is considerable debate as to the relative contribution of the social and economic factors that are present.
- Rather than being considered as competing theories, it is likely that selection, protection and stress all play a part to some extent in explaining the impacts of couple relationship breakdown. Although the relative contribution of each has yet to be fully understood, there is a general consensus that the causal or more protective effects are more prominent than selection in our understanding of why relationship breakdown leads to the impacts observed. This is a particularly significant finding.
- The physiological pathways derived from stress (cardiovascular function, neuroendocrine function and immune function) supports evidence of a causal relationship between relationship breakdown and ill-health among adults. Levels of Vasoactive Intestinal Peptide and Th2 cytokine IL-4 in the blood (indicating health impacts) among children of divorced parents supports this inference.
- Based on observing these physiological responses, parental divorce or separation is shown to be more harmful to children compared to the severe disease or death of a family member.

- There is some indication that the physiological pathways show more detriment to women compared to men (supporting the morbidity statistics but opposing the greater marriage advantage seen among men in the mortality data in Chapter 3).
- Divorce following low pre-divorce conflict, compared to high pre-divorce conflict, is shown to be more detrimental to the health and well-being of children. This is because levels of low conflict mean children have little time to anticipate the separation, and may result in some children blaming themselves for the break-up.
- Factors that protect children from the negative impact of relationship breakdown on children include: low levels of pre-divorce and post-divorce parental conflict, low levels of economic hardship, parental repartnership and stepfamily formation, positive parenting and parent-child relationships, good maternal mental health, sharing information with children about the separation, age, support from grandparents and ensuring children's views are incorporated into effective ways of smoothing transitions. Age effects show that older children find it harder to reintegrate into stepfamilies, although younger children find it more confusing and anxious which may lead to self-blaming.
- When considering all the various stresses faced by children after separation there is an argument that all are mediated through the influence on parent-child relationships. Therefore, good and effective parenting may be the most potent means of diffusing the negative impacts on children, and the role of the couple relationship in affecting parenting must be recognised.
- Mechanisms behind the negative impacts of relationship breakdown can also be drawn from examining the positive effects of marriage. From substantial review evidence, these positive effects include improved physical health, better relationships with children (compared to those not married), and less psychological distress.
- For these benefits of marriage to exist, the relationship must be satisfying and of high quality. Being unhappily married is reported to be more disadvantageous than being single. Therefore, preventing relationships from breaking down (where appropriate and achievable) and improving relationship satisfaction are both key to maintaining the well-being of adults and children.
- The dissolution of couple relationships results in a loss of the benefits from being in a partnership, as well as further strains associated with the process of separation. This is illustrated by research showing that never-married women have been shown to report less detrimental health outcomes (in terms of psychological health and limiting long-standing illness) compared to those who have experienced the stressful events of divorce or separation.

Chapter 8
Couple relationship breakdown: Risk factors and effectiveness of interventions

8.1 Introduction

With the previous chapter helping to explain the largely detrimental impacts of couple relationship breakdown, this chapter advances the evidence towards developments in practice. To start this chapter, risk factors for couple relationship breakdown are highlighted. As a logical progression, this chapter examines the effectiveness of relationship support programmes. Finally, from an alternative but necessary perspective, this chapter closes by considering when couple relationship breakdown can have more positive impacts.

8.2 What are the risk factors for relationship breakdown?

The risk factors for relationship breakdown within this section are subdivided further according to the different depth of research. At the outset, broad socio-demographic risk factors will be detailed, followed by the more specific strains on a relationship (especially transition to parenthood) and, finally, by exploring in greatest detail the interactive behaviour of couples.

8.2.1 Socio-demographic risk factors

Of obvious interest to interventions seeking to reduce levels of couple relationship breakdown and/or the associated impacts, the risk factors for dissolved relationships are a necessary addition to this review. Starting at the broadest of levels, Chapter 2 noted some of the characteristics of marriages that were associated with a greater likelihood of divorce. Considering the proportion of marriages ending in divorce, UK census data has been used to show elevated divorce rates under three conditions (ONS, 2008e).

- Firstly, the associations between early age of marriage and increased divorce. For example, among previously unmarried spinsters aged under 20 at the time of marriage, 27% were divorced within five years, compared to 9% of 30 to 34-year-olds who married in the same year (2000).
- Secondly, there is an association between history of previous divorce and increased likelihood of future divorce. For example, 14% of marriages among previously married men aged between 30 and 34 end in divorce within five years compared to 10% of previously unmarried men of the same age. This repeated behaviour may be due to a number of reasons such as seeing marriage as less traditional or some of the psychological issues from the last marriage affecting the quality of the existing relationship.
- Thirdly, the likelihood of divorce also varies by duration of marriage. To illustrate, 21% of divorced marriages occur within the first five years of marriage, and around half of all divorces occur within the first 10 years. Once marriages survive for a decade, under 31% will end in divorce, and if marriage continued for 20 years this figure would decrease to 15%. There are very few divorces beyond 35 years of marriage (ONS, 2008e). It is likely that the first 10 years of marriage coincides with the transition to parenthood for many couples which may have a bearing on this particular statistic (see later).

Also at this broad level, there is evidence that those who cohabit are at greater risk of relationship breakdown than those who marry. This may be because of a selection effect (individuals who cohabit are also more likely to separate) or a possibility that cohabiting itself can make a relationship less stable. It appears that the type of commitment that underpins the cohabiting relationship is influential. To illustrate, Smart and Stevens (2000) identify two types of commitment seen among cohabiting couples. Firstly, 'mutual', whereby the long-term is considered and agreements about the future of the relationship and finances are made and, secondly, 'contingent', whereby a relationship is maintained despite the fact no mutual framework has been worked out. Intuitively, the second type of commitment may be associated with a greater likelihood of couple relationship breakdown.

In more detail to the evidence reported above, an influential review by Clarke and Berrington (1999) analysed the role of numerous socio-demographic predictors of divorce. In reviewing the various theoretical perspectives on marriage, they note that the risk of marital breakdown can be related to factors affecting the attractiveness of the marriage, barriers to marital dissolution and possible alternatives to marriage. However, in setting the scene for their review, they make the important observation that most studies have yet to fully understand what processes are apparent in influencing marital breakdown. Significantly, in appreciation of the difficulties in presenting causal associations, the authors use multivariate techniques to hold a range of factors constant to identify the more likely predictors of divorce. In light of the varying theoretical perspectives, Clarke and Berrington (1999) present a framework for identifying the socio-demographic predictors of divorce as follows (Figure 5):

Figure 5 – Framework for analysing socio-demographic determinants of divorce (Clarke and Berrington 1999, adapted from Berrington and Diamond 1997).

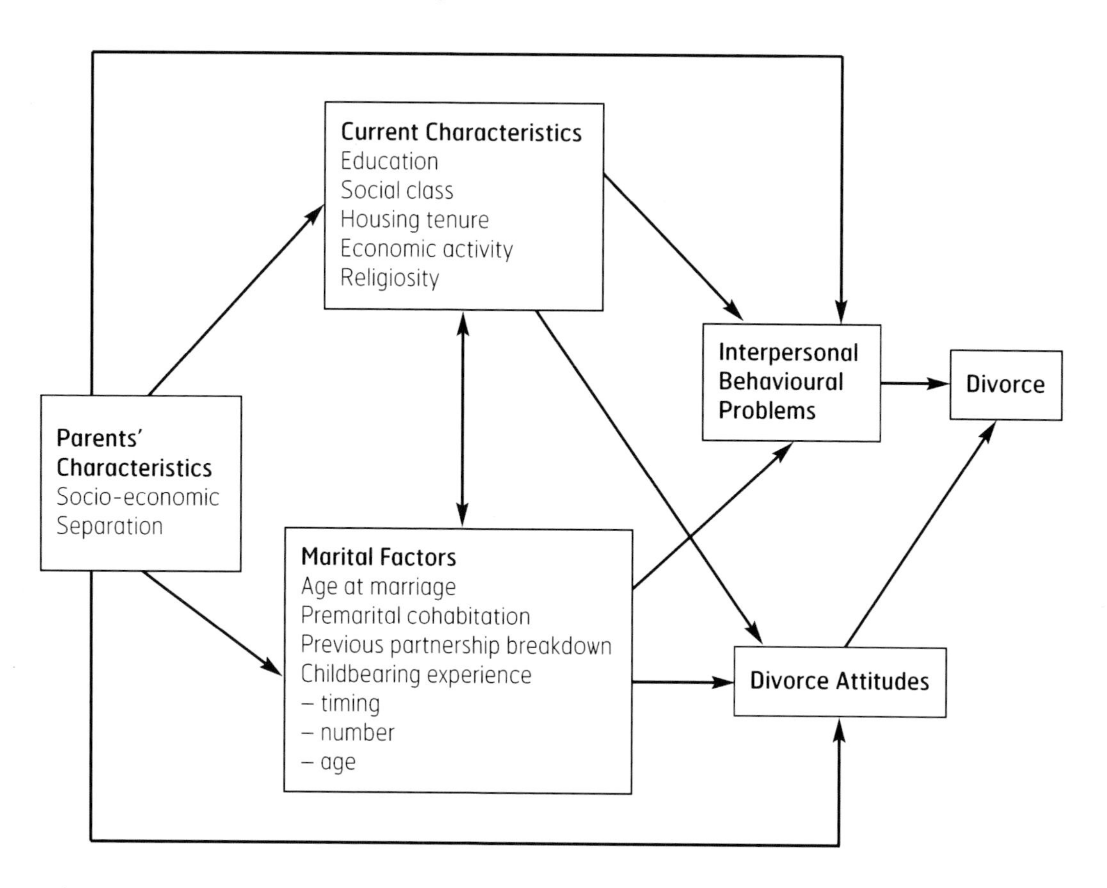

Their review details the role of a range of variables, and presents evidence where there is indication of a direct, causal relationship as opposed to indirect associations. For the latter, a prime example would be parents' socio-economic status, which affects marital breakdown indirectly: those from poorer social backgrounds are more likely to marry at a younger age which itself is more predictive of divorce (see later in this Section). Likewise, the review presents the inconsistent evidence between educational attainment and divorce. When studies control for age at marriage, the role of education becomes negligible illustrating how any association is mediated through age at marriage. Furthermore, there is inconsistent evidence on whether having children increases the risk of divorce, although some research suggests that the number of children has a role (with divorce being more likely if there are three or more children). In terms of social class, the multivariate analyses suggest this plays only a minor role in divorce patterns once age at marriage and childbearing experience has been taken into account.

In general, Clarke and Berrington's (1999) review concludes that demographic, and particularly the more volitional factors such as age at first marriage, play a more significant role in predicting marital breakdown compared to socio-economic factors. They highlight five key demographic factors and, for each, they present a brief synopsis of why these are important. These are highlighted below.

1. Early age at marriage – even when socio-economic characteristics are taken into account, people who marry at an early age have an increased risk of divorce. Explanations include insufficient time in seeking an appropriate marriage partner, a lack of knowledge of the longer-term characteristics of the future spouse, emotional immaturity, and the frequent change in outlook that occurs at a younger age which may drive relationships apart. There may also be less structural barriers to overcome for divorce, given that the majority of family and friends of a similar age may not be married.

2. Pre-marital conception – the authors cite plentiful evidence noting the importance of increased divorce among women experiencing a pre-marital conception. Those marrying after the birth of their first child have been shown to have an elevated risk of divorce in studies from Australia, UK, US, Canada and Sweden. Explanations include the experience of being an unmarried mother encourages less traditional attitudes to marriage and divorce.

3. Pre-marital cohabitation – the authors cite a wealth of research highlighting that those couples who cohabit prior to marriage have a higher risk of marital dissolution. Evidence suggests that these couples have less traditional attitudes to marriage and are more accepting of divorce. However, there is also evidence of a selection effect whereby those who cohabit beforehand possess other characteristics that may place them at higher risk of divorce.

4. Previous partnership breakdown – divorce rates tend to be higher among those who have been married previously. This may indicate a lower ability to remain married, more acceptance of divorce or the continued emotional or economic effects of the previous divorce. The same pattern of increased risk is observed among those who have cohabited with another partner prior to marriage.

5. Parental divorce – when controlling for early age at partnership, premarital cohabitation and pre-marital childbearing, those people experiencing parental divorce were still likely to have a relationship ending in divorce. The effect was only apparent among men.

Explanations for this inter-generational transmission of divorce includes a lack of married role models, and their parents' experience producing a more liberal attitude to divorce.

Finally, the Clarke and Berrington (1999) review concludes by noting the problems in resolving the independent associations between various demographic factors and divorce. This is primarily because of the difficulty in controlling for individual characteristics such as personality and attitudes that may also affect the likelihood of divorce. Indeed, Clarke and Berrington (1999) cite recent research into divorce noting the importance of pre-existing emotional and behavioural difficulties and poorer psychological well-being. They conclude their review by stating that "These demographic factors may reflect other, as yet unmeasured, differences in individuals' behavioural or psychological factors and attitudes towards marriage and divorce." (p.26). These differences are likely to persist, even if the general attitudes towards marriage may have changed through generations (see later in this section).

In relation to this, it is notable that there has been little investigation into the relationship dynamics across ethnic and religious groups within the UK, and how these may influence couple relationship formation and breakdown (Caballero et al., 2008). Recent research reported by Kiernan and Mensah (forthcoming), using data from the Millennium Cohort Study, revealed some notable differences in the partnership behaviours across different ethnic groups over an approximate five year time period. The most unstable families were seen among Black Caribbean mothers, regardless of their marital status when having their baby (who were all aged around 9 months at the time of the first survey sweep in 2001-2002). However, for the first five years of the child's life, there were minimal differences between the stability of White and Asian families. For example, of those parents married at the birth of their child, 12% of White parents had separated by the time the child was aged 5, compared to 14% of Pakistani parents and 11% of Bangladeshi parents. Twenty-one per cent of Black Caribbean parents had separated across this time period. Nonetheless, there still remains uncertainty as to how (and why) attitudes towards relationships and marriage may differ within and across contrasting ethnicities and cultures. In the UK context, this is an important area requiring more research (see Chapter 10).

With their interest in pre-divorce levels of conflict, the work of Booth and Amato (2001) (cited in chapter 5) is able to extend this section of the review by examining the risk factors specifically leading to the breakdown of low-conflict marriages. They note the importance of this area as the breakdown of more high-conflict marriages are occurring for more obvious reasons due to the severe level of discord in these relationships. Their study reviews previous research that outlines three different forms of commitment within relationships: personal commitment (when one wants the relationship to continue); moral commitment (when one feels obligated to remain in a relationship); and structural commitment (when one feels a constraint to remain in the relationship). They argue that personal commitment is unlikely to differ among low conflict marriages that do and do not end in divorce, whereas the differences in moral and structural may be more apparent. With this in mind, they compared four groups of parents within their longitudinal study of 2,033 married persons (not couples) from the US: low-conflict couples not ending in divorce, high-conflict couples not ending in divorce, high-conflict couples ending in divorce and low-conflict couples ending in divorce. The specific characteristics of the low-conflict couples ending in divorce indicate the main risk factors for these relationships breaking down. There were five interesting characteristics of the low-conflict divorced couples, as follows.

- Firstly, people divorcing from low-conflict marriages reported a lack of strong ties to the local community, home and friends (indicative of low levels of structural commitment).
- Secondly, those without shared assets (such a house) were more likely to divorce, again facilitated by the low level of structural commitment.
- Thirdly, those with more favourable attitudes to divorce, perhaps obtained through previous marriages or relationships, had a lower moral commitment to remain in a relationship.
- Fourthly, those more prone to risk-taking were also more likely to divorce.
- As a fifth and final reason, the authors note the greater likelihood of divorce among low-conflict couples who had not experienced a parental divorce compared to those who had (unlike the Clarke and Berrington, 1999, study reviewed above). This suggests that the low-conflict couples who had not experienced their own parental divorce were more likely to take risks and seek divorce, perhaps underestimating the effects this may have on their own children.

Collectively, these findings "...suggest that individuals in low-conflict marriages who divorced tended to have weak moral and structural commitment to marriage." (Booth and Amato, 2001, p.210).

Booth and Amato (2001) also found that child outcomes were worse when low-conflict marriages broke down (compared to high-conflict marriages) due to it being more unexpected, unwelcome and unpredictable. From an intervention point of view, Booth and Amato (2001) note the irony of their findings in terms of poor child outcomes: "Curiously, our results suggest that divorces with the greatest potential to harm children occur in [low-conflict marriages] that have the greatest potential for reconciliation or for managing a divorce such that it is less detrimental to their children." (p.211). More points in relation to this are made under the more positive effects of divorce outlined later in this chapter (Section 8.5).

8.2.2 Relationship strains including transition to parenthood

To further this chapter, events that are known to cause relationship strain are of clear importance. Transition points in a relationship are considered to place various strains on a relationship. Although these may include children starting school or children leaving home, or milestones such as moving into a shared home, one of the most widely reported strains involve events during the transition to parenthood. Research evidence has steadily developed since the 1980s where prospective longitudinal designs have investigated the issue of parenthood and relationship satisfaction in greater depth. For example, Cowan and Cowan (2000) reviewed 15 longitudinal studies and showed that the transition to parenthood is a stressful period for parents, with the decreased quality of the relationship proving to be detrimental to the development of the infant. The problems are often associated with the presence of post-natal depression (Simons et al., 2001). The Simons et al. study (2001 – see later in this chapter) found that around one-fifth of UK mothers reported relationship problems at their six to eight week development check for their baby. Furthermore, although difficult to attribute directly to the transition to parenthood, it is known that in 2007 around 117,000 under-16-year-olds have experienced the divorce of their parents in England and Wales, with one-fifth of these aged under five years (ONS, 2008c).

In terms of the specific strains following the birth of an infant, Shapiro and Gottman (2005) report that the "phenomena of the transition to parenthood are fairly consistent across studies" (p.2). They include increased marital conflict, reduced quality (first for wives and then later for husbands), managing the balance between work and family, less time available for conversation and sex, and increased sleeplessness, fatigue, irritability, and depression. More involvement of the family of origin has also been reported as a stressor to the relationship following the transition to parenthood (Cowan and Cowan, 2000).

As further evidence, Twenge et al. (2003) undertook a predominantly US review of 90 studies (involving 31,331 participants) that investigated the relationship between parenthood and marital satisfaction. Their meta-analysis (a statistical analysis combining the results of all the studies) indicated that parents had significantly lower marital satisfaction than non-parents, and that this was particularly marked for women with infants. Only 38% of women with infants had higher than average marital satisfaction compared with 62% of childless women. The Twenge et al. review (2003) indicated that more contemporary samples showed increased marital dissatisfaction after the birth of a child. This may be due to, in recent years, an even greater contrast between the lifestyle and choices open to young childless adults compared to those available to parents of young children.

More recently, Lawrence et al. (2008) demonstrated the decline in marital satisfaction after becoming parents. They followed 156 US couples in a longitudinal survey and assessed marital satisfaction (Quality of Marriage Index) at first six months of marriage, one month prior to the birth of the child and at six and twelve months post-partum. All couples were in their first marriage, had their first child, had this child within the first five years of marriage, and recorded whether this was planned or not planned. They also compared these to a control group of voluntarily childless couples who were similar in mean number of days married. By using this control group they were able to demonstrate that the decline in marital satisfaction was not just associated with the length of time married but due to the transition to parenthood.

Of interest, and from an intervention point of view, Lawrence et al. (2008) outline that a number of moderating factors affect the impact of this transition to parenthood on the couple relationship. Factors likely to exacerbate the impact include pre-existing problems, poor conflict management skills, post-natal depression, high socio-economic group, young parenthood, and unplanned parenthood. Indeed, Lawrence et al. (2008) conclude that "In sum, parenthood hastens marital decline – even among relatively satisfied couples who select themselves into this transition – but planning status and prepregnancy marital satisfaction generally protect marriages from these declines." (Lawrence et al., 2008, p.41). In addition, the characteristics of the child may prove to have a moderating effect on the couple relationship, with Cowan and Cowan (2003) noting how a fretful and demanding baby may have a more detrimental impact on parental equilibrium and mood. Furthermore, from a review of parents of disabled children, Glenn (2007) found that the experiences of the transition to parenthood were similar, although more intense and stressful where a child was disabled. Specific pressures encountered in parenting a disabled child included coping with constraining roles and responsibilities with extensive care demands, financial impacts and possible grief over the loss of the 'hoped-for' baby.

Most recently of all, Doss et al. (2009) confirm the evidence noted above though examining the impact of having a first child. Derived from 218 couples (US) over the course of the first eight years of marriage, the study reports:

"Compared with pre-birth levels and trajectories, parents showed sudden deterioration following birth on observed and self-reported measures of positive and negative aspects of relationship functioning. The deterioration in these variables was small to medium in size and tended to persist throughout the remaining years of the study." (Doss et al, 2009, p.601).

Interestingly, and in similar fashion to the Lawrence et al. (2008) study, Doss et al. (2009) noted a number of influences on the post-birth deterioration. Factors furthering the decline included history of parental divorce or conflict, pre-marital cohabitation, having the child soon after marriage, having lower financial incomes, and a history of poor conflict management. Interestingly, having female children increased the extent of relationship deterioration, possibly due to fathers having less interaction with a daughter when compared to having a son. The study showed that couples who were not parents reported a gradual decline in their relationship functioning over the same time period, but without the sudden change characteristic of parents.

8.2.3 Interactive behaviour of couples

In a different manner to identifying specific socio-demographic predictors or life events such as the transition to parenthood, research has also focused on the interactive behaviour of couples to understand why relationships may break down. This section includes relationship factors that are more changeable compared to some predictors such as personality, attachment styles (see Chang and Barrett, 2009, for a useful synopsis) and socio-economic characteristics that, although affecting the likelihood of relationship breakdown, are considered to be less amenable to such change. This point is made by Stanley (2001) who argues that "....risk factors that are relatively dynamic and changeable..." (p.276) and likely to increase the risk of divorce include the following: communication style problem-solving ability, communication positivity versus negativity, defensiveness and withdrawal, higher ratios of hostility to warmth and willingness to negotiate.

One of the leading specialists in this field, Dr. John Gottman, has worked extensively in the area of marriage, couples and family relationships for over 30 years in the US. Gottman argues that the onset of divorce is a product of the negative and positive balance between the perceptual, behavioural and physiological domains. He argues that the best predictor of marital breakdown is 'negative affect reciprocity', whereby a partner's response to their partner's negativity will be met with negative affect (Gottman, 1999). He notes that certain negatives are particularly damaging to the relationship, namely criticism, contempt, defensiveness and stonewalling (otherwise known as the 'Four Horsemen of Apocalypse', Gottman, 1999). Reviewing the work of Gottman, Hicks et al. (2004) summarise the role of these three domains and the Four Horsemen as follows:

"In sum, the core triad of alliance (behaviour flow, perception and physiology) has a bi-directional relationship. This triad determines flooding which leads to the distance isolation cascade (mediated by the Four Horsemen), which in turn leads to distress and frequently dissolution." (Hicks et al., 2004, p.99).

Conversely, a more stable relationship is determined by the overall level of positive affect and an ability to reduce negative affect during conflict. As outlined in Gottman's 'Sound Marital House' (Gottman, 1999), the 'floors' constituting a stable relationship consist of marital friendship, positive sentiment override, regulation of conflict through problem-solving, supporting one another's dreams and a 'top floor' of shared meaning. Essentially, understanding the factors that erode a relationship as well as those that create a more solid relationship enables relationship support interventions to address these important concepts. Used in Gottman's 'love lab' the impacts for relationship stability and quality are convincing (Gottman, 1999). Gottman (Gottman and Silver, 1999) claims he can predict, with 91% accuracy, which newly-wed couples will remain married and which will divorce four to six years later. He also claims from his 'love lab' intervention a relapse rate of 20% derived from a nine-month follow-up of 640 couples, which he compares to the higher than average nationwide relapse-rate of between 30% and 50% from standard therapy. From this study of 640 couples, Gottman (Gottman and Silver, 1999) reports that 27% were at a very high risk of divorce at the start of the workshops. At three months this had reduced to 6.7% and at nine months to 0%. In addition, the workshops helped those couples who were at a slight risk of divorce too (Gottman and Silver, 1999).

As a final note to this section, although the above offers some broad insight into the reasons for relationship breakdown, there is still a dearth of research into the precise details of why relationships break down and, in particular, why this is more apparent in today's society. However, of relevance to this area, Cherlin (2004) highlights the 'Deinstitutionalization of American Marriage', noting a significant shift in the 1960s and 1970s from the 'companionate' marriage to the 'individualized' marriage. This shift is associated with a greater emphasis on personal choice, characterised by rising divorce trends and declines in modern day marriage (see Chapter 2). However, although there may be various psychological, structural and societal forces at work that make relationship breakdown more evident, the precise mechanisms within individual relationships are clearly complex and highly varied from one situation to another. The issue of tracking couples throughout their relationship career, to record such in-depth data, clearly lends itself to a qualitative approach. However, the resources required to achieve this would clearly be excessive and compounded further by doing this level of investigation on a scale that would allow reasonable generalisations to be made.

8.3 Evidence for effective relationship support interventions – prevention and therapy

Having outlined why relationship breakdown leads to predominantly negative outcomes (Chapter 7), and the factors increasing the likelihood of this breakdown (Chapter 8), this next section progresses to examine the evidence for effective relationship support interventions. This section reviews a number of studies to illustrate the effectiveness of a number of relationship support interventions; however, readers seeking more comprehensive evidence of this area should be referred to a recent research review conducted by Chang and Barrett (2009). Chang and Barrett (2009) review the effectiveness of adult couple relationship support in terms of prevention, relationship counselling and therapy, and those experiencing parental separation or divorce. It should be noted that most evidence is derived from the US with very little few preventative programmes (especially) having been evaluated in the UK.

The studies reviewed in this section have been categorised as prevention or treatment based. Although prevention is seen as a more efficient approach than treatment, it must be recognised that uptake is generally lower due to a combination of lack of motivation, inability to recognise benefits and lack of service availability (Chang and Barrett, 2009).

One of the most significant and timely studies into the prevention of relationship breakdown has been published by Hawkins and colleagues (2008). They report findings from a meta-analysis (a statistical analysis combining the results of the preceding studies) of Marriage and Relationship Education (MRE) programmes on a couple's relationship quality and communication skills. In total, they analysed 86 previous reports (dating back to 1976), that provided data on 117 predominantly US studies and more than 500 effect sizes. The extensive nature of this study is clearly of great significance to this review.

Hawkins et al. (2008) point out how their paper on MRE effectiveness is innovative by including quasi-experimental studies (that, unlike experimental designs, may not have included random allocation or a control group), unpublished data, and also by assessing whether several variables (age, gender, etc.) moderate effectiveness. The inclusion of unpublished studies is particularly interesting in that those with larger effect sizes may be more likely to be published and, therefore, an exclusive focus on published studies may inflate the true effect size.

Both outcome measures (relationship quality and communication skills) were assessed in various ways, using a combination of different scales and questions. Most studies that were reviewed examined one or both of these measures before the intervention, immediately after and up to six months later. Very few had recorded longer-term impacts of MRE which is a distinct limitation in assessing effectiveness (see later in this section). From the 117 studies analysed, there were notable variations in relationship length, although the majority included White, middle-class and married couples reporting minimal distress.

In terms of results, Hawkins et al. (2008) describe the MRE effects on relationship quality in experimental studies as "modest but generally significant – ranging from .24 to.36" (p.726), with smaller effects in quasi-experimental studies from .15 to .29. The results included those studies that had follow-up assessments indicating that the effects of the intervention had not reduced substantially over the (albeit limited) time frames of the studies reviewed. For communication skills, the effects sizes were again greater in experimental studies, ranging from .36 to .54, compared to quasi-experimental studies (.14 to.29).

These results show that the impacts on communication skills are more substantial than on relationship quality. Hawkins et al. (2008) suggest this may be because most of the programmes concentrated on communication skills and the effects were derived from observation (that may lead participants to demonstrate such skills to researchers which they may not use to such an extent in natural settings). For the experimental and quasi-experimental differences, the non-random allocation to the MRE programme or control condition in the quasi-experimental studies could have resulted in people with greater relationship need being more likely to chose the MRE intervention. Therefore, the pre-test differences between the MRE groups and the control group that were likely to be evident in the quasi-experimental studies (unlike in a random allocation situation) may have reduced the effect sizes. Moreover, although there was no difference in the MRE effects on men and women, moderate-dosage programmes tended to have a larger effect size than low-dosage programmes. The authors conclude as follows:

"Our primary analyses, which focused on experimental studies that clearly address efficacy, demonstrated that MRE produces significant, moderate effect sizes on two different outcomes that were commonly examined in MRE studies [relationship quality and communication skills]......Moreover, when follow-up assessments were employed and evaluated, there was not much evidence of diminishing effects". (Hawkins et al., 2008, p. 730).

Hawkins et al. (2008) also note similar effect sizes for other programmes such as teenage pregnancy prevention and alcohol and drug use prevention. Finally, although a clearly influential study in demonstrating the effectiveness of MRE, the authors also note the limitations of the study and provide suggestions for further research in order to extend this evidence beyond their predominantly White, middle-class couples. They suggest more research is needed to assess the effectiveness of MRE on more ethnically diverse, disadvantaged and relationship distressed couples, and over a greater period of time. They also stress the importance of research in understanding how these changes in relationship quality and communication skills occur to support the development of more effective interventions. The importance of longer-term outcomes from preventative and therapeutic interventions, to assess whether the commonly reported short-term impacts from both are sustained, is echoed by the earlier mentioned review by Chang and Barrett (2009).

Also centred around the prevention of relationship distress or decline Halford et al. (2008) present a recent review of Couple Relationship Education (CRE) which they define as the "provision of structured education to couples about relationship knowledge, attitudes and skills" (p.497). In light of the wider dissemination of these programmes throughout the US, the authors assess the state of the current evidence for CRE whilst noting new opportunities for evaluation with more programmes being implemented. In reviewing the curriculum-based CRE that focuses on key relationship skills such as conflict management (typically 12-15 programme hours), they outline how many of the programmes have distinct overlap. To illustrate, they report that the Prevention and Relationship Enhancement Programme (PREP – Markman et al., 2004), Couple Commitment and Relationship Enhancement (Couple CARE – Halford et al., 2004) and Couple Communication – (Miller et al., 1975) all include developing realistic expectations, positive communication and effective conflict management. They state the evidence of effectiveness as follows:

"Meta-analyses consistently show that skills-training CRE is associated with large effect size increases in relationship skills (d>0.7)......Skills-training CRE is also associated with small to moderate short-term effect size increases in relationship satisfaction, with larger effects evident in couples that initially have lower levels of satisfaction." (Halford et al., 2008, p.500).

These meta-analytic data tend to be limited to the short-term impacts in similar fashion to the observation made by Hawkins et al. (2008) earlier in this section. Consequently, Halford et al. (2008) document three main ways in which the evidence for the effectiveness of CRE is "modest" (p.500) as follows:

- The limited number of Randomised Control Trials (RCTs) reporting long-term effects of CRE beyond 12 months (especially important as the aims of CRE is to prevent relationship problems which may only become observable over the long-term given that the majority entering the programmes have reasonable quality at the outset).
- No testing through RCTs whether CRE reduces divorce rates.
- Studies confined largely to White and well-educated people.

In concluding that there are "substantial limitations in our knowledge of the efficacy of CRE" (p.503), Halford et al. (2008) highlight the opportunities for future evaluation to address some of the limitations noted above. As described earlier, these limitations apply to other studies reviewing the effectiveness of programmes aiming to prevent relationship breakdown.

A further significant meta-analysis has been undertaken by Wood et al. (2005) which focuses specifically on marital therapy. With MRE and CRE programmes described above offering more of a preventative approach, this paper reports findings from couples who are experiencing marital distress. The paper opens by citing evidence for the effectiveness of Marriage and Family Therapy (MFT) as derived from previous meta-analyses (e.g. Butler and Wampler, 1999; and Dunn and Schwebel, 1995). In view of this, Wood et al. (2005) state that "Because of these meta-analyses, we can claim that what we do matters and that we do make a difference" (p.273-274). However, the Wood et al. (2005) study extends this evidence by standardising the various measures of marital distress that have been used as outcome measures (for example, the Marital Adjustment Test – Locke and Wallace, 1959, and the Dyadic Adjustment Scale – Spanier, 1976) and also by assessing the types of therapy that are most effective according to levels of distress. Their analysis of previous studies was extensive. The studies analysed included those published and unpublished, dating back to 1963, experimental and quasi-experimental (non-random assignment to treatment and control groups), and/or interventions that were primarily based on either Behavioural Marital Therapy or Emotionally Focused Therapy. From the 41 interventions analysed (derived from 20 published and three unpublished studies mainly from the US), they found that the therapy content made little difference for those mildly distressed. However, among couples facing moderate distress, the Emotionally Focused Therapy was more effective than Behavioural Marital Therapy. Wood et al. (2005) conclude:

"In reference to what works for whom, any intervention for mildly distressed couples is better than no intervention. No one intervention stood out against any other for mild distress. Moderately distressed couples should receive a full treatment model rather than isolated components or interventions. Emotionally Focused Therapy stood out in terms of treatment versus control comparisons when compared to isolated BMT [Behavioural Marital Therapy] Components.....Only BMT was used to treat a severely distressed group, but to great success." (Wood et al., 2005, p.285).

In a more specific context, a recent report by Cummings et al. (2008) outlines findings from a brief intervention programme for improving marital conflict in families. Families involved in the study were those who were not reporting clinically significant problems. The brief intervention consisted of a 4-session psychoeducational programme about marital conflict. Each session was between 30 and 45 minutes long and included up to five couples. The focus for the four sessions were as follows.

- Session 1. Identification of constructive and destructive conflict and their effects on couples, and the importance of maintaining emotional security in the context of this conflict.
- Session 2. Effects of marital conflict on children's emotional security.
- Session 3. Effects of constructive and destructive marital conflict on children.
- Session 4. Effects of marital conflict on parenting and parent-child attachments.

Couples were randomly assigned into one of two intervention groups: parent-only (n=24 couples) and parent-child (n=33). A third, self-study group did not receive the intervention (n=33) but were provided with written material. To assess the effects of the intervention couples completed the 'Marital conflict knowledge and family processes questionnaire' (19 questions) as well as ways in which parents responded to a list of topics that were often the subject of marital conflict (e.g. finance, parenting, etc.). Pre-intervention, post-intervention and 6-month and one-year follow-up assessments were conducted (note again, like earlier cited studies, the long-term outcomes of the intervention were not assessed). Shorter booster sessions were held at the 6-month and one-year follow-ups. For those parents in the two treatment groups, the intervention was found to be effective in meeting its aims of improving knowledge about marital conflict and the different ways of expressing disagreements (with more constructive rather than destructive conflict). The aim of the intervention was to improve ways of expressing disagreements rather than necessarily reducing the frequency of this conflict. Additional changes regarding conflict were also seen through improvements in marital satisfaction, parenting and child adjustment (furthering the link between couple relationships and parenting).

As a final note to this section, it is important to acknowledge the existence of interventions aiming to smooth the transition for children during and following parental separation. From a review of related research, Mooney et al. (2009) conclude that there has been little evaluation of these programmes assessing the long-term effect on child outcomes.

8.4 Evidence for effective relationship support interventions – transition to parenthood

In addition to MRE, CRE and marital therapy, interventions have also been developed to focus on times when strain on a relationship increases. As noted earlier on in this chapter, this is particularly evident during the transition to parenthood. Indeed, the earlier reviewed Halford et al. (2008) paper documents four RCTs supporting the evidence that relationships skills programmes can be effective in sustaining relationship satisfaction during the transition to parenthood.

As further evidence, also from the US, Schulz et al. (2006) immediately observe the "virtually nonexistent" (p.21) nature of programmes that help to improve the couple relationship during the transition to parenthood. Their paper makes a significant contribution to this area by including a control group of childless couples and by tracking intervention and control parents on five occasions from the final trimester in pregnancy to 66 months post-partum (when the child is 5.5 years). Long-term relationship interventions of this nature, as noted in the earlier Hawkins et al. (2008) and Halford et al. (2008) reviews, are extremely rare.

In more detail, married couples expecting their first child were randomly allocated to receive the 'couple groups' intervention (28 couples) or to a control comparison group (38 couples). In addition, recruited from the same community newsletters and clinics, 13 married childless couples were also included in the Schulz et al. (2006) study. All couples were asked to complete questionnaires, using the Marital Adjustment Scale (MAT – Locke and Wallace, 1959) in the last trimester of pregnancy and when the child was 6, 18, 42 and 66 months old. The intervention consisted of four couples meeting on a weekly basis alongside a co-leader couple. The co-leader couples were mostly clinical psychologists; the meetings were typically two and a half hours in length, began in the last trimester of pregnancy and continued for 24 weeks. The topics initiated by the co-leaders included how participants viewed their relationship, division of family labour, communication and problem-solving styles, and parenting styles. The informal discussions drew on a number of psychological principles such as attachment, accepting within-couple differences, preventing negative emotional exchanges from escalating, and normalising experiences. In summary, the analysis showed that all couples (including the childless ones) had similar levels of marital satisfaction at the outset indicating that random assignment had successfully created equivalent groups. However, those parents not assigned to the intervention group lost 16.4 units on the MAT or a 14% reduction (lower score equates to reduced relationship satisfaction) whereas the intervention group reported a decline of 4.1 units or a reduction of 4% of their initial marital satisfaction. Therefore, although the intervention couples had reported a decline in marital satisfaction, this was to a lesser extent than the control couples who did not receive the 'couple groups' intervention. This lower reduction in relationship satisfaction for the intervention group was evident among men and women. By contrast, the childless couples, reported a slight increase in their marital satisfaction.

In conclusion, Schulz et al. (2006) present evidence concurring with that presented throughout this entire review: that marital strain and breakdown can have damaging effects on adults and children. Their findings have clearly shown the transition to parenthood to be a time where these strains are intensified and their argument in favour of more resources to support parents at this time seems convincing. Moreover, they also state that these interventions could be particularly effective as an 'early intervention' approach given that couples at this time of new parenthood are particularly motivated towards becoming 'good parents' and may seek out information to support this intention. Interestingly, although they recognise that more research is required to find out why their intervention was effective, they suspect that the self-help approach and using information in a safe environment may have been key. Rather than purely providing educational resources or relationship skills training, their intervention helped,

"....men and women make sense of their changing experiences as partners and new parents in the key domains of their lives while these experiences were occurring." (Schulz et al., 2006, p.29).

Enabling parents to search for their own solutions in this manner, within a safe environment, ties in with innovative internet approaches to relationship skills enhancement. At the time of print, One Plus One has developed its own thecoupleconnection.net website to help people improve their relationship. Not designed as a counselling site, or for those couples in crisis, the approach is more early intervention-based and focuses on self-help activities and skills to support relationship improvements. Uniquely, the site offers information, allows people to share views and ideas with others and also provides a 'personal' space where people can work out solutions. In addition, a unique 'couple space', very much a safe environment on the site, allows these ideas to be shared with a partner.

Returning to the strains characteristic of the transition to parenthood, Simons et al. (2001) report findings from an RCT of training health visitors (in the London area) to identify and help couples with relationship problems. Nine pairs of clinics took part that were matched by the socio-economic level of the area, and one from each pair was randomly selected to receive the intervention with the other providing a matched control. There were five strands to the data collection, completed in 1998, as follows.

- At the six to eight weeks developmental check: mothers completed the Relationships Dynamics Scale in the intervention sites to assess relationship distress.
- At the six to eight weeks developmental check: health visitor response at both intervention and control sites to any relationship problems raised. Health visitors in the intervention sites were asked to invite mothers to discuss problems if their scores of the Relationship Dynamics Scale indicated relationship distress.
- At the 12-week immunisation check: mothers at the intervention and control sites were invited to complete a questionnaire that included the Relationship Dynamics Scale (for the second time for the intervention respondents) and the mothers' experience of any help received regarding relationship problems.

- Interviews with 25 randomly selected women, held 12 weeks after the six- to eight-week visit, who had been offered relationship support in the intervention sites.
- The 25 health visitors who implemented the intervention completed a questionnaire to record their experience.

The intervention had resulted in more mothers being identified as needing relationship support (21% of the 459 mothers in the intervention sites compared to 5% of the 502 from the control sites) and the percentage actually offered help (18% versus 3% respectively). At the 12-week visit, mothers from the intervention groups were twice as likely to have discussed relationship problems with their health visitor and 75% more likely to report having received help with a relationship problem (e.g. supportive listening, practical advice or referral), compared to the control group. The interviews with mothers and health visitors confirmed the value of the intervention.

In a further related paper, Simons et al. (2003) provide an "explanatory complement" (p.401) to this earlier publication. This paper adds detail about the intervention and some of the results that were derived from the intervention sample. The intervention was a training course, called 'Brief Encounters'®, developed and provided by One Plus One. The purpose of this course, now in its 15th year at the time of writing (having trained over 3,000 health practitioners), is to provide health visitors (primarily) with the knowledge and skills that enable them to act as a supportive and empathic listener and, when doing so, to possibly help relieve distress caused by discord in a relationship. More recent evaluation data collected during and immediately after the course confirms the "exceptional enthusiasm" (p.401) that Simons et al. (2003) document. The paper outlines that most of the support provided, in the intervention group, was 'listening/advice'. Also, the results at the 12-week follow-up among the intervention group showed that 40% (142/351) of mothers had discussed relationship problems with the health visitor, which was higher than for any other person (such as friends, partner, doctor, etc.). Also, around a quarter of the intervention mothers at the 12 week visit felt less depressed, anxious or worried and had felt better talking about their problems. However, few people (8%) had reported any positive changes in their relationship. The authors attribute this relatively low percentage to the stability of relationship scores during the period of study, which raises the issue of whether these changes could be more prominent if followed up for longer. During the interviews with mothers who were offered support, most were positively appreciative, and interviews with the health visitors drew a similar response towards the value of the intervention. The authors demonstrate the key role that a health visitor can play in identifying a need for, and providing support on, relationship issues to mothers during the transition to parenthood. Although the long-term impact of this support on the couple relationship remains unanswered, the importance of this skills enhancement is exacerbated given that few couples are likely to seek support from a relationship counsellor.

To expand on the mechanisms behind supporting couples during the transition to parenthood, a recent paper by Feinberg and Kan (2008) highlights the importance of co-parenting. In this context, co-parenting is defined "how parents co-ordinate their parenting, support or undermine each other and manage conflict regarding childrearing" (p.253). They cite research supporting the notion that co-parenting acts as a 'risk mechanism' or influence on parenting, parent-child relationships, infant well-being and also the couple relationship. By contrast, they categorise marital conflict and quality as a 'risk indicator' and thus an area that is less malleable to change. The link between co-parenting and the couple relationship is outlined as follows.

"The selection of co-parenting as the primary short-term target was based on a view of the co-parenting relationship as a key subset of the overall interparental relationship, which itself has been linked to parenting and child outcomes for 25 years" (Feinberg and Kan, 2008, p.260).

In view of this evidence, Feinberg and Kan (2008) review the impacts of their US-based Family Foundations (FF) intervention to enhance co-parenting quality on couples expecting their first child. The dimensions of co-parenting covered within FF were support (e.g. extent of agreement to "my partner supports my parenting decisions", p.256), undermining, and parenting-base closeness (joys of parenthood related to celebrating child's development, working together as a team, and witnessing one's partner developing as a parent). The outcome measures were improved co-parenting or increased co-parental support, parental adjustment/mental health (depression and anxiety during pregnancy and after birth), the parent-infant relationship (through parental self-efficacy and confidence) and infant well-being (indicated by regular sleep patterns, calming when distressed and sustained attention). Note that the impact on the satisfaction and quality of the couple relationship per se was not addressed.

The FF programme involved four pre-natal and four post-natal sessions among heterosexual couples who were expecting their first child. The 169 eligible couples were randomly assigned to the intervention (n=89) or control group (n=80). The study collected impact (rather than longer-term outcome data) with the pre-test measures undertaken during pregnancy and followed up when the baby was about six months old. Feinberg and Kan (2008) found that the FF programme demonstrated positive co-parenting, reduced maternal depression and anxiety, a positive parental relationship with the child and infant regulation, and they define its impact as moderate, with effect sizes ranging from .34 to .70. Interestingly, in citing evidence where relationship enhancement programmes showed limited impact on the couple relationship during the transition to parenthood (countered by research cited earlier in this section), they conclude that a focus on co-parenting, in this context in terms of parental support and managing conflict around parenting, may prove to be a fruitful approach to preserve relationship stability during this transition.

8.5 Are there any positive aspects of relationship breakdown?

As the final section to this chapter, evidence is presented outlining situations where relationship breakdown can have positive consequences for adults and children. Amato (2000), from his earlier cited review of studies in the 1990s, argues that the Divorce-Stress-Adjustment Perspective (Figure 4) can also be used to illustrate the positive effects of relationship breakdown (for example, forming a new identity and lifestyle). Although few studies have intended to research the positive effects of divorce, there are a number of instances where this has been detailed. Amato cites evidenced from Kitson (1992) and Marks (1996) where divorced individuals report higher levels of autonomy and personal growth than married people. Also, Acock and Demo (1994) found that divorced mothers tended to report improvements in career opportunities, social lives and general happiness after divorce. Amato (2000) concludes that "In summary, although the majority of studies document the negative consequences of divorce, a small number of studies indicate that divorce also has positive consequences for many individuals." (p.1,274). To place these findings into context, the imbalance in research is likely to reflect that most relationships break down due to insufficient satisfaction with the relationship rather than a result of severe problems such as intense, repetitive conflict or violence. The situations where breakdown occurs due to severe problems characterised by violence or abuse, although in the minority, are likely to be the ones where the more positive aspects of relationship breakdown are evident (Halford et al., 2008).

The nature of the relationship prior to the relationship breakdown, and how this affects the outcomes, has been further evidenced as follows. Wheaton (1990) found that adults who were unhappy in their marriage reported an increase in psychological well-being following divorce compared to those who were moderately happy in their relationship. Wilcox et al. (2005), from a review of social science literature in the US, notes that divorce or separation from a high-conflict marriage can provide an important "escape hatch" for adults and children (Wilcox et al., 2005, p.4). In relation to pre-divorce conflict, Booth and Amato (2001) used longitudinal data to show that the escape from high-conflict marriages was particularly beneficial for child outcomes (in contrast to the breakdown of marriages that were low conflict). The authors note how these findings concur with two previous longitudinal studies conducted by Amato et al. (1995) and Jekielek (1998), who also researched how the pre-divorce level of conflict was associated with child outcomes (see Chapter 5). Gruber (2004), in reviewing 40 years worth of census data in the US, also notes the benefits for children following the breakdown of high-conflict marriages.

More recently, a paper published by Gardner and Oswald (2006) presents a vivid challenge to the negative impacts of relationship breakdown. The title of the paper, 'Do divorcing couples become happier by breaking up?' clearly questions much of the research evidence presented in this review and, by this nature, warrants particular attention. At the outset, they outline the complexity that has been apparent throughout this review. That is by attributing the seemingly negative impacts of the relationship breakdown on parents and children to this breakdown, as opposed to other influences. Furthermore, they note that cross-sectional studies can only be suggestive of a causal relationship between relationship breakdown and outcomes (hence most of the evidence in this review is longitudinal in dimension). In their study, Gardner and Oswald (2006) use data from the first 11 waves of the 'British Household Panel Survey' (1991-2001) which records information from over 10,000 adults from over 5,000 households. The survey records marital status and thus identified 430 cases of divorce and 278 separations due to death during this period. The study essentially compared the outcomes for these cases in comparison to those married, through the 12-item 'General Health Questionnaire' score which is a well recognised indicator of psychological distress (see more reference to this study and additional psychological impacts in Chapter 3). Through the longitudinal dimension, the data could therefore record people's levels of psychological distress both before and after divorce. Their study found that divorce is traumatic in the short-term. However, by two years after the divorce, the levels of psychological well-being are better when compared to the levels of distress two years prior to the divorce. The conclusions derived from this study make for compelling reading.

"The study finds that divorce works. The longitudinal evidence in this paper suggests that marital dissolution eventually produces a rise in psychological well-being. Both men and women gain, and do so approximately equally. For those couples who take it, the leap in the dark seems to improve their lives." (Gardner and Oswald, 2006, p.324).

Gardner and Oswald (2006) present some final points in this paper that are of particular interest. They note that the timeframe for the mental distress during a divorce, with improvements two years on, is similar for bereaved people, but the distress itself is less intense than for the widowed. The psychological distresses are similar for men and women, and remarriage within two years does not bring forward the increase in psychological well-being from the reported two years after divorce. Finally, the impacts of divorce among adults with children seem to fare equally to those without children.

In further reference to the positive benefits of divorce, Strohschein (2007), in using two waves of longitudinal survey of Canadian children, finds that previous divorce does not diminish a person's ability to parent effectively. This challenges the widely held stereotype that previous divorce can impact on children through an inability to parent in the future. As a further, although unrelated benefit, rather than assuming a relationship breakdown negatively affects all adults and children, there is a case to support that the breakdown of relationships in the adolescent and teenage transition is an essential learning experience for later life.

The positive effects of divorce are also likely to tie in with the person who initiated the relationship break-up. Indeed, adults can experience different trajectories of stress from divorce according to this initiation. As an example, the effects of divorce may not be apparent until the legal separation is completed for a spouse who wanted the marriage to continue. Conversely, stress may be more apparent at an earlier stage for the initiating spouse who, by the time the divorce is legal, could be in a state of relief (Amato, 2000). As noted earlier in Chapter 1, most of the legal proceedings associated with divorce in the UK are initiated by women.

Finally, linked to the positive effects of divorce, Amato (2000) observes the ongoing debate and positioning over people's perceptions of marriage. For some, divorce is seen as a social evil and root cause of many social problems (see background policy in Chapter 1). For others, divorce is seen as providing people with a second chance for future happiness and removes adults and children from the effects of dysfunctional families (thus having a positive effect). This point, illustrating contrasting perspectives, is a fitting conclusion to this section.

8.6 Conclusion and key findings from Chapter 8

The risk factors for relationship breakdown, although notably under-researched, have highlighted situations where the largely detrimental impacts are more likely to be felt. As a logical progression, this chapter has reviewed 'what works' in terms of relationship interventions and therefore illustrates the types of prevention packages that are required when the risk for relationship breakdown is enhanced. Finally, and as an important caveat to this review, the cases where divorce and relationship breakdown have positive outcomes are fully acknowledged. This chapter concludes by outlining some key findings as follows.

- UK census data show an association between elevated divorce rates and early age at marriage, history of previous divorce, and duration of marriage (half of all divorces occur in the first 10 years of marriage).
- Cohabitation increases the likelihood of relationship breakdown. Explanations include a selection effect (cohabitants are more likely to separate), the instability of a cohabiting relationship (less barriers to separate), and cohabitants having less traditional attitudes to marriage and relationship stability. Whether the arrangement is mutual or contingent is likely to affect the future of the relationship.
- Review evidence on the predictors of relationship breakdown suggests that demographic factors (especially those more volitional) are more predictive of marital breakdown compared to socio-economic factors. These factors are: early age at

marriage, pre-marital conception, pre-marital cohabitation, previous partnership breakdown, and parental divorce. The latter is particularly important and maintains a predictive effect when controlling for early age at partnership, pre-marital cohabitation and pre-marital childbearing.

- Research on the breakdown of low-conflict marriages, where the mechanisms may be less apparent, suggests that weak moral and structural commitment (less barriers to breakdown) are facilitating factors. The breakdown of these low-conflict marriages is also shown to have worse outcomes for children, with the breakdown of high-conflict marriages often being more beneficial to children.
- Evidence from prospective longitudinal designs shows that the transition to parenthood is associated with relationship breakdown. The impacts are reported to have increased in contemporary samples due to the greater contrast between the lifestyle and choices open to young childless adults compared to those available to parents of young children.
- Reasons for the decline in relationship satisfaction through new parenthood include less time together, increased sleeplessness, increased depression (including post-natal depression), and increased fatigue. Protective factors include high pre-pregnancy relationship satisfaction, planned rather than unplanned pregnancy, and a low-demanding and fretful baby.
- Dr. John Gottman has worked extensively in the area of marriage, couples and family relationships for over 30 years in the US. He notes that certain negatives are particularly damaging to the relationship, namely criticism, contempt, defensiveness and stonewalling. (He terms these as the 'Four Horsemen of Apocalypse'.) Conversely, a more stable relationship is determined by the overall level of positive affect and an ability to reduce 'negative affect reciprocity' during conflict. As outlined in Gottman's 'Sound Marital House' (Gottman, 1999), the 'floors' constituting a stable relationship consist of marital friendship, positive sentiment override, regulation of conflict through problem-solving, supporting one another's dreams and a 'top floor' of shared meaning. Understanding the factors that erode a relationship as well as those that create a more solid relationship has enabled Gottman to incorporate these principles into his 'love lab'.
- In general, little is known about precisely why relationships break down or why contemporary relationships show more fragility. The complexities in accounting for personality and attitudinal differences makes this difficult to research. However, it is clear that attitudes to marriage have changed with shifts in the 1960s and 1970s from the 'companionate' marriage to the 'individualized' marriage of modern day. This shift is associated with a greater emphasis on personal choice, characterised by declines in marriage and divorce trends (see Chapter 2).
- A recent meta-analytic study (of 117 studies) has shown significant although moderate effects from Marriage and Relationship Education programmes on couple relationship quality and communication skills. The impacts are comparable to interventions focusing on pregnancy prevention and alcohol and drug use. Follow-up data, although limited, suggest the effectiveness does not diminish substantially through time.
- To further assess the effectiveness of MRE programmes, research is required among more ethnically diverse, disadvantaged and relationship-distressed couples. More research is also required to understand how changes in relationship improvements occur in order to

inform even more effective interventions. Perhaps most critically of all, the evidence for the effectiveness of relationships skills programmes has rarely extended beyond 12 months.

- A recent meta-analytic study (of 41 studies) has found that Marriage and Family Therapy interventions have some effectiveness, with Emotionally Focused Therapy shown to be more effective than Behavioural Marital Therapy among couples reporting moderate distress.
- Interventions focusing on reducing the couple relationship difficulties during the transition to parenthood have been shown to be effective in the long-term. Following up couples from the last trimester in pregnancy to 66 months after birth, Schulz et al. (2006) found the decline in relationship satisfaction was significantly less for those parents who attended discussion groups led by clinical psychologists compared to those who did not. No such decline was evident among childless couples.
- There are suggestions that self-help approaches in a 'safe environment' may be a particularly effective approach to improving couple relationships. One Plus One has developed a website, thecoupleconnection.net, to help people improve their relationship. The site includes self-help activities which people can do alone or with their partner.
- One Plus One also provides a 'Brief Encounters'® training course enabling practitioners, mainly health visitors, to respond more effectively to people reporting relationship difficulties. Results from a Randomised Controlled Trial have shown more mothers were identified as needing relationship support by health visitors who received the training (compared to the control group). Mothers in the intervention group (relative to the control group) were also more likely to report having received such support with a relationship problem in the form of supportive listening, practical advice or referral.
- Positive aspects of relationship breakdown have been identified as high levels of autonomy and personal growth, as well as the 'escape' from high-conflict relationships. In general, the more positive aspects of relationship breakdown are seen when the prior relationship involved severe problems (such as intense conflict or violence) rather than general dissatisfaction with the relationship.
- The likelihood of positive and negative outcomes following the relationship breakdown may also be affected by who initiated the separation. Adults can experience different trajectories of stress according to this initiation. As an example, for the spouse who wanted the marriage to continue, the impacts of the separation may become apparent at a later stage than the person who initiated the break-up.

Chapter 9
Issues for consideration in estimating the economic costs of couple relationship breakdown

9.1 Introduction

The statistics outlined in Chapter 2 show how couple relationship breakdown has become one of the more common life transitions in Britain. Government policy in this area has focused on the legal process, particularly with a view to making it less adversarial, and on ensuring that absent parents continue to take financial responsibility for their children. However, the decision to separate or divorce made by individuals has consequences for other members of society, and this is particularly evident in terms of economic costs. The consequences can be found in the areas of health, social services, education, childcare, care of elderly and disabled people, housing, transport, social security and the environment as well as the courts and associated services. This chapter draws specific attention to the factors that need to be considered in calculating the economic costs of relationship breakdown. The costs for the couple and society at large will be considered.

Studies which aim to estimate the cost of couple relationship breakdown generally either focus on the impact on the costs of public services, or on the immediate financial costs to the parties involved in the relationship (e.g. the legal costs incurred in divorce proceedings). They also tend to focus on the short-term costs over a singe year. As shown in Chapter 1, estimates of the annual costs to Great Britain have included five billion pounds (Hart, 1999), fifteen billion pounds (Lindsay et al., 2000), and more recently the Social Justice Policy Group (2007) estimate that within the UK "family breakdown costs the taxpayer £20-£24 billion each year" (p.11). Arriving at these economic costs encompasses many of the issues that have been discussed previously in this review. This includes reporting 'average' economic outcomes which may not reflect the wide variation in costs incurred by different individuals. Also, although the majority of instances involve economic costs, some groups also report economic gains from relationship breakdown (see next section). Finally, the same issues arise concerning the ability to attribute these economic costs to the relationship breakdown, with direct (causal) and indirect mechanisms at work.

9.2 Who bears the economic costs?

Couple relationships break down because either or both partners take the view that the advantages of remaining within a relationship are exceeded by the advantages of terminating it. This power of one of the parties to dissolve the relationship does not require them to consider the externalities that generate in the form of the economic costs to others.

There is consistent evidence that for women divorce and separation from a partner leads to a reduction in income and a markedly increased probability of living in poverty particularly if they have children (Jarvis and Jenkins, 1999). Women in Britain are 40% more likely to enter poverty if they divorce than if they remain married (Aassve et al., 2006). Their income falls by an average of 17% after divorce, with larger falls among younger women, particularly mothers, and smaller falls among older women (Jansen et al., 2007). Using data from the UK 'Millennium Cohort Study', Kiernan and Mensah (forthcoming) observe the increase in family poverty upon parental separation that occurred between when the child was around 9 months and age 5. Relative to consistently married and cohabiting families, mothers living without a partner since the birth of the cohort child were found to be the most economically disadvantaged with poverty[16] reported at 79% (Kiernan and Mensah,

16. Poverty in this context defined as living below 60% of the median income (median being the precise income level that separates the top-half income of the population to the lower-half).

forthcoming). Kiernan and Mensah (forthcoming) also note that subsequent partnership behaviours such as becoming married can change the financial outlook. Indeed, using data from the 'British Household Panel Survey', Jenkins (2008) notes reductions in income upon parental separation, but also shows (for five years following the separation) that women who remain in paid work or who have a new partner fare much better than those who do not have a job or a new partner. In addition, although the economic impacts can be felt by the separated couple and their children, others implicated can include their children's subsequent children, their parents, other family members and the wider community.

There is a difference between those who experience adverse outcomes and those who bear the economic costs. In part, individuals bear the costs of their adverse outcomes, but in many instances other members of the community bear part of the financial costs. Most importantly, although the couple involved in the relationship that has broken down bear part of the cost, other members of the family and the wider community are likely to bear a disproportionate share. This is known in economic jargon as an 'externality': an outcome which occurs as a result of decisions made by others, over which they have no means of control. This may mean that the wider community has a stronger incentive to reduce the incidence of relationship breakdown than do the couple themselves. It follows that if there is a reduction in the incidence of relationship breakdown, any savings in costs are likely to be widely dispersed across society.

However, it is also important to note that some groups benefit from relationship breakdown: divorce lawyers, mediators, counsellors and estate agents derive all or part of their income from the consequences of couple relationship breakdown. Although in the longer-term people in this type of work can move into other areas of work, in the short-term any reduction in couple relationship breakdown would translate into lower incomes for these groups.

9.3 Economic outcomes to consider

This review has shown an extensive literature on the consequences of relationship breakdown, particularly for the couple involved and their children. Broadly speaking, the main economic outcomes can be summarised as follows:

- financial costs in terms of legal fees, moving, the need to maintain two households rather than one, additional childcare costs;
- impact on employment and earnings prospects;
- impact on disposable income; and
- impact on services supporting the detrimental health and social impacts of relationship breakdown.

These factors can be influenced directly by the breakdown of the relationship, but they can also be influenced by how the parties to the breakdown conduct themselves subsequently (Flowerdew and Neale, 2003). In some cases the externalities are relatively straightforward to calculate. For example, if women who have experienced relationship breakdown are less likely to be employed than otherwise similar women in intact relationships, this has both a cost to the woman herself in terms of foregone earnings, and to the public purse in terms of providing social security and related benefits. Both these can be estimated using published average values.

In other cases, estimation is more difficult. Thus, the increase in the number of households as a consequence of divorce and separation has an impact on the demand for the stock of housing relative to the supply, driving up prices. This has an adverse impact on those trying to get on the housing ladder in terms of the prices they have to pay, and the costs of their mortgages, but actually provides a benefit in the form of an untaxed capital gain to those who are already established property owners (whether as owner-occupiers or landlords). Where the response to these extra households is to build, then there are some who gain (housebuilders and those who own land which is developed) and some who lose (those who experience loss of amenity and who have to pay for additional infrastructure costs). In these cases, it may be best to identify that there are potential costs, without necessarily trying to estimate the scale of these costs.

The costs also vary considerably according to timescale. Although there are some immediate costs of relationship breakdown (for example, legal and moving costs) many of the costs accrue over a lifetime. This is particularly true for the costs incurred by children. Lower school achievement (associated with parental separation – see Chapter 6), for example, translates into lower lifetime earnings. An initial earnings gap of only 5%, with similar increases thereafter, translates into a reduction in earnings over a forty-year working lifetime of around £16,000 after discounting inflation. Each year, in Britain, between 150,000 and 200,000 couples with children separate or divorce (see Chapter 2). If only a quarter of these children experience lower lifetime earnings, the cost could be more than £800 million at current values. Thus, each year, divorcing and separating parents may influence costs on their children in terms of lost earnings.

There is evidence that people whose parents' relationship broke up when they were children are more likely to experience early parenthood, parenthood outside marriage, and to have their own adult relationships break down, even after taking account of any other adverse circumstances in their childhoods that pre-dated their parents' divorce or separation (Kiernan, 2003). This implies that some of the consequences for this second generation of children can be attributed to the breakdown of their grandparents' relationship. Therefore, ideally, costs should be estimated over a forty-year time period. In practice it is unlikely that this will be feasible, but it remains the ideal.

The finance required to support the physical and psychological health impacts of divorce on parents and children play a significant part in estimating the economic costs, especially in the provision and use of health services as a consequence. Identifying the extent to which this ill-health is caused by couple relationship breakdown makes the economic costs attributed to health difficult to estimate. In addition to the health impacts detailed throughout this review, there is consistent evidence that for women divorce and separation from a partner leads to a reduction in income and a markedly increased probability of living in poverty (see earlier). Divorced and separated mothers also have lower employment rates than mothers with partners, even after taking account of differences in the age of their children. Their lack of access to childcare by the father, which is more common in couple families, and the fact that for most couple mothers moving into work is done from the baseline of already having an earner in the household, underpin this. Thus the cost of moving into work (in terms of foregone social security and housing benefit) is generally small and the net returns are positive. For single parents receiving income support and housing benefit, the option of starting to work for a few hours a week and build up gradually is not open to them. Their initial move into work has to be sufficient to qualify for working tax credits and to cover the cost of formal childcare. Furthermore, the time spent not working has an impact on subsequent income, probably because skills have a tendency to deteriorate with non-use.

Alongside the economic costs on former couples, this review has shown extensive evidence that divorce and separation adversely affects the outcomes for children in a range of different areas of their lives (Chapters 5 and 6). In economic terms, this is clearly apparent through the poverty and poorer housing they share with their mothers. A recent Department for Work and Pensions (DWP) study observed that "children in lone-parent families were much more likely to live in low-income households than those in families with two adults" (DWP, 2008, p.7). Poor health, behavioural problems, involvement in crime, anti-social behaviour, teenage parenthood, etc. can all impact on the social and health support services. More directly, poor educational attainment can lead to few job prospects and further poverty. Also, as children from separated parents are more likely to experience relationship breakdown themselves as adults, the economic effects may be long-lasting (Kiernan and Hobcraft, 1997).

There are also costs involved in the legal aspects of divorce and in terms of at least one partner moving house. However, these costs are income for the lawyers and the removal companies or for the Government (in terms of stamp duty on homes). In the longer-term if there were fewer divorces, those benefiting from divorce would develop new areas of business, but in the short term these costs are not costs to the wider economy, so should not be included in any calculation.

9.4 A framework for calculating the economic outcomes for adults and children over the short-, medium- and longer-term

The following Table 8 illustrates the range of economic costs that can be attached to the key outcomes for the partners to the relationship and Table 9 does the same for their children's outcomes. Immediate (first year), medium (up to 10-15 years) and longer-term (more then 15 years) costs are presented. For any calculation of the economic impact of couple relationship breakdown, these costs should be included. The tables outline costs affecting individuals (men and women), other family members, the public purse and the wider cost implications for society. As noted earlier, the ideal time frame for presenting the costs would be around 40 years to include impacts on the second generation of children affected by divorce.

Table 8: Costs incurred due to the outcomes for the partners

	Woman's costs[17]	Man's costs	Other family members' costs	Costs to public purse	Costs to wider society
Immediate costs (first year)	• Loss of income • Additional expenditure due to separate household • Reduction in opportunity to take paid employment • Cost of formal childcare	• Additional expenditure due to separate household	• Providing financial and in-kind support	• Social security and housing benefit costs for new households • Cost of additional use of health services by the partners • Cost of providing additional social housing units • Lower tax receipts	• Higher rents and house prices due to extra pressure on housing
Medium-term costs (up to 10-15 years)	• Continued loss of income, reinforced by impact of worklessness on future earnings • Higher household expenditure (mitigated by some repartnering) • Poorer health • Higher mortality • Cost of formal childcare	• Additional expenditure due to separate household • Poorer health • Higher mortality	• Less access to financial and other support as parents age	• Social security and housing benefit costs for extra households • Incapacity benefit costs for differential health • Cost of additional use of health services by the partners • Cost of substance misuse services • Lower tax receipts	• Higher rents and house prices due to extra pressure on housing
Longer-term costs (more than 15 years)	• Continued loss of income, reinforced by impact of worklessness on future earnings • Higher household expenditure (mitigated by some repartnering) • Poorer health • Higher mortality • Cost of formal childcare	• Additional expenditure due to separate household • Poorer health • Higher mortality	• Less access to financial and other support as parents age	• Social security and housing benefit costs for extra households • Incapacity benefit costs for differential health • Cost of additional use of health services by the partners • Cost of substance misuse services • Lower tax receipts	• Higher rents and house prices due to extra pressure on housing

17. Some of the woman's and man's costs (e.g. formal childcare) reflect the most common scenario of the majority of women caring for their children after separation. We acknowledge the exceptions where, for example, children may be living with their father following separation.

Table 9: Costs incurred due to the outcomes for the children

	Child's own costs	Costs to public purse	Costs to wider society
Immediate costs (first year)	• Increased poverty • Increased incidence of mental health problems • Poorer health generally • Poorer performance at school • Experience of abuse or neglec	• Cost of health services (particularly CAMHS)[18] • Cost of additional educational support • Cost of dealing with child abuse and neglect • Criminal justice system costs	• Costs to victims of crime
Medium-term costs (up to 10-15 years)	• Increased incidence of mental health problems • Poorer health generally • Poorer performance at school • Experience of abuse or neglect • Early pregnancy • Breakdown of own adult relationship • Lower earnings • Lower employment rate	• Cost of health services (particularly CAMHS) • Cost of additional educational support • Cost of dealing with child abuse and neglect • Criminal justice system costs • Benefit costs • Lower tax receipts	• Costs to victims of crime • Cost of voluntary sector support for young people in trouble
Longer-term costs (more than 15 years)	• Breakdown of own adult relationship • Lower earnings • Lower employment rate	• Criminal justice system costs • Benefit costs • Lower tax receipts	• Costs to victims of crime

It is unlikely that it will be possible to attach monetary values to all of these outcomes, although the framework serves as a useful template. Where possible it is desirable to estimate the impact of relationship breakdown using sources from longitudinal studies, in that these account for any differences in initial characteristics, and do provide evidence of the difference in trajectories of people with a similar starting position (see Chapter 1). In terms of estimating costs, the most useful general sources are as follows.

- The Audit Commission and National Audit Office.
- The Home Office produces useful estimates of criminal justice system costs, including costs to victims.
- 'Unit Costs of Health and Social Care' published annually by the Personal Social Services Research Unit at the University of Kent, which provides costs of GP visits, inpatient stays, outpatient consultations with different specialists, etc.
- Department for Work and Pensions for average benefit payments to different types of claimant.

9.5 Conclusion and key findings from Chapter 9

This chapter has outlined issues for consideration in estimating the economic costs of relationship breakdown. As for outcomes in previous chapters, the same caveats arise in attributing costs causally to the breakdown, how the costs are

18. CAMHS or Child and Adolescent Mental Health Services

presented as an 'average' that may not necessarily affect individual circumstances, and how the economic costs to some are economic gains to others. The chapter culminates in the presentation of the costs that need to be accounted for in estimating the economic impact of relationship breakdown. These tables encapsulate the necessary dimensions in any such calculation, i.e. costs for men, women, children, other family members, public purse and society. For all, the costs across the short-, medium- and longer-term (ideally up to 40 years after the breakdown) need to be considered. A summary of key findings from Chapter 9 are now presented.

- Women in Britain are 40% more likely to enter poverty if they divorce than if they remain married. Their income falls by an average of 17% after divorce, with larger falls among younger women, particularly mothers, and smaller falls among older women. Relative to married and cohabiting families, single mothers are also found to be the most economically disadvantaged although subsequent partnership behaviours such as becoming married can change the financial outlook.
- Although the economic impacts can be felt by the separated couple and their children, others implicated can include their children's subsequent children, their parents, other family members and the wider community.
- Although the couple involved in the relationship that has broken down bear part of the cost, other members of the family and the wider community are likely to bear a disproportionate share. This is known in economic jargon as an externality: an outcome which occurs as a result of decisions made by others, over which they have no means of control.
- It is important to note that some groups benefit from the costs of couple relationship breakdown: divorce lawyers, mediators, counsellors and estate agents derive all or part of their income from the consequences of couple relationship breakdown.
- The main economic outcomes of couple relationship breakdown can be summarised as: financial costs in terms of legal fees, moving, the need to maintain two households rather than one, additional childcare costs; impact on employment and earnings prospects; impact on disposable income; and impact on services supporting the detrimental health and social impacts of couple relationship breakdown.
- The ability to derive economic costs varies immensely. For example, if women who have experienced relationship breakdown are less likely to be employed than otherwise similar women in intact relationships, this has both a cost to the woman herself in terms of foregone earnings, and to the public purse in terms of providing social security and related benefits. In other cases, estimation is more difficult. For example, where there is pressure on housing (partly due to more separated families), then there are some who gain (housebuilders and those who own land which is developed) and some who lose (those who experience loss of amenity and who have to pay for additional infrastructure costs). In these cases, it may be best to identify that there are potential financial impacts.
- The costs also vary considerably according to timescale. Although there are some immediate costs of relationship breakdown (for example, legal and moving costs) many of the costs accrue over a lifetime. This is particularly true for the costs incurred by children (lower school achievement, for example, may translate into lower lifetime earnings).
- Ideally, economic costs should be estimated over a forty-year time period. This is because some of the consequences for a second generation of children can be attributed to the breakdown of their grandparents' relationship.

In practice it is unlikely that this will be feasible, but it remains the ideal.

- A framework for estimating the economic costs to ex-partners and children has been developed, and takes into account events over the short-, medium-, and longer-term. This framework includes costs to women, men, other family members, the public purse and wider society. This framework presents items that need to be included when calculating the economic cost of relationship breakdown. They include costs arising as a direct (e.g. additional expenditure due to separate household) and indirect result of relationship breakdown (e.g. reduced opportunity to take paid employment).

Chapter 10
The impact of couple relationship breakdown: Conclusions and implications for practice, policy and research

10.1 Introduction

This extensive review of international research has outlined the impacts that occur when couple relationships break down. The review has documented impacts on adults and children, alongside addressing a range of related issues such as the mechanisms behind these impacts. The resounding conclusion is the apparent association between couple relationship breakdown and disadvantage, evident through a wide range of health and socio-economic indicators. In light of the increased fragility of couple relationships in today's society, this chapter seeks to extend the review by drawing out some concluding points and ultimately deriving significant implications for practice, policy and research.

10.2 Key findings

The preceding chapters have provided valuable insights into the impact of couple relationship breakdown on adults and children. This review has been innovative by including the breakdown of a range of couple relationship statuses (where possible), and thus reflecting the changes in relationship formation that have been evident over the last 40 years or so. Today's climate of couple relationships is one of declining rates of marriage and divorce, with married partnerships arguably becoming more homogenous than ever. Alongside these trends, there has been an increased diversity in relationship forms with, for example, greater numbers of cohabiting and 'closely involved' relationships. Nonetheless, with married and divorced people being more easily identified than other relationship forms, most of the reviewed research has been confined to the effects of marital breakdown.

A theme running throughout this review, and one to be borne in mind during this final chapter, is the precise contribution that relationship breakdown has on the reported impacts. The key to establishing whether the association between relationship breakdown and outcome is causal, is to assess the extent to which 'selection' effects are occurring. Selection bias occurs when comparing samples (e.g. married and divorced) that differ in a number of ways (e.g. history of mental health problems) such that any reported impacts that are directly attributed to the breakdown are difficult to discern. The possibility of reverse causation, for example alcohol use causing relationship breakdown rather than vice versa, and the inability to rule out other influences such as behaviour, genetics and personality, bring further complications (see later in this chapter). In appreciation of these complexities, priority in this review has been given to prospective longitudinal cohort studies where, essentially, sample members serve as their own control group with the impact of relationship breakdown observed by comparing outcomes pre- and post-breakdown. It is indeed fortunate that this review has been able to draw upon a number of sizeable longitudinal studies.

This review is underpinned by recognising the importance of strengthening couple relationships and the benefits this has for adult and child well-being, as well as effective parenting. In acknowledging the detrimental effects of couple relationship breakdown, this review is able to support the importance of developments in policy and practice that can either help prevent relationship breakdown or minimise the negative effects on adults and children when the relationship is irretrievable. It is important to emphasise that there is convincing evidence that some relationships can be repaired, improved and prevented from breaking down (see Chapter 1).

In view of these points, this chapter will now outline what are arguably the most significant 10 findings from this review. Reference to the relevant chapters from where they are derived is provided. These findings have distinct relevance to the implications for practice, policy and research that follow in a later section.

1. There is an unequivocal association between couple relationship breakdown and adult ill-health (Chapter 3). Mortality statistics for England and Wales (in 2007) show elevated mortality rates for non-married (single, widowed and divorced) males and females for all age groups between 25 and 64 years. From middle age (45 years onwards) the single (never-married) group show the highest rates of mortality. Overall, the elevation of mortality rates among unmarried groups is greatest among men of all ages. Office for National Statistics data from England and Wales show that, between the ages of 30 and 50, single men have death rates about three times that of married men, and single women have rates about double those of married women. There is also evidence of an 'accumulative' effect, with the strength of these mortality associations increasing by number of years non-married. Associations between marital status and general health status and more specific health conditions such as Coronary Heart Disease and blood pressure are also evident. Unlike the mortality rates (from middle age), there is evidence from morbidity data that the divorced and separated fare the worst out of all marital status groups. Studies indicate that the protective effect of marriage may be predominant in explaining these health differences, rather than the effect of people being selected out of marriage, or being more predisposed to relationship breakdown due to their poor health status. Nonetheless, and in light of the earlier mentioned note prior to these findings, evidence of a causal relationship between relationship status and the mortality statistics cannot be confirmed.

2. In studying couple relationships and health, it is clear that the marriage must be of a high quality to be advantageous (Chapter 3). Indeed, evidence suggests that the health outcomes for some single people are more positive than those reporting unhappy marriages. Therefore, preventing relationships from breaking down and improving relationship satisfaction are both key to maintaining the well-being of adults and children.

3. Couple relationship breakdown is associated with poorer adult mental health (Chapter 4). Research suggests that these impacts are observed from two years prior to breakdown, with a peak at the time of separation. Some research has shown, by two years post-separation, that psychological strain drops below the level of stress before the separation indicating a relief from stress over the longer-term.

4. Evidence from extensive reviews of other studies has reported associations between couple relationship breakdown and poor child outcomes (Chapters 5 and 6). These include: poverty and socio-economic disadvantage (especially); physical ill-health; psychological ill-health; lower educational achievement; substance misuse and other health-damaging behaviours; and behavioural problems including conduct disorder, anti-social behaviour and crime. Longitudinal, cohort studies have shown that these effects may be long-term for some children, and include socio-economic disadvantage, cohabitation or marriage at an early age, teenage pregnancy, a child born outside of marriage, and increased risk of their own marital breakdown. However, these negative impacts of relationship breakdown on children are far from universal. Some are able to adjust to a changing situation after a period of instability whilst others are less fortunate with negative impacts extending into adulthood (see Point 10).

5. The impact of multiple relationship transitions are particularly detrimental to children (Chapter 5). Changes in family structure (e.g.

from marriage to divorce, to remarriage, involving new half-siblings, etc.) may be more disruptive to children than maintaining a stable family structure, even if that is with a single parent. The effects are also considered to be accumulative, with the increased number of transitions leading to greater consequences for children. Younger children experiencing parental separation have a greater potential to face multiple transitions (because of their age) and therefore are more likely to experience the detrimental effects that may result compared to older children.

6. Divorce following low pre-divorce conflict, compared to high pre-divorce conflict, is shown to be more detrimental to the health and well-being of children (Chapter 5). This is because levels of low conflict often mean children have little time to anticipate the separation, and may result in some blaming themselves for the separation (noted as being quite ironic given that the relationships with least conflict, although having a greater chance of reconciliation or a less stressful separation, appear to have more harm for children). Therefore, although interventions need to foster a continued parent-child relationship to alleviate the impact of relationship breakdown on children, they also need to consider ways in which children perceive and attribute the conflict and breakdown. This also illustrates that couple relationship breakdown should be viewed as a 'process' with events prior, during and after the breakdown affecting the impacts. Research also indicates that it is not whether parents are in conflict that is key, but the issue of how this conflict occurs. For example, 'destructive' conflict can be particularly harmful to children, although 'constructive' conflict can be important in children learning how to resolve disputes in an effective manner.

7. Even though divorce is more common nowadays, there is evidence to suggest that the adverse outcomes for adults and children are still equally apparent (Chapter 5). This opposes the argument that increasing divorce rates diminish the negative impacts in line with reduced stigma and more acceptance of couple relationship breakdown. Furthermore, the difference in adult mortality rates by marital status, in England and Wales, has actually increased since divorce has become more common.

8. There are three main theories to explain the association between couple relationship breakdown and its impacts – selection, protection and stress (Chapter 7). Selection applies where unhealthy people (for example) are less likely to marry or stay married since ill-health is thought to interfere with establishing and maintaining relationships. Selection theory argues that poorly functioning people (predisposed to score low on well-being after a relationship breakdown) are especially likely to divorce. This predisposition, rather than the divorce itself, contributes to a lowering of well-being and therefore is not indicative of a causal relationship between couple relationship breakdown and well-being. The second theory concerns the protective effects of marriage that can provide a buffer against stress and other changes in life (through social interaction, intimacy, companionship, financial reward, etc.). The third concerns the effects of stress that are faced due to a relationship breakdown or through the bereavement felt due to the death of a partner. Theories two and three are more supportive of a causal relationship between couple relationship breakdown and impact. The physiological pathways derived from stress (cardiovascular function, neuroendocrine function and immune function) support evidence of a causal relationship between relationship breakdown

and ill-health. Based on observing these physiological responses among children, parental divorce or separation is shown to be more harmful compared to the severe disease or death of a family member. Moreover, the general consensus is that although selection effects may be apparent in explaining some of the impacts of couple relationship breakdown, it is argued that the protective and stress effects operate over and above these selection effects, thus indicating the role that relationship breakdown can have in causing negative outcomes.

9. The dissolution of a relationship results in a loss of the protective benefits from being in a partnership (such as effects on physical and psychological health), as well as further strains associated with the process of separation (Chapter 7). This is illustrated by research showing that never-married women have been shown to report less detrimental health outcomes in terms of psychological health and limiting long-standing illness compared to those who have experienced the stressful events of divorce or separation. However, this does not apply when observing mortality data that show single (never-married people) reporting higher death rates from middle age than those who were divorced or widowed.

10. There are a number of moderating factors that can determine the impact of couple relationship breakdown and why, for some, the impacts are worse than for others (Chapter 7). For children, these include: parenting quality; financial resources; maternal mental health; children's age (older children tend to face more problems adjusting to new family forms than younger children, although for a younger child who cannot recognise the distress, the removal of one parent may cause confusion and anxiety, and lead to self-blaming); sex (mixed evidence); pre-divorce conflict (low levels may mean children have little time to anticipate the separation); communication between parent and child about the separation, child relationship and contact with both parents after separation, supportive other family members; new family setting after separation (see multiple transitions point earlier); and whether one parent is repartnering at any one time (rather than at the same time) with the latter more difficult to adjust to. When considering all the various stresses faced by children after separation that may influence how much they are affected, there is a strong case for all being mediated through the parent-child relationship. Therefore, good and effective parenting may be the most potent means of reducing the negative impacts on children. In addition, with the unequivocal link between couple relationship satisfaction and supportive parenting, the role of supporting couple relationships (including new, post-separation relationships) in order to minimise the impacts on children is clear. In view of these various risk and protective factors, there is a powerful argument that the way a family functions, rather than the family type, may be more important in shaping child outcomes. Moderating factors affecting the psychological impact on adults include social and economic support, maternal mental health, ability to forgive, and consideration to who initiated the separation. Relative to the evidence establishing the impact of couple relationship breakdown, defining and understanding the factors that can help prevent or reduce the detrimental impacts reflect some of the more innovative findings from this review (see forthcoming implications).

10.3 Implications for practice and policy

There are a number of ways in which the reported evidence has clear implications for practice and policy. Key points to observe for practice and policy include: evidence demonstrating that couple relationships can be strengthened and that breakdown can be prevented; the opportunities available to minimise the burden when breakdown occurs (in light of factors that moderate the impacts); the importance of maintaining relationship quality; and recognising opportune moments where relationship strain is more pronounced (e.g. transition to parenthood, the birth of a disabled child, etc.). With the detrimental impacts associated with relationship breakdown, this evidence supports the case for more investment to help strengthen family relationships and to minimise the burden when relationship breakdown does occur.

Evidence outlined in this review illustrates instances of where, and how, couple relationships can be strengthened and prevented from breaking down. Although long-term evidence of effectiveness is still required, one of the key studies in this area was that undertaken by Schulz et al. (2006). Evaluating a relationship enhancement intervention during the transition to parenthood, some of the findings have far reaching consequences. Reviewed in detail in Chapter 8, Schulz et al. (2006) followed new parents for five and a half years beyond the birth of their first child. Central to the effectiveness of their 'couple groups' intervention, they found that rather than purely providing educational resources or relationship skills training, their intervention helped couples to make sense of their changing experiences themselves.

Enabling parents to search for their own solutions in this manner, within a safe environment, ties in with innovative internet approaches to evidence-based relationship skills enhancement such as the thecoupleconnection.net site created by One Plus One during 2008. The approach offered through this interactive website is early intervention-based and focuses on self-help activities and skills to support relationship improvements. The site follows the principles of the 'Helping Process' (Braun et al., 2006) with five key stages: exploring the issue through information;

developing understanding; making plans; making changes; and reviewing. Uniquely, the site offers information, allows people to share views and ideas with others and also provides a 'personal' and 'couple' space where people can work out solutions through a safe environment. It is clear that innovative approaches such as thecoupleconnection.net present a new means of accessing a population that is traditionally less likely to seek out professional support. Ongoing evaluation data will report the extent to which thecoupleconnection.net has helped people to improve their couple relationship. Aside to innovative approaches to preventing the breakdown of couple relationships, this review has also shown a need for improved awareness about couple relationships, the importance of recognising relationship difficulties at an early stage, and the general necessity for the wider availability of relationship support services in the UK involving new technological solutions to improve reach.

Nonetheless, in light of earlier reviews that have covered elements of the impact of couple relationship breakdown (McAllister, 1995; Lindsay, 2000), it is clear that research examining the protective factors following a relationship breakdown has been particularly enhanced in recent years. Indeed, while much of the evidence on impacts is relatively well established, arguably one of the more innovative strands for practice and policy has been the factors known to prevent long-term detrimental outcomes for children in particular. The parent-child relationship appears instrumental in such a scenario (see next paragraph). With couple relationship breakdown becoming more widespread, establishing the protective factors for adults and children may reflect the primary direction for ongoing research and practice developments in this field. The recent policy directive from the DCSF, 'The Children's Plan: One Year On' (DCSF, 2008b), outlines the importance of minimising harmful outcomes as a priority for 2009:

"Introduce new ways to support parents at times when their relationships come under strain, and give more support to children when family relationships break down" (DCSF, 2008b, p.7).

A further theme central throughout this review is evidence outlining the link between couple relationships and parenting. Poor quality parental relationships are associated with poor parenting and poor quality parent-child relationships as a consequence (Reynolds et al., 2001; Strohschein, 2005). Conversely, children raised by parents reporting high relationship quality and satisfaction tend to have high levels of well-being (e.g. Cummings and Davies, 1994; Hawthorne et al., 2003; Hetherington and Kelly, 2002; Reynolds et al., 2001). Also, improvements in co-parenting (supporting a partner during parenting) have been shown to improve partner- and parent-infant relationships and their well-being (Feinberg and Kan, 2008). This association is also summarised through the 'vicious' and 'virtuous' cycles of parenting whereby the degree of support for the mother affects the criticism of the father, which affects the father's satisfaction of their relationship with the mother, which affects the father's involvement with the child, which affects the support for the mother, etc. (One Plus One, 2006).

With this link between couple relationships and parenting, it is worth emphasising that effective parenting and a strong parent-child relationship has been argued to be the most potent means of reducing the negative impact of couple relationship breakdown on children, should this occur. However, this evidence also demonstrates that it is not just a case of preventing marriages or relationships from breaking down where appropriate that is key, but improving the quality of those relationships that do exist will enhance parenting and ultimately child well-being. Collectively, this evidence demonstrates the need for parenting interventions to acknowledge the importance of the couple relationship in improving adult and child outcomes. To illustrate, Feinberg and Kan (2008) outline that co-parenting (as illustrated by couple relationship elements of parenting support, lack of undermining, and parenting-base closeness) acts as a 'risk mechanism' or influence on parenting and one that is more malleable to change compared to focusing on marital conflict or parenting itself. Therefore, practice-based developments on co-parenting may prove to be an effective means of improving the couple relationship, parenting, and ultimately the well-being of both adults and children.

Within this review there have been instances where the impacts of relationship breakdown differ by gender. Gender differences have clear implications for practice and policy. Perhaps most notable are the mortality differences seen in Chapter 3 between those married and divorced. These statistics clearly show how the marriage advantage is more pronounced among men. These differences are difficult to explain as, especially in this example, the outcome is likely to occur years after the divorce. Nonetheless, the evidence is rather uncertain given the reverse gender differences observed through the morbidity data in Chapter 3 (where divorced or separated women fare slightly worse than men in terms of psychological ill-health and limiting long-standing illness).

To help understand these gender differences, a suitable starting point would be to recognise that men and women differ in their views and experiences of relationships. To illustrate, Hetherington and Kelly (2002) provide great detail in how some of their five relationship types reflect the gender differences, for example, in the male breadwinner and female homemaker roles in the 'traditional' marriage. Hetherington and Kelly (2002) also show how men and women perceive relationship problems differently and vary in reaching their decision to divorce. Their contribution, entitled 'The his and her marriage; the his and her divorce', encapsulates the gender differences that may underpin the mortality and morbidity variations detailed in this review. In relation to this, there are distinct changes in gender roles that may have a future bearing on these disproportionate impacts of couple relationship breakdown. For example, Gershuny et al. (2005), in using data from three national household surveys (Britain, US and Germany), show how the gender roles in the family have changed with an increase in married women's employment and a more egalitarian division of domestic labour as a consequence. It is intuitive to argue that the dissolution of marriages of this nature may have different impacts on those of a more 'traditional' marriage, particularly in terms of economic disadvantage.

Finally, as for adults, there is mixed evidence over whether the impacts are affected by the gender of children. There is some evidence to suggest that boys find parental separation more disturbing although girls show greater long-term impact. Also, boys find adjustment to stepfamilies easier than girls, especially when girls are in early adolescence. Although acknowledging the complexities in this evidence, among adults and children, there is some suggestion that practice and policy developments in couple relationship enhancement need to be aware of these gender differences. As to be shown next, more research to clarify these gender differences would be welcome.

10.4 Implications for research

The presentation of the concluding points and implications for practice and policy gravitates readers towards areas where more research is required.

1. In general, little is known about precisely why couple relationship breakdown or why contemporary relationships show more fragility. The complexities in accounting for personality and attitudinal differences makes this difficult to research. However, it is clear that attitudes to marriage have changed with shifts in the 1960s and 1970s from the 'companionate' marriage to the 'individualized' marriage of modern day. This shift is associated with a greater emphasis on personal choice, characterised by long-term declines in marriage and rising divorce trends. The attitudinal and personality-based origins of couple relationship breakdown, relative to the broader socio-demographic predictors, are still under-researched. There is a clear role for studies adopting qualitative methodologies to provide this greater insight.

2. It is arguable that couple relationship support needs to differ among subsets of the population, be they younger, older, expecting parents, new parents, of mixed heritage, etc. Understanding more about the needs and unique experiences that these subgroups face is key to providing tailored support. To illustrate, the relationships between teenage parents is particularly fragile, with relationship breakdown having consequences for both parents and the child. Young people face the challenge of securing a sound economic footing, balancing work and home-life pressures, as well as contending with the strains associated with the transition through adolescence to parenthood. In addition, although a more obvious subset, the male/female differences in the impact of relationship breakdown still requires more clarification (take the mortality and conflicting morbidity data in Chapter 3 as evidence). In the

UK, research is also sparse in defining and understanding the relationship dynamics across different ethnic, religious and cultural groups. More research on these subsets would clearly be valuable.

3. There is more research required to assess the effectiveness of Marriage and Relationship Education programmes on couple relationship quality. Research is required among more ethnically diverse, disadvantaged and relationship distressed couples. More research is also required to understand how changes in relationship improvements occur in order to inform even more effective interventions. Research into the effectiveness of such programmes in the UK is particularly in need as most evidence, at present, is derived from the US. Perhaps most critically of all, the evidence for the effectiveness of relationships skills programmes has rarely extended beyond 12 months and so the long-term effectiveness of these programmes is not yet known. In relation to this, research evidence assessing the effectiveness of relationship enhancement programmes during the transition to parenthood, a known time of increased relationship tension, are virtually non-existent. Also, although interventions aimed at helping children through a family separation have been implemented in the UK, more research is required to ensure all are evidence-based and evaluated in a robust and long-term fashion.

4. Several studies in this review have used standardised measures of relationship quality and satisfaction (e.g. Dyadic Adjustment Scale – Spanier, 1976; Marital Adjustment Test - Locke and Wallace, 1959). Although internationally recognised, there is some argument that these scales need to be refined in order to reflect the contemporary nature of relationships and those that increasingly exist outside of marriage. In addition, especially as is the case in the UK, there is no readily available or standardised way for practitioners to quickly and opportunistically assess the relationship support needs of adults. Therefore, research to develop robust but concise measures for assessing relationship support need would allow practitioners to identify problems and provide appropriate support. Moreover, using such measures over time could be an effective means of assessing the impact of the support offered including that through a more formal relationships support intervention.

Nonetheless, arguably the greatest need for research brings us back to the association/causation debate that is central to the evidence presented in this review. It has already been sufficiently emphasised that there is no definitive answer to this. However, we are able to gain a degree of confidence from longitudinal study designs and multivariate analytical techniques, as to whether such a causal relationship can be inferred. The reality is, in some instances a causal relationship can be more strongly inferred (e.g. child mental health impacts from parental separation) compared to other instances (e.g. mortality impacts), although never for absolute certainty. This issue stems from that fact that laboratory experiments or Randomised Controlled Trials are considered by some to be the only means to derive acceptable evidence of causation. In noting that this is not acceptable for ethical and practical reasons, particularly in the case of couple relationship breakdown, Rutter (2009) outlines recent statistical advances where evidence of causation can be derived with more certainty. The wider adoption of these statistical techniques in new research will advance our understanding of the extent to which impacts outlined in this review are a result of relationship breakdown.

Rutter (2009) notes statistical advances that "go beyond the traditional multivariate regression techniques that seek to 'control' for confounders" (p.4) that have predominated in this review. Although the full details of these techniques are beyond the scope of this review, they serve as important developments for new research. Also, on the occasions where these statistical techniques have been used in this review, evidence can be categorised above that derived from the more common traditional multivariate techniques. The first advance is the growth curve trajectories that are used to classify individuals according to their propensity towards an impact of relationship breakdown (in this instance). They are essentially used to assess whether some event (i.e. relationship breakdown) alters the identified trajectory. As an example, they have been used in Strohschein's (2005) study of child-related longitudinal data in Canada (1994, 1996 and 1998), as reviewed in Chapters 6 and 7. Using a growth curve model to control for the range of variables specified, these studies found that children whose parents divorced during the study reported higher than average anxiety and depression prior to divorce, followed by an increase in these outcomes after the divorce. Using such statistical advances increases the inference of a causal relationship in this instance. The second technique is propensity scores which seek to negate the effects of selection bias by calculating the conditional probability of being exposed to a causal agent. The third is by using Direct Acyclic Graphs which involve predicting how possible confounders (that may influence the causal relationship) would operate. The fourth and final advance involves mediation, whereby the focus is on identifying a variable that may mediate a relationship between two further variables. If such a mediating variable is found to exist, then there can be no evidence of a causal relationship between the original two variables. Of additional interest, the paper moves on to discuss scenarios whereby 'natural experiments' can be conducted to elicit a more causal effect (e.g. in the use of twin studies and whole population comparisons where societies differ substantially, for example in their extent of couple relationship breakdown – see Rutter, 2007).

Aside to the statistical advances, there is also a need to consider innovative research designs that can help to advance our understanding of causal inference. One significant contribution to this has been through the work of Sampson and colleagues (2006) who used a counterfactual life-course approach to clarify the relationship between marriage and criminal activity. Using longitudinal data, they essentially compare the causal effect of a person being married, to this same person being unmarried, throughout their life course. Their advances are stated as follows:

"By weighting for time-varying propensities to marriage over each year of the life course, our counterfactual strategy "thinks" like an experiment and provides an alternative to the static between-individual comparisons that dominate the marriage and outcome literature." (Sampson et al., 2006, p.466-7).

In relation to these statistical and design issues, there is also a need to adopt a wider variety of measures to further clarify the relationships documented throughout this report. With longitudinal data, argued as being the most widely available and promising design to assess the evidence, there is still further scope to use other means to triangulate the data and assess whether findings are concordant to those documented elsewhere. One example would be to adopt more qualitative studies which can provide useful and plausible explanations behind some of the quantitative relationships, as well as unearthing mechanisms that can be subject to quantitative verification.

Nonetheless, although these statistical and design advances have led to strong claims for the role of protective (causal) effects to dominate over selection (non-causal) effects in explaining health variations (Murphy, 2007), the relative contribution of these explanations still remains unanswered.

10.5 Final comments

This final chapter has advanced the review by highlighting ten key findings, presenting avenues for developments in practice and policy, and noting areas in need of more research. In light of these points, although the evidence demonstrating the impact of couple relationship breakdown is highly complex, the overriding conclusion is the apparent association it has with adult and child disadvantage. This association remains strong despite the fact that divorce and separation is more widespread in today's society with research showing that the impacts have not diminished through time (e.g. Ely et al., 1999; Gruber, 2004; Sigle-Rushton et al., 2005). Rather, the increased exposure of adults and children to couple relationship breakdown means that more people are affected compared to those of a previous generation. Hence the urgency and increased policy emphasis on family functioning and stability outlined in Chapter 1.

Although the 'protection' offered by couple relationships (in terms of social support, companionship and intimacy) has been shown to explain the association between relationship breakdown and health "over and above selection effects" (Murphy, 2007, p.66), the relative contribution of this to economic support still remains unanswered. Indeed, the issue of poverty and economic resource remains central to our understanding of the impacts of relationship breakdown. There is a case for well-being being affected mostly by a decline in economic resources which, in turn, have arisen from relationship breakdown. For example, Chapter 9 has reported that women in Britain are 40% more likely to enter poverty if they divorce than if they remain married (Aassve et al., 2006). However, independent of relationship breakdown, poverty and financial hardship are likely to be two of many different factors affecting well-being. As one example of the multifaceted influences at work, Farrington (1996) notes that parental separation sits alongside "thousands of factors" (p.2) that may affect youth crime. Therefore, although relationship breakdown per se may play a role, it is recognised that financial disadvantage itself alongside a whole host of other factors may be integral in affecting adult and child well-being (regardless of the couple relationship).

Nonetheless, although many factors may affect well-being, some of which are unknown and unmeasured, the role of poverty and financial disadvantage must not be understated. Turning the evidence outlined in this review 'on its head', if one was to outline factors that affect well-being, there is a powerful argument that poverty and financial disadvantage play a more significant role than couple relationship breakdown. For example, Wilcox et al. (2005) states that the influence of socio-economic status and poverty may be particularly powerful influences on child well-being, with the latter proving to be a better predictor of educational attainment, for example, over that of relationship breakdown. Also, Mooney et al. (2009) outlines that when compared with peers from more advantaged backgrounds, children from poorer backgrounds, whether from intact or non-intact families, generally do less well across a number of measures, such as health and educational attainment. This point, supported by these two illustrations, places the role of couple relationship breakdown into its correct context. Furthermore, with the economic recession at the time of writing, it may well be that rising unemployment and financial uncertainty places enhanced pressures on couple relationships. Future practice, policy and research will need to establish how much this may impose more worry and relationship strain among families, whilst also recognising that the financial pressures may increase the structural barriers connected to relationship dissolution.

Therefore, although economics and finance may play a significant role in affecting well-being independent of couple relationship breakdown, the final point in this review should acknowledge how the two are inextricably linked. It must be reiterated that financial capability (often reduced following a separation) acts as a powerful protective factor against the potential harmful outcomes from relationship breakdown. With positive parenting, linked to the quality of the couple relationship, offering an additional protective factor, it is clear that family functioning and within-family effects (from finance and parenting) are particularly significant alongside couple relationship breakdown in affecting outcomes. Moreover, although the impact of couple relationship breakdown can be considered detrimental as an 'average effect' (which may disguise instances of differing impacts), the financial situation and positive parenting are important influences on adult and child outcomes that must be integrated in any related practice and policy.

References

Aassve, A., Betti, G., Mazzuco, S. & Mencarini, L. (2006). *Marital Disruption and Economic Well-Being: A Comparative Analysis.* Colchester: Institute for Social and Economic Research.

Acock, A.C. & Demo, D.H. (1994). *Family Diversity and Well-Being.* Thousand Oaks, CA: Sage.

Afifi, T.O., Cox, B.J. & Enns, M.W. (2006). Mental Health Profiles among Married, Never-Married, and Separated/Divorced Mothers in a Nationally Representative Sample. *Social Psychiatry and Psychiatric Epidemiology,* **41** (2), 122-129.

Ahrons, C.R. (2007). Family Ties after Divorce: Long-term Implications for Children. *Family Process,* **46** (1), 53-65.

Aldous, J. & Ganey, R.F. (1999). Family Life and the Pursuit of Happiness: The Influence of Gender and Race. *Journal of Family Issues,* **20**, 155-180.

Amato, P., Loomis, L. & Booth, A. (1995). Parental Divorce, Marital Conflict and Offspring Well-Being During Early Adulthood. *Social Forces,* **73**, 895-915.

Amato, P. & Cheadle, J. (2005). The Long Reach of Divorce: Divorce and Child Well-Being across Three Generations. *Journal of Marriage and Family,* **67**, 191-206.

Amato, P.R. & Keith, B. (1991). Parental Divorce and Adult Well-Being: A Meta-Analysis. *Journal of Marriage and Family,* **53**, 43-58.

Amato, P.R. (2000). The Consequences of Divorce for Adults and Children. *Journal of Marriage and Family,* **62** (4), 1,269-1,287.

American Psychiatric Association. (1980). *The Diagnostic and Statistical Manual of Mental Disorders, Third Edition.* Washington, DC: American Psychiatric Association.

American Psychiatric Association. (1987). *The Diagnostic and Statistical Manual of Mental Disorders, Third Edition - Revised.* Washington, DC: American Psychiatric Association.

Ashby, S. & Step, J. (2004). *NHS Patient Experiences - Patient Survey.* London: National Audit Office. [online]
Available from: **http://www.nao.org.uk/publications/nao_reports/05-06/survey_experiences.pdf** [cited 10th November 2008]

Barrett, A.E. (2000). Marital Trajectories and Mental Health. *Journal of Health and Social Behaviour,* **41** (4), 451-464.

Bellis, M.A., Downing, J. & Ashton, J.R. (2006). Adults at 12? Trends in Puberty and Public Health Consequences. *Journal of Epidemiology Community Health,* **60**, 910-911.

Benson, H. (2006). *The Conflation of Marriage and Cohabitation in Government Statistics – a Denial of Evidence Rendered Untenable by an Analysis of Outcomes.* Bristol: Bristol Family Trust.

Benzeval, M. (1998). The Self-Reported Health Status of Lone Parents. *Social Science and Medicine,* **46** (10), 1,337-1,353.

Bergman, K., Sarkar, P., O'Connor, T.G., Modi, M. & Glover, V. (2007). Maternal Stress During Pregnancy Predicts Cognitive Ability and Fearfulness in Infancy. *Journal of the American Academy of Child and Adolescent Psychiatry*, **46** (11), 1-10.

Berrington, A. & Diamond, I. (1997). Marital Dissolution among the 1958 British Birth Cohort: The Role of Cohabitation. *Population Studies*, **53**, 19-38.

Booth, A. & Amato, P. (2001). Parental Pre-divorce Relations and Offspring Post-Divorce Well Being. *Journal of Marriage and Family*, **63** (1), 197-212.

Braun, D., Davis, H. & Mansfield, P. (2006). *How helping works: Towards a shared model of process.* London: The Centre for Parent and Child Support, One Plus One, Parentline Plus. Available from: **http://www.oneplusone.org.uk/Publications/How-helping-works.pdf** [cited 2nd April 2009]

Brennan, K.A., Clark, C.L. & Shaver, P.R. (1998). Self-report measurement of adult romantic attachment: An integrative overview. In J. A. Simpson & W. S. Rholes (Eds.) *Attachment theory and close relationships.* New York: Guilford Press.

Brinig, M.F. & Nock, S.L. (2003). "I only want trust": Norms, trust, and autonomy. *Journal of Socio-Economics*, **32** (5), 471-487.

Burgess, S., Propper, C. & Aassve, A. (2003). The Role of Income in Marriage and Divorce Transitions among Young Americans. *Journal of Population Economics*, **16** (3), 455-475.

Butler, M.H. & Wampler, K.S. (1999). A Meta-Analytic Update of Research on the Couple Communication Program. *American Journal of Family Therapy*, **27**, 223-239.

Caballero, C., Edwards, R. & Puthussery, S. (2008). *Parenting 'Mixed' Children: Negotiating Difference and Belonging in Mixed Race, Ethnicity and Faith Families.* York: Joseph Rowntree Foundation.

Cabinet Office. (2008). *Social Exclusion Definition.* [online]
Available from: **http://www.cabinetoffice.gov.uk/social_exclusion_task_force/context.aspx**
[cited 9th October 2008]

Chang, Y-S. & Barrett, H. (2009). *The nature and effectiveness of support services targeting adult couple relationships: A literature review.* London: Family and Parenting Institute.

Chase-Lansdale, P.L., Cherlin, A.J. & Kiernan, K. (1995). The Long-term Effects of Parental Divorce on the Mental Health of Young Adults: A Developmental Perspective. *Child Development*, **66**, 1,614-1,634.

Cherlin, A. (2004). The Deinstitutionalization of American Marriage. *Journal of Marriage and Family*, **66**, 848-861.

Cherlin, A.J., Furstenberg, F.F., Chase-Lansdale, P.L., Kiernan, K.E., Robins, P.K., Morrison, D.R. & Teitler, J.O. (1991). Longitudinal Studies of Effects of Divorce on Children in Great Britain and the United States. *Science*, **252**, 1,386-1,389.

Cheung, Y.B. (2000). Marital Status and Mortality in British Women: A Longitudinal Study. *International Journal of Epidemiology*, **29** (1), 93-99.

Clarke, L. & Berrington, A. (1999). *Socio-Demographic Predictors of Divorce*. London: One Plus One.

Cohen, S., Klein, D.N. & O'Leary, D. (2007). The Role of Separation/Divorce in Relapse into and Recovery from Major Depression. *Journal of Social and Personal Relationships*, **24** (6), 855-873.

Collingwood Bakeo, A. & Clarke, L. (2006). *Risk Factors for Low Birth Weight Based on Birth Registration and Census Information, England and Wales: 1981-2000*. London: Office for National Statistics.

Corney, R. (1998). *Evaluation of the Brief Encounters Training Course*. London: One Plus One.

Cowan, P. & Cowan, C. (2000). *When Partners Become Parents: The Big Life Change for Couples*. Mahwah, NJ: Erlbaum.

Cowan, P. & Cowan, C. (2003). Normative Family Transitions, Normal Family Process, and Healthy Child Development. In F. Walsh. (Ed.) *Normal Family Processes*. New York: Guilford Press.

Coyne, J.C., Rohrbaugh, M.J., Shoham, V., Sonnega, J.S., Nicklas, J.M. & Cranford, J.A. (2001). Prognostic Importance of Marital Quality for Survival of Congestive Heart Failure. *American Journal of Cardiology*, **88** (5), 526-529.

Crosier, T., Butterworth, P. & Rodgers, B. (2006). Mental Health Problems among Single and Partnered Mothers: The Role of Financial Hardship and Social Support. *Social Psychiatry and Psychiatric Epidemiology*, **42** (1), 6-13.

Cummings, E.M. & Davies, P. (1994). *Children and Marital Conflict: The Impact of Family Dispute and Resolution*. London: Guilford.

Cummings, E.M. & Davies, P.T. (2002). Effects of Marital Conflict on Children: Recent Advances and Emerging Themes in Process-Oriented Research. *Journal of Child Psychology and Psychiatry*, **43** (1), 31-63.

Cummings, E.M., Faircloth, W.B., Mitchell, P.M., Cummings, J.S. & Schermerhorn, A.C. (2008). Evaluating a Brief Prevention Program for Improving Marital Conflict in Community Families. *Journal of Family Psychology*, **22** (2), 193-202.

Darton, K. (2005). *Children and Young People and Mental Health*. London: Mind.

Davies, P.T. & Cummings, E.M. (1998). Exploring Children's Emotional Security as a Mediator of the Link between Marital Relations and Child Adjustment. *Child Development*, **69** (1), 124-139.

DCSF (2007). *The Children's Plan: Building Brighter Futures*. London: HMSO.

DCSF (2008a). *The Child Health Promotion Programme: Pregnancy and the First Five Years of Life*. London: Department of Health.

DCSF (2008b). *The Children's Plan: One Year On*. London: HMSO.

Del Bono, E., Ermisch, J. & Francesconi, M. (2008). *Intrafamily Resource Allocations: A Dynamic Model of Birth Weight*. IZA Discussion Paper 3,704. Germany: IZA.

Department of Health (1991). *The Health of the Nation: a consultative document for health in England.* London: HMSO.

De Vogli, R., Chandola, T. & Marmot, M.G. (2007). Negative Aspects of Close Relationships and Heart Disease. *Archives of International Medicine*, **167** (18), 1,951-1,957.

DfES (2003). *Every Child Matters Green Paper*. London: HM Government.

DfES (2004). *Every Child Matters: The Next Steps*. Nottingham: Department for Education and Skills.

DfES (2006). *Respect Task Force: Action Plan*. London: HM Government.

DfES (2007a). *Aiming High for Children: Supporting Families*. London: HMSO.

DfES (2007b). *Every Parent Matters*. Nottingham: Department for Education and Skills.

DWP (2008). *Households Below Average Income: an analysis of the income distribution 1994/95-2006/07*. London: Department for Work and Pensions.

Donkin, A. (2001). Does Living Alone Damage Men's Health? *Health Statistics Quarterly*, **Autumn**, 11-17.

D'Onofrio, B.M., Turkheimer, E., Emery, R.E., Maes, H.H., Silberg, J. & Eaves, L.J. (2007). A Children of Twins Study of Parental Divorce and Offspring Psychopathology. *Journal of Child Psychology and Psychiatry*, **48** (7), 667-675.

Doss, B.D., Rhoades, G.K., Stanley, S.M. & Markman, H.J. (2009). The Effect of the transition to Parenthood on relationship Quality: An 8-Year Prospective Study. *Journal of Personality and Social Psychology*, **96** (3), 601-619.

Drew, L. & Smith, P. (1999). The Impact of Parental Separation/Divorce on Grandparent-Grandchild Relations. *International Journal of Aging and Human Development*, **48** (33), 191-216.

Dunn, J. (2008). *Family Relationships: Children's Perspectives*. London: One Plus One.

Dunn, R.L. & Schwebel, A.I. (1995). Meta-Analytic Review of Marital Therapy Outcome Research. *Journal of Family Psychology*, **9**, 58-68.

Eaker, E.D., Sullivan, L.M., Kelly-Hayes, M., D'agostino, R.B. & Benjamin, E.J. (2007). Marital Status, Marital Strain, and Risk of Coronary Heart Disease or Total Mortality: The Framingham Offspring Study. *Psychosomatic Medicine*, **69** (6), 509-513.

Earls, F. & Jung, K.G. (1987). Temperament and Home Environment Characteristics as Causal Factors in the Early Development of Childhood Psychopathology. *Journal of the American Academy of Child and Adolescent Psychiatry*, **26** (4), 491-498.

Ebrahim, S., Wannamethee, G., Mccallum, A., Walker, M. & Shaper, A.G. (1995). Marital Status, Change in

Marital Status, and Mortality in Middle-Aged British Men. *American Journal of Epidemiology*, **142** (8), 834-842.

Elliot, J. & Vaitilingam, R. (2008). *Now We Are 50: Key Findings from the National Child Development Study*. London: The Centre for Longitudinal Studies.

Ellis, B.J. & Essex, M.J. (2007). Family Environments, Adrenarche and Sexual Maturation: A Longitudinal Test of a Life History Model. *Child Development*, **78** (6), 1,799-1,817.

Ely, M., Richards, M.P.M., Wadsworth, M.E.J. & Elliott, B.J. (1999). Secular Changes in the Association of Parental Divorce and the Children's Educational Attainment: Evidence from Three British Birth Cohorts. *Journal of Social Policy*, **28** (3), 437-455.

Ewing, J.A. (1984) Detecting Alcoholism: The CAGE Questionnaire. *Journal of the American Medical Association*, **252**, 1,905-1,907.

Farrington, D.P. (1996). The Explanation and Prevention of Youthful Offending. In J.D. Hawkins. (Ed.) *Delinquency and Crime: Current Theories*. Cambridge: Cambridge University Press.

Feinberg, M.E. & Kan, M.L. (2008). Establishing Family Foundations: Intervention Effects on Co-Parenting, Parent/Infant Well-Being and Parent-Child Relations. *Journal of Family Psychology*, **22** (2), 253-263.

Feinstein, L. & Symons, J. (1999). Attainment in Secondary School. *Oxford Economic Papers*, **51**, 300-321.

Flowerdew, J. & Neale, B. (2003). Trying to Stay Apace: Children with Multiple Challenges in Their Post Divorce Family Lives. *Childhood*, **10** (2), 147-161.

Formby, P. & Cherlin, A.J. (2007). Family Instability and Child Well-Being. *American Sociological Review*, **72**, 181-204.

Fragile Families. (2008). *Mothers' and Children's Poverty and Material Hardship in the Years Following a Non-Marital Birth*. Princeton, NJ: Centre for Research on Child Wellbeing.

Frech, A. & Williams, K. (2007). Depression and the Psychological Benefits of Entering Marriage. *Journal of Health and Social Behaviour*, **48** (2), 149-163.

Gallo, L.C., Troxel, W.M., Matthews, K.A. & Kuller, L.W. (2003). Marital Status and Quality in Middle-Aged Women: Associations with Levels and Trajectories of Cardiovascular Risk Factors. *Health Psychology*, **22** (5), 453-463.

Gardner, J. & Oswald, A.J. (2006). Do Divorcing Couples Become Happier by Breaking Up? *Journal of the Royal Statistical Society: Series A*, **169** (2), 319-336.

Gershuny, J.I., Bittman, M. & Brice, J. (2005). Exit, Voice, and Suffering: Do Couples Adapt to Changing Employment Patterns? *Journal of Marriage and Family*, **67**, 656-665.

Glenn, F. (2007). *Growing Together, or Drifting Apart?* London: One Plus One.

Goldberg, D. (1992). *General Health Questionnaire (GHQ-12)*. Windsor, UK: NFER-Nelson.

Golombok, S. (2000). *Parenting: What really counts?* London: Routledge.

Golombok, S. (2006). New Family Forms. In A. Clarke-Stewart & J. Dunn. (Eds.) *Families count: effects of child and adolescent development.* Cambridge: Cambridge University Press.

Gottman, J.M. (1999). *The Marriage Clinic: A Scientifically-Based Marital Therapy.* New York: W.W.Norton.

Gottman, J.M. & Silver, N. (1999). *The Seven Principles for Making Marriage Work.* New York: Three Rivers Press.

Government Actuary Department. (2005). *Non-Married Mortality Rates Compared to Married Mortality Rates.* London: HM Government.

Gregg, P. & Machin, S. (1998). *Child Development and Success or Failure in the Youth Labour Market.* London: London School of Economics.

Grewen, K.M., Girdler, S.S. & Light, K.C. (2005). Relationship Quality: Effects on Ambulatory Blood Pressure and Negative Affect in a Biracial Sample of Men and Women. *Blood Pressure Monitoring,* **10** (3), 117-124.

Gruber, J. (2004). Is Making Divorce Easier Bad for Children? The Long-Run Implications of Unilateral Divorce. *Journal of Labour Economics,* **22** (4), 799-833.

Grundy, E.M.D., Butterworth, S., Henretta, J., Wadsworth, M.E.J. & Tomassini, C. (2005). *Partnership and Parenthood History and Health in Mid and Later Life.* London: Economic and Social Research Council.

Grych, J.H. & Fincham, F.D. (1990). Marital Conflict and Children's Adjustment: A Cognitive-Contextual Framework. *Psychological Bulletin,* **108** (2), 267-290.

Grych, J.H., Fincham, F.D., Jouriles, E.N. & Mcdonald, R. (2000). Interparental Conflict and Child Adjustment: Testing the Mediational Role of Appraisals in the Cognitive-Contextual Framework. *Child Development,* **71** (6), 1,648-1,661.

Hadju, P., Mckee, M. & Bojan, F. (1995). Changes in Premature Mortality Differentials by Marital Status in Hungary and in England and Wales. *European Journal of Public Health,* **5** (4), 259-264.

Halford, W.K., Moore, E.M., Wilson, K.L., Dyer, C. & Farrugia, C. (2004). Benefits of a Flexible Delivery Relationship Education: An Evaluation of the Couple Care Program. *Family Relations,* **53**, 469-476.

Halford, W.K., Markman, H.J. & Stanley, S. (2008). Strengthening Couples' Relationships with Education: Social Policy and Public Health Perspectives. *Journal of Family Psychology,* **22** (4), 497-505.

Hansagi, H., Brandt, L. & Andreasson, S. (2000). Parental Divorce: Psychosocial Well-Being, Mental Health and Mortality During Youth and Young Adulthood: A Longitudinal Study of Swedish Conscripts. *European Journal of Public Health,* **10** (2), 86-92.

Hanson, R.L., Imperatore, G., Bennett, P.H. & Knowler, W.C. (2002). Components of The "Metabolic Syndrome" And Incidence of Type 2 Diabetes. *Diabetes,* **51** (10), 3,120-3,127.

Harold, A.T., Aitken, J.J. & Shelton, K.H. (2007). Inter-Parental Conflict and Children's Academic

Attainment: A Longitudinal Analysis. *Journal of Child Psychology and Psychiatry,* **48** (12), 1,223-1,232.

Hart, G. (1999). *The Funding of Marriage Support: Review.* London: Lord Chancellor's Dept.

Haskey, J. (1996). The Proportion of Married Couples Who Divorce: Past Patterns and Current Prospects. *Population Trends,* **83**, 25-36.

Haveman, R. & Wolfe, B. (1995). The Determinants of Children's Attainments: A Review of Methods and Findings. *Journal of Economic Literature,* **33**, 1,829-1,878.

Hawkins, A.J., Blanchard, V.L., Baldwin, S.A. & Fawcett, E.B. (2008). Does Marriage and Relationship Education Work? A Meta-Analytic Study. *Journal of Consulting and Clinical Psychology,* **76** (5), 723-734.

Hawthorne, J., Jessop, J., Pryor, J. & Richards, M. (2003). *Supporting Children through Family Change: A Review of Interventions and Services for Children of Divorcing and Separating Parents.* London: Joseph Rowntree Foundation.

Heinz, A.J., Wu, J., Witkiewitz, K., Epstein, D.H. and Preston, K.L. (in press). Marriage and Relationship Closeness as Predictors of Cocaine and Heroin Use. *Addiction Behaviors.*

Herberth, G., Weber, A., Roder, S., Elvers, H.D., Kramer, U., Schins, R.P.F., Diez, U., Borte, M., Heinrich, J., Schafter, T., Herbarth, O. & Lehman, I. (2008). Relation between Stressful Life Events, Neuropeptides and Cytokines: Results from the Lisa Birth Cohort Study. *Paediatric Journal of Allergy and Immunology.* Online First.

Hetherington, E.M. & Kelly, J. (2002). *For Better or for Worse? Divorce Reconsidered.* London: W.W.Norton.

Hicks, M., Mcwey, L., Brendon, K. & West, S. (2004). Using What Premarital Couples Already Know to Inform Marriage Education: Integration of a Gottman Model Perspective. *Contemporary Family Therapy,* **26** (1), 97-113.

HM Government. (1969). *Divorce Reform Act.* London: HMSO.

HM Government. (1996). *Family Law Act.* London: HMSO.

HM Government. (2004). *Civil Partnership Act.* London: HMSO.

Holt-Lunstad, J., Birmingham, W. & Jones, B.Q. (2008). Is There Something Unique About Marriage? The Relative Impact of Marital Status, Relationship Quality, and Network Social Support on Ambulatory Blood Pressure and Mental Health. *Annals of Behavioural Medicine,* **35** (2), 239-244.

Hope, S., Power, C. & Rodgers, B. (1998). The Relationship between Parental Separation in Childhood and Problem Drinking in Adulthood. *Addiction,* **93** (4), 505-514.

House of Representatives Legal and Constitutional Affairs Committee. (1998). *To Have and to Hold: Strategies to Strengthen Marriage and Relationships.* Canberra, Australia: House of Representatives Legal and Constitutional Affairs Committee.

Jacob, T. & Johnson, S.L. (2001). Sequential Interactions in the Parent-Child Communications of Depressed Fathers and Depressed Mothers. *Journal of Family Psychology*, **15** (1), 38-52.

Jansen, M., Snoeckx, L. & Mortelmans, D. (2007). *Repartnering and Re-Employment: Strategies to Cope with the Economic Consequences of Partnership Dissolution British Household Panel Survey 2007.* Colchester, University of Essex: Institute for Social and Economic Research.

Jarvis, S. & Jenkins, S.P. (1999). Marital Splits and Income Changes: Evidence from the British Household Panel Survey. *Population Studies*, **53** (2), 237-254.

Jatoi, A., Novotny, P., Cassivi, S., Clark, M.M., Midthun, D., Patten, C.A., Sloan, J. & Yang, P. (2007). Does Marital Status Impact Survival and Quality of Life in Patients with Non-Small Cell Lung Cancer? Observations from the Mayo Clinic Lung Cancer Cohort. *Oncologist*, **12** (12), 1,456-1,463.

Jekielek, S. (1998). Parental Conflict, Marital Disruption and Children's Emotional Well-Being. *Social Forces*, **76**, 905-936.

Jenkins, S.P. (2008) *Marital splits and income changes over the longer-term. Working Paper of Institute for Social and Economic Research.* Colchester: University of Essex.

Jeynes, W.H. (2001). The Effects of Recent Parental Divorce on Their Children's Sexual Attitudes and Behaviour. *Journal of Divorce and Remarriage*, **35** (1/2), 115-133.

Johnson, A.M., Wadsworth, J., Wellings, K. & Field, J. (1994). *Sexual Attitudes and Lifestyles.* Oxford: Blackwell Scientific Publications.

Johnson, D.R. & Wu, J. (1996). *An Empirical Test of Crisis, Social Selection and Role Explanations of the Relationship between Marital Disruption and Psychological Distress: A Pooled Time Series Analysis of Four Wave Panel Data.* Paris, France: International Conference on Social Stress Research.

Johnson, N.J., Backlund, E., Sorlie, P.D. & Loveless, C.A. (2000). Marital Status and Mortality: The National Longitudinal Mortality Study. *Annals of Epidemiology*, **10** (4), 224-238.

Joung, I.M., Stronks, K., Van De Mheen, H., Van Poppel, F.W.A, Van Der Meer, J.B.W. & Mackenbach, J.P. (1997). The Contribution of Intermediary Factors to Marital Status Differences in Self-Reported Health. *Journal of Marriage and Family*, **59**, 476-490.

Juby, H. & Farrington, D.P. (2001). Disentangling the Link between Disrupted Families and Delinquency. *British Journal of Criminology*, **41**, 22-40.

Kalmijn, M. & Monden, C.W.S. (2006). Are the Negative Effects of Divorce on Well-Being Dependent on Marital Quality? *Journal of Marriage and Family*, **68** (5), 1,197-1,213.

Kaplan, R.M. & Kronick, R.G. (2006). Marital Status and Longevity in the United States Population. *Journal of Epidemiological Community Health*, **60**, 760-765.

Kendler, K.S., Thornton, L.M. & Prescott, C.A. (2001). Gender Differences in the Rates of Exposure to

Stressful Life Events and Sensitivity to Their Depressogenic Effects. *American Journal of Psychiatry*, **158** (4), 587-593.

Kessler, R.C., Andrews G., Colpe L.J., Hiripi, E., Mroczek, D.K., Normand, S.-L. T., Walters, E.E. & Zaslavsky, A.M. (2002). Short screening scales to monitor population prevalences and trends in non-specific psychological distress. *Psychological Medicine*, **32** (6), 959–976.

Kiernan, K. & Hobcraft, J. (1997). Parental Divorce During Childhood: Age at First Intercourse, Partnership and Parenthood. *Population Studies*, **51** (1), 41-55.

Kiernan, K. & Pickett, K.E. (2006). Marital Status Disparities in Maternal Smoking During Pregnancy, Breastfeeding and Maternal Depression. *Social Science and Medicine*, **63** (2), 335-346.

Kiernan, K.E. (2003). *Cohabitation and Divorce across Nations and Generations*. London: London School of Economics and Political Science.

Kiernan, K.E. & Mensah, F.K. (forthcoming 2010). Unmarried Parenthood, Family Trajectories, Parent and Child Well-Being. In, K. Hansen, H. Joshi & S. Dex. (Eds.) *Children of the 21st Century: From birth to age 5*. Bristol: Policy Press.

Kissman, K. (2001). Interventions to Strengthen Non-Custodial Father Involvement in the Lives of Their Children. *Journal of Divorce and Remarriage*, **35** (1/2), 135-146.

Kitson, G.C. (1992). *Portrait of Divorce: Adjustment to Marital Breakdown*. New York: Guilford Press.

Kposowa, A.J. (1999). Suicide Mortality in the United States: Differentials by Industrial and Occupational Groups. *American Journal of Industrial Medicine*, **36** (6), 645-652.

Kposowa, A.J. (2000). Marital Status and Suicide in the National Longitudinal Mortality Study. *Journal of Epidemiological Community Health*, **54** (4), 254-261.

Krumrei, E., Coit, C., Martin, S., Fogo, W. & Mahoney, A. (2007). Post Divorce Adjustment and Social Relationships. *Journal of Divorce and Remarriage*, **46** (3/4), 145-166.

Lakka, H.M., Laaksonen, D.E., Lakka, T.A., Niskanen, L.K., Kumpusalo, E., Tuomilehto, J. & Salonen, J.T. (2002). The Metabolic Syndrome and Total and Cardiovascular Disease Mortality in Middle-Aged Men. *Journal of the American Medical Association*, **288** (21), 2,709-2,716.

Lawrence, E., Rothman, A.D., Cobb, R.J., Rothman, M.T. & Bradbury, T.N. (2008). Marital Satisfaction across the Transition to Parenthood. *Journal of Family Psychology*, **22** (1), 41-50.

Ledoux, S., Miller, P., Choquet, M. & Plant, M. (2002). Family Structure, Parent-Child Relationships, and Alcohol and Other Drug Use among Teenagers in France and the United Kingdom. *Alcohol and Alcoholism*, **37** (1), 52-60.

Leonard, K.E. & Rothbard, J.C. (1999). Alcohol and the Marriage Effect. *Journal of Studies on Alcohol*, **13**, 139-146.

Lillard, L.A. & Waite, L.J. (1995). Till Death Do Us Part: Marital Disruption and Mortality. *American Journal of Sociology,* **100** (5), 1,131-1,156.

Lindsay, D. (2000). *The Cost of Family Breakdown.* Bedford: Family Matters.

Locke, H. & Wallace, K. (1959). Short Marital Adjustment and Prediction Tests: Their Reliability and Validity. *Marriage and Family Living,* **2**, 251-255.

Lucas, R.E. (2005). Time Does Not Heal All Wounds: A Longitudinal Study of Reaction and Adaptation to Divorce. *Psychological Science,* **16** (12), 945-950.

Lund, R., Christensen, U., Holstein, B.E., Due, E. & Osler, M. (2006). Influence of Marital History over Two and Three Generations on Early Death. A Longitudinal Study of Danish Men Born in 1953. *Journal of Epidemiological Community Health,* **60** (6), 496-501.

Lund, R., Holstein, B.E. & Osler, M. (2004). Marital History from Age 15 to 40 Years and Subsequent 10-Year Mortality: A Longitudinal Study of Danish Males Born in 1953. *International Journal of Epidemiology,* **33** (2), 389-397.

Macintyre, S. (1992). The Effects of Family Position and Status on Health. *Social Science and Medicine,* **35** (4), 453-464.

Maclean, M. (2004). *Together and Apart: Children and Parents Experiencing Separation and Divorce.* London: Joseph Rowntree Foundation.

Mansfield, P. (1996). Marrying for Children? In C. Clulow. (Ed.) *Partners Becoming Parents.* London: Sheldon Press.

Margolin, G., Oliver, P. & Medina, A. (2001). Conceptual Issues in Understanding the Relation between Inter-Parental Conflict and Child Adjustment: Integrating Developmental Psychopathology and Risk/Resilience Perspectives. In J. Grych & F. Fincham. (Eds.) *Inter-Parental Conflict and Child Development.* New York: Cambridge University Press.

Markman, H., Stanley, S., Blumberg, S., Jenkins, N. & Whaley, C. (2004). *Twelve Hours to a Great Marriage.* San Francisco: Jossey-Bass.

Marks, N.F. (1996). Flying Solo at Midlife: Gender, Marital Status and Psychological Well-Being. *Journal of Marriage and Family,* **58**, 917-932.

Martikainen, P., Martelin, T., Nihtila, E., Majamaa, K. & Koskinen, S. (2005). Differences in Mortality by Marital Status in Finland from 1976 to 2000: Analyses of Changes in Marital-Status Distributions, Socio-Demographic and Household Composition, and Cause of Death. *Population Studies,* **59** (1), 99-115.

McAllister, F. (1995). *Marital Breakdown and the Health of the Nation (2nd Edition).* London: One Plus One.

McIntosh, J. (2003). Enduring Conflict in Parental Separation: Pathways of Impact on Child Development. *Journal of Family Studies,* **9** (1), 63-80.

McLanahan, S. & Garfinkel, I. (2003). Strengthening Fragile Families. In I. Sawhill. (Ed.) *One Percent for the Kids: New Policies, Brighter Futures for America's Children.* Washington DC: Brookings Institution.

Meadows, S.O. (2007). *Family structure and fathers' well-being: Trajectories of mental and physical health.* Centre for Research on Child Wellbeing: Working Paper #2007-19-FF. NJ: Princeton University.

Meltzer, H., Gatward, R., Goodman, R. & Ford, T. (2000). *The Mental Health of Children and Adolescents in Great Britain.* London: Office for National Statistics.

Miller, P. (1997). Family Structure, Personality, Drinking, Smoking and Illicit Drug Use: A Study of UK Teenagers. *Drug and Alcohol Dependence,* **45** (1-2), 121-129.

Miller, S., Nunnally, E. & Wackman, D. (1975). Minnesota Couples Communication Program: Premarital and Marital Groups. In D. Olsen. (Ed.) *Treating Relationships.* Lake Mills, IA: Graphic.

Mooney, A., Oliver, C. & Smith, M. (2009). *Impact of Family Breakdown on Children's Well-Being: Evidence Review.* London: Department of Children, Schools and Families (RB113).

Moos, R. H. (1993). *Coping Response Inventory.* Odessa, FL: Psychological Assessment Resources.

Murphy, M., Glaser, K. & Grundy, E. (1997). Marital Status and Long-term Illness in Great Britain. *Journal of Marriage and Family,* **59**, 156-164.

Murphy, M. (2007). Family Living Arrangements and Health. In Office for National Statistics. (Ed.) *Focus on Families.* Hampshire: Palgrave Macmillan.

Murphy, M., Grundy, E. & Kalogirou, S. (2007). The Increase in Marital Status Differences in Mortality up to the Oldest Age in Seven European Countries 1990-1999. *Population Studies,* **61** (3), 287-298.

Nilsson, C.J., Lund, R. & Avlund, K. (2007). Cohabitation Status and Onset of Disability among Older Danes: Is Social Participation a Possible Mediator? *Journal of Aging and Health,* **20**, 235-253.

Noller, P., Feeney, J.A., Peterson, C. & Atkin, S. (2000). Marital Conflict and Adolescents. *Family Matters,* **55** (Autumn), 68-73.

O'Connor, T.G. & Jenkins, J.M. (2000). *Marital Transitions and Children's Adjustment: Understanding Why Families Differ from One Another and Why Children in the Same Family Show Different Patterns of Adjustment.* Quebec: Human Resources Development Canada.

Office for National Statistics. (2006). *Divorces: 1957-2003, Couples, and children of divorced couples, numbers, age of child.* London: Office for National Statistics. [online]
Available from: **http://www.statistics.gov.uk/STATBASE/xsdataset.asp?vlnk=7079**
[cited 19th November 2008].

Office for National Statistics. (2007a). *Focus on Families.* Hampshire: Palgrave Macmillan.

Office for National Statistics. (2007b). *Divorces Fall by 7 Per Cent in 2006.* London: Office for National Statistics.

Office for National Statistics. (2007c). *Social Trends 37. Households and Families.* Hampshire: Palgrave Macmillan.

Office for National Statistics. (2007d). *Mortality Statistics: Review of the Registrar General on Deaths in England and Wales, 2005.* London: HMSO.

Office for National Statistics. (2008a). *Marriage, divorce and adoption statistics: Review of the Registrar General on marriages and divorces in 2005 and adoptions in 2006, in England and Wales. Series, FM2, no. 33.* London: The Stationery Office.

Office for National Statistics. (2008b). Age Differences at Marriage and Divorce. *Population Trends,* **132**, 17-25.

Office for National Statistics. (2008c). *Divorce rate lowest for 26 years.* London: Office for National Statistics. [online]
Available from: **http://www.statistics.gov.uk/pdfdir/div0808.pdf**
[cited 19th November 2008]

Office for National Statistics. (2008d). The Proportion of Marriages Ending in Divorce. *Population Trends,* **131**, 28-36.

Office for National Statistics. (2008e). *Civil Partnerships: Numbers Almost Halved in 2007.* London: Office for National Statistics. [online]
Available from: **http://www.statistics.gov.uk/cci/nugget.asp?id=1685**
[cited 24th July 2008]

Office for National Statistics. (2008f). *Social Trends 38. Households and Families.* Hampshire: Palgrave Macmillan.

Office for National Statistics. (2008g). Trends in Suicide by Marital Status in England and Wales, 1982-2005. *Health Statistics Quarterly,* **37**, 8-14.

Office for National Statistics. (2009). *Marriages: UK marriages decrease by 2.7%.* London: Office for National Statistics. [online]
Available from: **http://www.statistics.gov.uk/cci/nugget.asp?id=322**
[cited 9th March 2009]

One Plus One (2006). *The Transition to Parenthood: The 'magic moment'.* London: One Plus One.
Available from:
http://www.oneplusone.org.uk/Publications/InformationSheets/Transitiontoparenthood.pdf
[cited 1st July 2009]

Orth-Gomer, K., Wamala, S.P., Horsten, M., Schenck-Gustafsson, K., Schneiderman, N. & Mittleman, M.A. (2000). Marital Stress Worsens Prognosis in Women with Coronary Heart Disease: The Stockholm Female Coronary Risk Study. *Journal of American Medical Association,* **284** (23), 3,008-3,014.

Pevalin, D.J. & Ermisch, J. (2004). Cohabiting Unions, Repartnering and Mental Health. *Psychological Medicine*, **34** (8), 1,553-1,559.

Phares, V., Duhig, A.M. & Watkins, M. (2002). Family Context: Fathers and Other Supports. In S.H. Goodman & I.H. Gotlib. (Eds.) *Children of Depressed Parents: Mechanisms of Risk and Implications for Treatment*. Washington DC: American Psychological Association.

Power, C., Rodgers, B. & Hope, S. (1999). Heavy alcohol consumption and marital status: disentangling the relationship in a national study of young adults. *Addiction*, **94**, 1,477-1,487.

Prior, P.M. & Hayes, B.C. (2003). The Relationship between Marital Status and Health: An Empirical Investigation of Differences in Bed Occupancy within Health and Social Care Facilities in Britain 1921-1991. *Journal of Family Issues*, **24** (1), 124-148.

Raschke, H.J. (1987). Divorce. In M.B. Sussman & S.K. Steinmetz. (Eds.) *Handbook of Marriage and the Family*. New York: Plenum.

Reynolds, J., Harold, G. & Pryor, J. (2001). *Not in Front of the Children? How Conflict between Parents Affects Children*. London: One Plus One.

Richards, M., Hardy, R. & Wadsworth, M. (1997). The Effects of Divorce and Separation on Mental Health in a National UK Birth Cohort. *Psychological Medicine*, **27** (5), 1,121-1,128.

Robins, L.N., Helzer, J.E., Croughan, J.L., Williams, J.B. W. & Spitzer, R.L. (1981). *The NIMH Diagnostic Interview Schedule, Version III*. Washington, DC: Public Health Service.

Robles, T.F. & Kiecolt-Glaser, J.K. (2003). The Physiology of Marriage: Pathways to Health. *Physiology and Behaviour*, **79** (3), 409-416.

Rodgers, B. (1994). Pathways between parental divorce and adult depression. *Journal of Child Psychology and Psychiatry*, **35**, 1,289-1,308.

Rodgers, B. & Pryor, J. (1998). *Divorce and Separation: The Outcomes for Children*. York: Joseph Rowntree Foundation.

Rogers, S.J. & Deboer, D.D. (2004). Changes in Wives' Income: Effects on Marital Happiness, Psychological Well-Being, and the Risk of Divorce. *Journal of Marriage and Family*, **63** (2), 458-472.

Rotermann, M. (2007). Marital Breakdown and Subsequent Depression. *Health Reports*, **18** (2), 33-44.

Royal College of Psychiatrists. (2008). *Ways to Reduce the Impact of Parental Separation on Children*. [online]
Available from: **http://www.rcpsych.ac.uk/default.aspx?page=0**
[cited 16th December 2008]

Rutter, M., Tizard, J. & Whitmore, K. (1970). *Education, Health and Behaviour*. London: Longman.

Rutter, M. (2007). Proceeding from observed correlation to causal inference: the use of natural experiments. *Perspectives on Psychological Science*, **2**, 377-395.

Rutter, M. (2009). Epidemiological methods to tackle causal questions. *International Journal of Epidemiology*, **38**, 3-6.

Rye, M.S., Loiacono, D.M., Folck, C.D., Olszewski, B.T., Heim, T.A. & Madia, B.P. (2001). Evaluation of the psychometric properties of two forgiveness scales. *Current Psychology*, **20**, 260-277.

Rye, M.S. & Pargament, K.I. (2002). Forgiveness and romantic relationships in college: can it heal the wounded heart? *Journal of Clinical Psychology*, **58** (4), 419-441.

Rye, M.S., Folck, C.D., Heim, T.A., Olszewski, B.T. & Traina, E. (2004). Forgiveness of an Ex-Spouse: How Does It Relate to Mental Health Following a Divorce? *Journal of Divorce and Remarriage*, **41** (3/4), 31-51.

Saffrey, C. & Ehrenberg, M. (2007). When Thinking Hurts: Attachment, Rumination and Post Relationship Adjustment. *Personal Relationships*, **14**, 351-368.

Sakraida, T.J. (2008). Stress and Coping of Midlife Women in Divorce Transition. *Western Journal of Nursing Research*, Online First, 1-19.

Sampson, R.J., Laub, J.H. & Wimer, C. (2006). Does Marriage Reduce Crime? A Counterfactual Approach to Within-Individual Causal Effects. *Criminology*, **44**, 465-508.

Sanz-De-Galdeano, A. & Vuri, D. (2007). Parental Divorce and Students' Performance: Evidence from Longitudinal Data. *Oxford Bulletin of Economics and Statistics*, **69** (3), 321-338.

Schoenborn, C.A. (2004). Marital Status and Health: United States, 1999-2002. *Advance Data*, **351**, 1-32.

Schulz, M.S., Cowan, C.P. & Cowan, P.A. (2006). Promoting Healthy Beginnings: A Randomised Controlled Trial of a Preventive Intervention to Preserve Marital Quality During the Transition to Parenthood. *Journal of Consulting and Clinical Psychology*, **74** (1), 20-31.

Seltzer, J.A. (1994). Consequences of Marital Dissolution for Children. *Annual Review of Sociology*, **20**, 235-266.

Shapiro, A.F. & Gottman, J.M. (2005). Effects on Marriage of a Psycho-Education Intervention with Couples Undergoing the Transition to Parenthood, Evaluation at 1-Year Post-Intervention. *Journal of Family Communication*, **5** (1), 1-24.

Shiner, R.L. & Marmorstein, N.R. (1998). Family Environments of Adolescents with Lifetime Depression: Associations with Maternal Depression History. *Journal of the American Academy of Child and Adolescent Psychiatry*, **37** (11), 1,152-1,160.

Sigle-Rushton, W., Hobcraft, J. & Kiernan, K. (2005). Parental Divorce and Subsequent Disadvantage: A Cross Cohort Comparison. *Demography*, **42** (3), 427-446.

Simon, R.W. (2002). Revisiting the Relationships among Gender, Marital Status and Mental Health. *American Journal of Sociology*, **107**, 1,065-1,096.

Simons, J., Reynolds, J. & Morison, L. (2001). Randomised Controlled Trial of Training Health Visitors to

Identify and Help Couples with Relationship Problems Following a Birth. *British Journal of General Practice*, **53**, 793-799.

Simons, J., Reynolds, J., Mannion, J. & Morison, L. (2003). How the Health Visitor Can Help When Problems between Parents Add to Postnatal Stress. *Journal of Advanced Nursing*, **44** (4), 400-411.

Smart, C. & Stevens, P. (2000). *Cohabitation Breakdown*. York: Joseph Rowntree Foundation.

Smyth, C. & Maclachlan, M. (2004). The Context of Suicide: An Examination of Life Circumstances Thought to Be Understandable Precursors to Youth Suicide. *Journal of Mental Health*, **13** (1), 83-92.

Social Exclusion Taskforce. (2008). *Reaching Out: Think Family*. London: Social Exclusion Taskforce.

Social Justice Policy Group. (2006). *The State of the Nation Report: Fractured Families*. London: Social Justice Policy Group.

Social Justice Policy Group. (2007). *Breakthrough Britain: Ending the Costs of Social Breakdown. Volume 1: Family Breakdown*. London: Social Justice Policy Group.

Spanier, G.B. (1976). Measuring Dyadic Adjustment: New Scales for Assessing the Quality of Marriage and Similar Dyads. *Journal of Marriage and Family*, **38**, 15-28.

Spector, A.Z. (2006). Fatherhood and Depression: A Review of Risks, Effects, and Clinical Application. *Issues in Mental Health Nursing*, **27** (8), 867-883.

Spreeuw, J. & Wang, X. (2008). *Modelling the Short Time Dependence between Two Remaining Lifetimes*. [online]
Available from: **www.actuaries.org.uk/__data/assets/pdf_file/0006/128832/Spreeuw_modelling.pdf**

Stanley, S.M. (2001) Making a Case for Pre-marital Education. *Family Relations*, **50**, 272-280.

Statistics Canada (1999). Psychological Health – Depression. *Health Reports*, **11** (3), 63-76.

Stewart, J.A. (2005). Women's Satisfaction with Life Following Marital Separation: Coping Resources and Adjustment of Lone-Parent Women. *Journal of Divorce and Remarriage*, **43** (1/2), 89-107.

Strohschein, L. (2005). Parental Divorce and Child Mental Health Trajectories. *Journal of Marriage and Family*, **67**, 1,286-1,300.

Strohschein, L. (2007). Prevalence of Methylphenidate Use among Canadian Children Following Parental Divorce. *Canadian Medical Association Journal*, **176** (12), 1,711-1,714.

Talge, M.N., Neal, C. & Glover, V. (2007). Antenatal Maternal Stress and Long-term Effects on Child Neurodevelopment: How and Why? *Journal of Child Psychology and Psychiatry*, **48** (3/4), 245-261.

Troxel, W.M., Matthews, K.A., Gallo, L.C. & Kuller, L.H. (2005). Marital Quality and Occurrence of the Metabolic Syndrome in Women. *Archives of Internal Medicine*, **165** (9), 1,022-1,027.

Tucker, J.S., Friedman, H.S., Wingard, D.L. & Schartwz, J.E. (1996). Marital History at Midlife as a Predictor of Longevity: Alternative Explanations to the Protective Effect of Marriage. *Health Psychology*, **15** (2), 91-101.

Twenge, J.M., Campbell, K.W. & Foster, C.A. (2003). Parenthood and Marital Satisfaction: A Meta-Analytic Review. *Journal of Marriage and Family*, **65**, 574-583.

Van Poppel, F. & Joung, I. (2001). Long-term Trends in Marital Status Mortality Differences in the Netherlands 1850-1970. *Journal of Biosocial Science*, **33** (2), 279-303.

Wade, T.J. & Pevalin, D.J. (2004). Marital Transitions and Mental Health. *Journal of Health and Social Behaviour*, **45** (2), 155-170.

Waite, L. & Gallagher, M. (2000). *The Case for Marriage*. New York: Broadway Books.

Wallerstein, J.S. & Kelly, J.B. (1980). *Surviving the Break-up: How Children and Parents Cope with Divorce*. London: Grant McIntyre.

Wallerstein, J.S. (1991). The Long-Term Effects of Divorce on Children: A Review. *Journal of the American Academy of Child and Adolescent Psychiatry*, **30** (3), 349-360.

Weihs, K.L., Enright, T.M. & Simmens, S.J. (2007). Close Relationships and Emotional Processing Predict Decreased Mortality in Women with Breast Cancer: Preliminary Evidence. *Psychosomatic Medicine*, **70** (1), 117-124.

Wellings, K., Nanchahal, K., Macdowall, W., Mcmanus, S., Erens, B., Mercer, C.H., Johnson, A.M., Copas, A.J., Korovessis, C., Fenton, K.A. & Field, J. (2001). Sexual Behaviour in Britain: Early Heterosexual Experience. *Lancet*, **358** (9296), 1,843-1,850.

Wheaton, B. (1990). Life Transitions, Role Histories and Mental Health. *American Sociological Review*, **55**, 209-223.

Wilcox, W.B., Doherty, W., Glenn, N. & Waite, L. (2005). *Why Marriage Matters, Second Edition: Twenty Six Conclusions from the Social Services*. New York: Institute for American Values.

Williams, K. (2003). Has the Future of Marriage Arrived? A Contemporary Examination of Gender, Marriage, and Psychological Well-Being. *Journal of Health and Social Behavior*, **44**, 470-487.

Willett, J.B. (1994). Measurement of change. In, T. Husen & N.T. Postlethwaite. (Eds.), *The International Encyclopedia of Education*. 2nd ed., 671-678. Oxford, England: Pergamon Press.

Wilson, C.M. & Oswald, A.J. (2002). *How Does Marriage Affect Physical and Psychological Health? A Survey of the Longitudinal Evidence*. Warwick: University of Warwick.

Wood, N.D., Crane, D.R., Shaalje, G.B. & Law, D.D. (2005). What Works for Whom: A Meta-Analytic Review of Marital and Couples Therapy in Reference to Marital Distress. *The American Journal of Family Therapy*, **33**, 273-287.

Wood, R.G., Goesling, B. & Avellar, S. (2007). *The Effects of Marriage on Health: A Synthesis of Recent Research Evidence.* Washington DC: Mathematical Policy Research.

World Health Organisation. (2008). *Mental Health.* [online]
Available from: **http://www.who.int/topics/mental_health/en/index.html**
[cited 12th May 2008]

Wu, L.L. & Martinson, B.C. (1993). Family Structure and the Risk of a Pre-Marital Birth. *American Sociological Review,* **16**, 386-406.

Wyke, S. & Ford, G. (1992). Competing Explanations for Associations between Marital Status and Health. *Social Science and Medicine,* **34** (5), 523-532.

Zubrick, S.R., Silburn, S.R., Garton, A., Burton, P., Dalby, R., Carlton, J., Shepherd, C. & Lawrence, D. (1995). *Western Australian Child Health Survey: Developing Health and Wellbeing in the Nineties.* Perth, WA: Australian Bureau of Statistics and the Institute for Child Health Research.

Appendix 1
Legislative landmarks of relevance to this review

Marriage

1970 People who have undergone gender reassignment surgery are not allowed to marry.

1982 'Forced' marriages, as opposed to arranged marriages, are declared to be against the law where either the husband or the wife has been forced to get married against their will, and has been placed under considerable physical or emotional pressure to do so.

2002 The ban on marriages of transsexuals is challenged successfully at the European Court of Human Rights.

2004 English law changes to allow those who have undergone gender reassignment surgery to have their new identities recognised by the law. This means they can now lawfully get married.

2005 The Home Office declares that forced marriages are a form of domestic violence and are an abuse of human rights.

Civil Partnerships

2004 The law changes to allow same-sex couples to register their relationships with the State from December 2005. This means that they will receive almost exactly the same rights and responsibilities as heterosexual couples when they get married.

Cohabitation

2006 The Law Commission recommends the Government reform the law so as to protect the financial interests of those who live together without getting married or registering their civil partnerships. The Commission proposes an 'opt-out' scheme whereby those who share a home or have a child together and make a contribution to the relationship which has long-lasting consequences when the relationship breaks down will be entitled to a share in property. Couples can opt-out by agreeing in writing to do so.

Divorce Law Reform

1969 The previous grounds for divorce are replaced with a single requirement: that the marriage has broken down irretrievably. This moves divorce law away from its religious roots.

1973 The Government introduces a 'no-fault' system of divorce. This means that, for the first time, couples can get a divorce where they have lived separately for two years or more, and this has led to the breakdown of their marriage.

1973 The law changes to allow couples to get a divorce quickly and in a more amicable manner by introducing a 'special procedure'. Where the divorce is straightforward and neither side contests it, the parties need not go to court; instead, a judge can decide whether to grant the divorce based on the paperwork sent by the couple and their lawyers.

1977 The 'special procedure' is extended to all divorces that are not contested by either the husband or the wife.

2005 Civil partners are allowed to dissolve their partnerships in almost exactly the same way as married couples get divorce.

Financial Consequences of Divorce

1973 The needs and means of the husband and wife are taken into account by courts who decide how much each should receive when they get a divorce.

1973 It becomes possible to arrange that one of the parties can stay in the family home for a certain period of time, but that the house must be sold when a certain event takes place, e.g. when the youngest child of the family reaches the age of 21.

1977 It becomes possible to postpone the sale of the family home whilst either the husband or the wife needs it, until they die, remarry or cohabit with someone else.

1979 The courts begin to consider that, in certain circumstances, a 'clean break' is appropriate, so that all ties between the couple are ended when they divorce.

1980 When considering whether a clean break is appropriate, the courts start to take into consideration the welfare of any children involved who may be affected.

1990 Courts start to prefer to order a clean break between the couple where there are other financial resources that either side can rely on, e.g. income support. The income of a husband or wife's new partner can be taken into account where they are now living together.

1996 The courts start to move away from the idea of awarding what either side needs, and look at what their reasonable requirements are, now and in the future, instead.

2001 After a number of landmark cases, the overriding objective of the courts is to achieve a fair split of the couple's finances, taking into consideration the contributions the husband and the wife have made to the marriage, their health, the way of life they have become accustomed to leading and so on.

Appendix 2
Family-type definitions for Table 7 (Chapter 6)

Family Type	
Both natural parents	Couple family where all children live with both natural parents (i.e. children from both biological [natural] parents only).
Natural mother and stepfather	Couple family where all children are natural children of the female partner only (i.e. children born to natural mother now live with a stepfather). The couple do not have any children between them and the stepfather is not the natural parent of any child in the family.
Natural father and stepmother	Couple family where all children are natural children of the male partner only (i.e. children born to natural father now live with a stepmother). The couple do not have any children between them and the stepmother is not the natural parent of any child in the family.
Natural parents and stepfather	Couple family where some children are natural children of both partners together and some children are the natural children of the mother only (i.e. some children in the family are half-siblings). The natural children of the mother only are effectively the stepchildren of the male partner (making him a stepfather).
Natural parents and stepmother	Couple family where some children are natural children of both partners together and some children are the natural children of the father only (i.e. some children in the family are half-siblings). The natural children of the father only are effectively the stepchildren of the female partner (making her a stepmother).
Stepmother and stepfather	Couple family with no children of both partners together. The family contains children who are the natural children of the female partner (and not the male) as well as children who are the natural children of the male partner (and not the female). This means that both partners will be step-parents to one or more of the children in the family and that no child lives with both natural parents.
Natural parents and stepmother and stepfather	Couple family with some children of both partners together (i.e. natural children of both members of the couple) as well as some natural children of the mother only and some natural children of the father only. This means the family will contain at least three children and that each partner will be a step-parent to at least one child in the family.
Lone mother	Family with child headed by mother alone.
Lone father	Family with child headed by father alone.
Not in a family	Children in care, etc.

Definitions taken from Great Britain Census, 2001

Notes

Notes

Notes

Notes